THE
GARDEN
OF
AMERICAN
METHODISM

The Delmarva Peninsula,

1769–1820

Best wishes
to Gary
the co-director
of the N.E.H. Summer
Seminar and a good friend

Bill Willer

THE GARDEN OF AMERICAN METHODISM

The Delmarva Peninsula, 1769–1820

by

William Henry Williams

The Peninsula Conference of the
United Methodist Church

SR *Scholarly Resources Inc.*
Wilmington, Delaware

To Helen

Published for the
Peninsula Conference of the United Methodist Church,
139 North State Street, Dover, DE 19901
by Scholarly Resources Inc.

ISBN 0-8420-2227-9

Table of Contents

Acknowledgements vii

Preface ix

Introduction xi

Chapter 1: The Coming of Enthusiasm 1

Chapter 2: The Coming of Methodism 19

Chapter 3: Methodism Victorious, 1781–1820 57

Chapter 4: The Attractions of Methodism 89

Chapter 5: The Broadcasters of Methodism 121

Chapter 6: The Impact of Methodism 147

Some Afterthoughts 179

Notes 181

Selected Bibliography 210

Acknowledgments

Many people have made contributions to this study of Peninsula Methodism. I am particularly grateful to John A. Munroe, H. Rodney Sharp Professor Emeritus, University of Delaware, who suggested the topic, offered encouragement and advice at crucial times, and read the manuscript. Allen Clark of Wesley College, and the archivist at Barratt's Chapel, helped in so many ways that they are impossible to list. Others from the academic world who deserve mention include Harold Hancock of Otterbein College, Ken Rowe of Drew University, Gary Nash of U.C.L.A., Kenneth Carroll of Southern Methodist University, and James May of Candler School of Theology, Emory University. Archivists who have been particularly helpful include Phebe Jacobsen, Maryland Hall of Records; S. Garner Ranney, Maryland Diocesan Archives, Historical Society of Maryland; and Edwin Schell, Lovely Lane U. M. Church Archives. Morris Library, University of Delaware, and the Delaware Technical and Community College Library, Georgetown, have been very cooperative in meeting the needs of the author.

The process of transforming this manuscript into a book was supported by the Peninsula Conference Council on Ministries and the Peninsula Conference Bicentennial Committee of the United Methodist Church. Glenn Catley, the chairperson of the latter committee, has worked hard to bring this study to print, as have Barbara Beidler and James L. Preston of Scholarly Resources Inc. The typing was done by Jean Maloney. Others who have helped along the way with their advice and encouragement include Kirk Mariner, Sterling Green, Felton May, J. Gordon Stapleton, Charles Carpenter, and Cleo Henry. Many others have given generously of their time and books. The University of Delaware supported this project with financial aid and a sabbatical leave.

Preface

Nineteen eighty-four marks the bicentennial of American Methodism as an independent religious movement. Unfortunately, this very significant religious movement has attracted less scholarly interest than it deserves. Although some attention has been paid to Methodism along the American frontier, regional studies that deal solely with the Wesleyan movement are surprisingly rare. The development of Methodism along the settled Eastern Seaboard and, more specifically, in the Mid-Atlantic Region cries out for particular attention.

This study attempts to fill part of this scholarly void with an examination of the growth and development of early Methodism in a specific part of the Mid-Atlantic Region—the Delmarva Peninsula. What it meant to be a Methodist in a particular place and time is explored as exhaustively as the available sources permit. Although the evidence indicates a certain uniqueness in Peninsula Methodism, it also points to a commitment to most of the same activities, attitudes, and values that characterized Methodism across the United States. Indeed, because local is often universal, a close look at Peninsula Methodism opens a window to a clearer perception of Methodism's character and its impact on American history. Moreover, some of the issues and developments that originated on the Delmarva Peninsula ultimately helped shape the nature of American Methodism.

Unlike some historical monographs, this study is not woven around a particular framework that inevitably champions one ideological or unifying historical perspective. Rather, it merely attempts to tell as much of the story of early Peninsula Methodism as possible in a chronological and then in an analytical manner.

Introduction

In 1859, retired Methodist itinerant John Lednum published
A History of the Rise of Methodism in America. The former circuit rider
could only marvel at the story. What faith and courage those early
Wesleyan itinerants had shown in riding in the vanguard of the
American frontier as it pushed through the Appalachians into the
great Mississippi Valley beyond. Now even the far-off towns of the
Pacific Coast and the Willamette Valley of Oregon rang out on
Sunday mornings with the hymns and sermons of America's largest
Protestant denomination.

What a grand success story it was, and John Lednum had
certainly done his part. He hadn't been a great orator—some
maintained that Lednum's preaching was marred by "distracting"
mannerisms—but then neither was Francis Asbury an exceptional
speaker and look at what, with God's help, he had accomplished.
Indeed, it seemed like only yesterday that Asbury and the other
pioneer Methodist itinerants were spreading the Wesleyan message
up and down the Eastern Seaboard.

The American Revolution had been a trying time for those
early itinerants; most American revolutionaries thought them to be
Tories, because of their pacifist beliefs. As an Englishman, Asbury
felt particularly insecure and sought political refuge in Delaware
at the home of Judge Thomas White. There, Asbury expressed the
hope that Delaware would "become a garden of the Lord filled
with the plants of his own planting." Lednum smiled to himself as
he turned to page 211 in his newly published work and read

> and it came to pass, for in the beginning of the present century,
> not only Delaware, but the whole Peninsula was the garden
> of the Lord, with plants of his own planting.

A few years later Henry Boehm, another former circuit rider, put
it more succinctly: "The Peninsula that lies between the Delaware

The Delmarva Peninsula

and Chesapeake bays ... was the garden of Methodism in America."[1]

The Peninsula

The Delmarva Peninsula begins about fifteen miles south of Philadelphia and pushes southward for more than two hundred miles. Bounded on the west by the mouth of the Susquehanna River and the full length of the Chesapeake Bay, and on the east by the mouth of the Delaware River, the Delaware Bay, and the Atlantic Ocean, it includes all of Delaware and the Eastern Shore of Maryland and Virginia, taking its name from these three states. The Peninsula gradually widens as it proceeds south, reaching a breadth of almost seventy miles before receding to a long, narrow neck that finally ends with the confluence of bay and ocean at Cape Charles. In the extreme north, piedmont meets coastal plain along a line extending from the mouth of the Susquehanna to Wilmington, Delaware. South of the fall line, only an occasional hill or swale interrups the flatness of the land. The Peninsula's western edge, serrated by hundreds of rivers, creeks, and marshes, is a waterman's paradise.

Although Europeans began settling the Peninsula in the first half of the seventeenth century, at the beginning of the American Revolution there remained unsettled pockets that kept alive the ambiance of frontier life. In the swamps of Dorchester on Maryland's Eastern Shore, bears were hunted as late as 1770. During the late eighteenth century approximately two-thirds of the Peninsula's population was white and, except for the extreme north where the Scotch-Irish predominated, was overwhelmingly of English ancestry. Blacks made up the other one-third of the population and, in 1790, approximately 80 percent were slaves.

Despite the presence of mills, particularly along the Brandywine and other fast-flowing streams of the north, the economy of the Peninsula was overwhelmingly agrarian. As late as 1820, more than 80 percent of the whites and probably a higher percentage of the blacks made their living from the land.[2] Over this rough, semiliterate and illiterate population of subsistence farmers, watermen, and black slaves ruled a gentry class intent on maintaining its dominant position and in producing a veneer of culture that reflected its own peculiar values and concerns. The gentry's economic, social, and political prominence rested on large land holdings along rivers and inlets which, worked by slave labor, produced cash crops for a trans-Atlantic economy.

It was here on the Delmarva Peninsula, with its diverse and deferential population, that the Methodist message stirred a warmer response than anywhere else in early America. This book examines how and why this happened, and the impact it had on the Peninsula and on Methodism beyond the Peninsula.

Chapter One

The Coming of Enthusiasm

George Whitefield

On October 30, 1739, the ship *Elizabeth* dropped anchor in the Delaware Bay just off Lewes. A pilot boat came along side and took off three men. The youngest, George Whitefield, was a slender, pale, blue-eyed Englishman of twenty-four. There was a peculiar cast to his left eye which would lead, in later years, to the sobriquet "Dr. Squintum."[1] But being cross-eyed had its advantages. When Whitefield spoke to a large gathering, he seemed to be looking at everyone at once.

The voyage had lasted eleven weeks and Whitefield was eager to go ashore. At 5:00 P.M. the pilot boat tied up at Lewes, and Whitefield and his two companions proceeded to the local inn. While there, Whitefield was approached by a small delegation of Lewes's leading citizens requesting that he preach a sermon the next day.[2]

It was a natural request because George Whitefield, despite his youth, was already a famous evangelist in England and Wales. An ordained Anglican clergyman, he had aligned himself with a group of Oxford University religious reformers, headed by John and Charles Wesley, called Methodists. Although Methodists insisted that they were Anglicans, they got little cooperation and a good deal of opposition from the Anglican establishment. In England and Wales, Methodists were often denied pulpits in Anglican churches and, of necessity, turned to preaching in open fields. It was in these open fields that Whitefield developed the techniques that swayed thousands at a time. The news of Whitefield's pending arrival had reached Lewes two weeks earlier.

At two the following afternoon, in St. Peter's Anglican Church, the people of Lewes and its hinterland got a taste of the Whitefield preaching style. The gestures and timing of an actor combined with the voice of a great orator that had, it was said, the range of one mile. Benjamin Franklin would later attest to the power of Whitefield's vocal chords by figuring out, mathematically, that Whitefield could be heard by more than thirty thousand people at one time. In a day when sermons and prayers were usually read, Whitefield rarely used notes as he pointedly reminded his audiences that they were "half beast and half devil."[3] The Anglican rector in Lewes, William Becket, would later accuse Whitefield of acting the part of the "mountebank" and of preaching "Hell and damnation, fire and brimstone enough to have burnt a wooden frame." This was strong stuff indeed, though not by the standards of some other colonial evangelists; Jonathan Edwards in western Massachusetts and William Tennent and his four sons in the middle colonies were even more concerned and more graphic about the judgement to come.[4]

For most Anglicans, the Whitefield style was typical of a movement they labeled, with considerable contempt, "enthusiasm." Along with some non-Anglicans, they regarded "enthusiasts" with horror, and "enthusiam" became a synonym for disorder, irreverence, and fanaticism. Whitefield and other "enthusiasts" found, at best, a very cool reception in most of colonial America's Anglican churches. By contrast, Whitefield found a warmer reception among Presbyterians and Congregationalists.

The first Whitefield sermon preached on the Peninsula was to a Lewes crowd made up of "persons of different denominations." Whitefield then proceeded overland to Philadelphia, not bothering to preach along the way. On Thursday, November 29, 1739, he returned to the Peninsula, preaching twice the next day to an estimated five thousand in Wilmington. On Saturday he spoke to "about 2,000 people from a balcony," in New Castle, Delaware, and to about the same number in Christiana. On Sunday, December 2, eight to ten thousand gathered at White Clay Creek to hear Whitefield preach twice with only a half-hour break between sermons. It rained most of the time, but that didn't seem to bother the huge crowd as it "stood in the open air." Next was Northeast, Maryland, but little advance notice had been given and there were only "about fifteen hundred people" present. Whitefield then crossed the Susquehanna to Maryland's Western Shore.[5]

On May 13, 1740, Whitefield returned to Delmarva and preached at Nottingham in Cecil County, Maryland, and at Wilmington, White Clay Creek, and New Castle in northern Delaware. By his own estimates the crowds ranged from two to five thousand.

George Whitefield as he looked in his later years.
(Courtesy, Library of Congress)

He left New Castle on May 16, boarding the ship *Savannah* bound for Georgia. Lack of wind caused the *Savannah* to drop anchor off Reedy Island, about ten miles south of New Castle, and Whitefield spent the next few days preaching to sailors and others who gathered on the island.

Friday, May 23, found the *Savannah* anchored off Lewes, and Whitefield again preached at St. Peter's. By Saturday the crowds had become so large that many couldn't get into the sanctuary. On Sunday Whitefield "preached twice from a balcony to about two thousand, the church not being capable of holding them."

Whitefield left for Georgia but returned to the Peninsula in late November, stopping at the familiar places as well as at Bohemia Manor in Cecil County and at St. George's in northern Delaware. He would return a number of times in subsequent years and Bohemia Manor, the home of the Bayards, became his favorite resting place. Further details are sketchy, but we know that he preached in Lewes, Delaware, and in Cecil, Kent, and Queen Anne's counties, Maryland, in 1746. Although crowds that year were large on Maryland's Eastern Shore, Whitefield thought it best not to go further south on the Peninsula because of the summer heat. The following year Bohemia Manor served, for one month, as an anchor for a three-hundred-mile circuit that stretched all the way south to Somerset County, Maryland. Whitefield's last visit to Bohemia Manor was in 1757, and his last recorded visit to the Peninsula was at New Castle in 1765, only five years before his death.[6]

Although Whitefield was labeled a Methodist and he was an ordained Anglican clergyman, his theology was most closely attuned to the Calvinism of the Presbyterians. In 1740 in Lewes, for example, he was accused of preaching predestination. This Calvinist bent was further accentuated through Whitefield's subsequent contacts with American Presbyterians. One Sussex man recalled the impact of Whitefield's Calvinism on his own family. His father had heard Whitefield preach several times and consequently had wedded himself to the concept of "the elect, and once in grace always in grace." But even more important, Whitefield also preached the necessity of the new birth in Christ. Men had to recognize that only by accepting Christ as their personal savior was there hope for salvation.[7]

Anglicans objected to Whitefield's preaching style and Calvinist theology, but were even more offended by his attacks on Church of England clergy. After all, Whitefield charged that most of the Anglican missionaries sent to the colonies were "corrupt in their principles and immoral in their practices."[8]

Whitefield's enemies were quick to admit his ability to draw crowds, but were even quicker to agree with the Reverend William Becket of Lewes that it was the "vulgar everywhere" who were inclined to turn out. Many on the Peninsula who flocked to hear Whitefield did have little or no religious background, but they were joined by some Anglicans and large numbers of Presbyterians, particularly in northern Delaware.[9]

Presbyterianism had a long history on the Peninsula, but it wasn't until the great influx of Scotch-Irish immigrants into New Castle County, Delaware, during the early and mid-eighteenth century that Presbyterians became numerous. Descended from Presbyterian Scotsmen who immigrated to northern Ireland during the seventeenth century, many Scotch-Irish left for the New World and its better economic prospects a century later. In 1741, an Anglican cleric wrote from lower New Castle County that Presbyterians in his area were "by far the greatest party, and are still increasing, multitudes of them coming in and settling from the North of Ireland."[10]

Being the most numerous religious body in northern Delaware did not make the Presbyterians immune to internal discord. Presbyterian ministers William Tennent and his four sons were leaders in the Great Awakening in New Jersey, Pennsylvania, and Delaware. The Tennent preaching technique, emphasizing Hell, damnation, and rebirth, was controversial and split Presbyterianism into two warring camps. Those supporting the Tennents and their methods were called "New Side" or "New Light." Those who rejected "enthusiasm" were called "Old Side" or "Old Light." This great schism among the Presbyterians, ostensibly healed in 1758, continued below surface until after the American Revolution.

Whitefield's arrival on the scene strengthened the New Side party, and the New Side, in turn, supported Whitefield's work on the Peninsula. William Tennent's son, the Reverend Charles Tennent of the White Clay Creek Presbyterian Church, for example, was one of Whitefield's hosts and supporters when the great evangelist toured northern Delaware in 1739 and 1740.[11]

George Whitefield's impact was considerable. The crowds that he attracted on the Peninsula, as elsewhere in colonial America and England, were enormous. Though his own accounts of attendance were sometimes suspect—he reported a crowd of over ten thousand at White Clay Creek when that figure probably exceeded the entire population of New Castle County—there is evidence supporting his figures. The *Pennsylvania Gazette* reported two thousand less than Whitefield's estimate at White Clay Creek, but at

New Castle and Christiana, the *Gazette*'s estimates actually surpassed his own. A surprising source gives further credence to Whitefield's counts. When he spoke from a balcony in Lewes in 1740, he estimated the crowds at about two thousand. His strong critic the Reverend Becket admitted that those same crowds were "not less than 1400 or 1500."[12]

Whitefield was a genius at stirring religious feelings, but too often this excitement cooled after his departure. To keep alive religious enthusiasm on a long-term basis, Whitefield encouraged his followers to form religious societies whenever possible. In 1740 in Lewes, a society of Whitefieldites was organized to "meet, to sing Psalms and hymns etc. twice a week." Made up of Anglicans, Presbyterians, and Quakers, and never numbering more than thirty, the Lewes society has been called by some the first Methodist society in America.[13] By 1742 this society ceased meeting, and the Reverend Becket reported that "Mr. Whitefield's proselytes have recanted, some of them (the most considerable) in print." That same year a society organized in New Castle "upon Whitefield's plan" was facing difficulties. Despite the fact that it was supported by New Side ministers who "preach loud, long and thunder out Hell and damnation," one observer noted that the society's "heat seems to cool."[14]

The Anglican clergy of the Peninsula reviled Whitefield at every opportunity. They maintained that the money Whitefield raised was not, as Whitefield claimed, to support an orphanage in Georgia, but rather was spent on "a company of fellows and gadding young women who follow him to Georgia." The bitterness was understandable. Not only had Whitefield openly criticized the Anglican clergy, his revival preaching caused a decline in attendance at regular Anglican services. After Whitefield's visits to New Castle in 1739–40, no more than half the regular Anglican communicants bothered to receive communion. At Appoquinimi (St. Anne's), less than a mile south of Middletown, in lower New Castle County, attendance was also down.[15]

By 1742, however, a peculiar development was taking place in some of the areas touched by Whitefield's preaching. That summer, in four Anglican churches in Sussex County, the congregations became so large that the Reverend Becket was forced to preach outside. At Appoquinimi, too, attendance had actually increased over what it was before Whitefield's visit. But eighteen years later, the Anglican cleric at Appoquinimi did admit that the "New Light phrenzy which broke out at Mr. Whitefield's first appearance . . . took deep root and occasioned some defection from the Church."

As divisive as Whitefield's preaching was to Anglicans, he created even more controversy among the Peninsula's Presbyterians. According to George Ross, Anglican rector at New Castle, Whitefield added to the ill will between the New Side and the Old Side by insisting that a group of young ministers "as unruly as himself" were "the only ministers fit to be heard and followed."[16]

Whitefield's evangelical message produced dramatic crowd responses in Lewes and across the northern sector of the Peninsula. Typical was the crowd reaction at White Clay Creek on November 21, 1740. "The melting soon began, and the greatest part of the congregation was exceedingly moved. Several cried out, and others were to be seen weeping bitterly." In subsequent years this evangelical fever would cool, only to be revived by itinerant preachers on horseback during the American Revolution. As these itinerant preachers roamed up and down the Peninsula, they found that some of their converts had been prepared by George Whitefield's sermons some twenty or thirty years before.[17]

Whitefield never preached on Virginia's Eastern Shore, in some areas of Maryland's Eastern Shore, or in parts of central and southern Delaware. His impact, nevertheless, was profound. In 1815, Methodist Bishop Francis Asbury stopped at Bohemia Manor. In a reflective mood he wrote in his journal that Bohemia Manor was where "the Whitefield Methodists, called New Lights, laboured with success; the Wesleyan Methodists are heirs to this, according to the gospel."[18]

To Asbury, the Whitefieldites were useful because they helped prepare the Peninsula for the coming of Wesleyan Methodism. Asbury had less use for the Nicholites, followers of evangelist Joseph Nichols, because they tried to steal some "lazy, backsliding Methodists."[19]

Joseph Nichols

Joseph Nichols is a shadowy figure who has left us little biographical information. Unlike Whitefield, whose evangelical calling carried him far from his native England, Nichols only occasionally ventured beyond his native Delmarva Peninsula, and then only short distances. Born near Dover in 1730, Nichols had little formal education. Early on he turned to farming, owning at one time as much as 224 acres in southern Kent County, Delaware.

As a young man Nichols spent his leisure time in dancing, attending parties and horse races, and general merriment. During

the 1750s—we don't know the exact date—he married Mary Tumlin, daughter of Nathaniel Tumlin of Kent County, Delaware. At
least three children were born to the couple, but two died in their
teens.

Evidently a gifted musician and an entertaining raconteur,
Nichols was the center of a lively social circle. His gay social life
abruptly came to a halt when, at a party he was attending, a close
friend suddenly became ill and died. This death transformed
Nichols's life. Previously he had shown little outward interest in
religion. Now he became spiritually oriented, and drastically changed
his life-style. Self-denial replaced hedonism because, Nichols insisted, that which exalts the individual must be regulated and
subdued.

Unlike others in history who have undergone similar spiritual
awakenings, Nichols did not withdraw from his social circle. Rather,
he gradually transformed its gatherings to contemplative sessions
focusing on Scripture readings. A charismatic leader, Nichols drew
many of his friends along on his religious pilgrimage.

By the early 1760s Nichols felt impelled to preach. At first he
called himself a "Primitive Quaker" and his followers would often
be called or refer to themselves as "New Quakers." The Nicholites
attended some Quaker meetings but also conducted their own worship services. Nichols was quite dogmatic and several times disturbed Quaker meetings with controversial statements. At his own
meetings, Nichols would sit in silence, Quaker style, until moved
to preach. If he didn't feel moved, entire meetings were silent.

Nichols's cardinal belief was that an inward light—similar to
the Quaker inner light—enabled men and women to recognize and
therefore choose between good and evil. He broke from the Quakers,
however, by preaching his own "sinless perfection." Nichols did
leave the Peninsula on occasion in order to preach, going as far
north as Philadelphia and as far west as the Western Shore of
Maryland before his death in 1770. His critics charged that in order
to support his itinerant preaching, Nichols gave up farming and
left his wife and children "to shift as they can."[20]

In 1766, Quaker abolitionist John Woolman toured Delaware
and parts of the Eastern Shore of Maryland. Nichols, according to
one source, had earlier taken a strong stand against slavery. Woolman's presence reinforced Nichols's position, and even before most
Quakers, the Nicholites became abolitionists. Following the example of Woolman, the Nicholites wore undyed clothes, usually white,
in protest against human bondage. Dyes were produced by plantations practicing slavery, and to boycott dyed clothing was an
economic and symbolic gesture.[21]

Nichols's preaching produced significant numbers of converts in upper Dorchester and Caroline counties in Maryland, and lower Kent and upper Sussex counties in Delaware. In 1764 Charles Inglis, the Anglican rector at Dover, railed against "a mad enthusiast" who had been preaching along the Kent-Sussex boundary. The rector compared this man, who was Nichols, to James Naylor (1617–60), an English Quaker who had aroused emotional mysticism in his followers. Inglis went on to complain that the "ignorant, mad, and impious" Nichols had stirred up considerable interest in the area. Inglis's petulance is understandable. In a public debate between the two, Nichols evidently acquitted himself so well that he made converts of some of the onlookers. Two years later along the Kent-Sussex border, Anglican vestries of three churches desperately petitioned England for a missionary to fill their empty pulpits. The situation was critical because, the vestrymen noted, they were "surrounded with numbers of enthusiasts lately sprung up, who are indefatigable in seducing the members of our excellent Church."[22]

Apparently Nichols's preaching dramatically changed lives. John Woolman heard that some who had been irreligious had become Nichols's followers "and were become sober, well-behaved men and women." In 1797 another Quaker observer remarked on the growing economic prosperity enjoyed by the Nicholites. No doubt economic success was linked to their "sober, orderly, honest and remarkably industrious and punctual" character.

Like Whitefield, Nichols's messages were followed by outpourings of emotion—Woolman called them "irregularities"—by members of the congregation. Indeed, Woolman thought that the Nicholites needed the advice of "some skillful fathers." Unlike Whitefield, however, Nichols placed little emphasis on rebirth through the acceptance of Christ as a personal savior.[23]

After Nichols's death in 1770, the Nicholites were faced with a crisis. Some migrated to Guilford County, North Carolina. The number of Nicholite emigrants from the Peninsula is unclear but tradition maintains that seventy-five left for North Carolina in 1774–75, and many others followed later. The reasons for leaving are best left to conjecture, but certainly the death of Nichols and cheaper land in North Carolina were contributing factors.

While a minority of Nicholites were making ready to head for North Carolina, the rest, deciding to codify the informally understood principles of Joseph Nichols, drafted formal rules and regulations in 1774. Monthly meetings along Quaker lines were set up. Initially, Nicholites continued to hold their meetings at members' homes while often attending nearby Quaker meetings. Eventually,

Nicholite meeting houses were built. By 1785 there were three in use, all in Caroline County. The location of the meeting houses reflected the now heavy concentration of leadership and membership in that county. Religious services conducted at monthly meetings were open to the public and often drew a thousand people.

In 1780, Methodist leader Francis Asbury found Nicholites as far north as Jones Neck, southeast of Dover. They were up to their old tricks of trying to convert Methodists. They dressed in white and were accused by Asbury of being intolerant of singing, prayer, the wearing of a colored coat, or any other outward sign of nonconformity to their principles. To be fair, Asbury should have noted that the Nicholites were only opposed to prayers that weren't spontaneous. According to Asbury, the Nicholites were experiencing a revival in 1780, and he intimated that the revival was somehow sparked by the Methodist presence.[24]

Toward the end of the eighteenth century it became evident to most Nicholites that they should unite with their Quaker cousins. Nicholite leader James Harris had long been in favor of the merger. In 1796, an itinerant Quaker attended a Nicholite meeting at Marshyhope Creek, Caroline County, and noted that there was "an apprehension" that the Nicholites "would not be long a distinct society from Friends." In 1798, 122 Nicholites joined the Third Haven monthly meeting. In the next few years probably three hundred other Nicholites became Quakers, but it wasn't until the Civil War that the last independent Nicholite died. Although Nicholites were encountered in eastern Tennessee as late as 1804, most who had migrated to the south probably followed the merger path of their Delmarva brethren. But even after becoming Quakers, former Nicholites often stood out because of their ascetic ways.

Whitefield and Nichols demonstrated that the Peninsula was responsive to "enthusiasm." Nichols also demonstrated that Delmarva was responsive to a call for a more ascetic and industrious life-style.[25] Prior to the American Revolution, however, no Peninsula-wide religious denomination was able to tap these two religious wellsprings.

Quakers

The Society of Friends established itself on the Peninsula in the seventeenth century but failed to increase membership in dramatic fashion during the eighteenth century. Part of the problem was the lack of proselytizing zeal, traceable to the change Quakers had undergone in less than a century. Branded "enthusiastic" during the seventeenth century, the Friendly approach to divine truth had moved from "enthusiasm" to a calm mysticism by the mid-eighteenth century. Quakers became reserved and introverted in their religious exercises, traits that went along comfortably with their rise to social respectability.[26]

Quakers like John Woolman were comfortable with some of Joseph Nichols's positions, but the emotionalism that Nichols stirred up at meetings was upsetting. Indeed, the comparison of Nichols to seventeenth-century Quaker "enthusiast" James Naylor is very significant. Perhaps the unsympathetic view that Benjamin Mifflin and other Quakers had of Nichols is traceable to the fact that his "enthusiasm" reminded Friends only too well of their own roots.[27]

Presbyterians

By 1750 there were more than thirty Presbyterian congregations on the Peninsula. Most were organized under the New Castle Presbytery New Side or the New Castle Presbytery Old Side. The heaviest concentration of Presbyterians was in New Castle and Cecil counties, where the recent Scotch-Irish immigration had been so large. Presbyterians were also scattered the length and width of the Peninsula, with clusters of congregations in Sussex County (where some Scotch-Irish had immigrated), in Kent County, Delaware, and in present-day Wicomico County, Maryland.[28] From all indications, membership in most congregations south of New Castle County was not very large.

One of the problems that the Presbyterians couldn't overcome was the shortage of qualified clergy. The New and Old Sides didn't see eye to eye on a number of issues, including the spiritual prerequisite to becoming a clergyman. The New Side insisted on a conversion experience that could be assigned a specific time and place, while the Old Side didn't agree that a rebirth experience was that essential. Both camps, however, agreed that an advanced education was necessary to enter the ministry. Although New Side and Old Side disagreed over what institutions could best provide the necessary education, their insistence on an educated clergy limited the number of qualified ministers available to meet the needs of an expanding church on the Peninsula.

In the struggle between Old and New Side forces, the New Side seemed to have the upper hand in the north end of the Peninsula, while the Old Side had the edge further south where Presbyterians were less numerous.[29] A concentration of New Side

preachers in the north brought an emotional message to predominantly Scotch-Irish ears. South of New Castle and Cecil counties,
where the white population was overwhelmingly English and had
demonstrated its responsiveness to Englishman George Whitefield's
revival efforts, there were only a few New Side clergy to tap the
reservoir of Anglo-Saxon emotionalism. From time to time, itinerant New Side preachers would ignite revivals, such as in Somerset
County, Maryland, in 1745, and in Accomack County, Virginia,
in 1765. But, on the whole, these were generally short-lived affairs.[30]

Moravians

To the north of the Peninsula, Pennsylvania's Moravians had
been stirred to action by the Great Awakening. During the 1740s
and 1750s, Moravian itinerants spoke at Smyrna, Dover, and Lewes,
Delaware, but left no permanent organizations to institutionalize
the results of their revivals.[31]

Baptists

Although Baptists would later be regarded as "enthusiasts,"
during the colonial era Delmarva Baptists did not exhibit strong
evangelistic tendencies. This was in contrast to Virginia, where
Baptists increased in dramatic fashion in the decade prior to the
American Revolution. Indeed, with the exception of the Welsh
Tract Baptist Church, the lack of Baptist activity on the Peninsula
was notable.

In 1703, a congregation of fifteen or twenty Baptist families
from Wales, via Pennsylvania, settled on the Welsh Tract, a few
miles south of Newark, Delaware. Still standing is a brick church
built by this congregation in 1746. Thanks to an influx of more
Welsh settlers and a few converts, the congregation grew to 108 by
1790. In 1736, a portion of the membership moved to South Carolina and established a church on the banks of the Peedee River.
Periodically, offshoots of the Welsh Tract Church would crop up
in other areas of the Peninsula. In 1750, for example, there was
probably a small Baptist congregation at Duck Creek Cross Roads
(Smyrna), Delaware, and one in Cecil County, Maryland. Except
for Welsh Tract, however, no strong Baptist congregations developed on the Peninsula until after the close of the colonial period.[32]

During the colonial era, being a Baptist on the Peninsula was as much a reaffirmation of ethnic identity as it was religious preference. Just as probably 50 percent of the Peninsula's Presbyterian clergy preached with Irish or Scotch accents, perhaps 80 percent of the Baptist preachers preached in Welsh or in Welsh accents. Indeed, the records of the Welsh Tract Church were kept in Welsh until 1732. No doubt the same accents were as prevalent among the members of the respective congregations as in the pulpits.[33] To the Peninsula's predominantly English ears, those foreign accents were unattractive. It is not surprising that relatively few Anglo-Saxons found their way into Scotch-Irish Presbyterian congregations, and even fewer became Baptists during the colonial era.

Anglicans

Anglo-Saxons were most comfortable in their ancestral church, the Church of England. The first Anglican clergyman arrived at the southern end of the Peninsula shortly after the Pilgrims landed at Plymouth. By 1634 an Anglican church had been built in Northampton County, Virginia, just west of Cheriton. By 1750 there were upward of forty Anglican churches and chapels scattered throughout the Peninsula.[34]

During and after the heavy Scotch-Irish immigration, northern Irish began to occupy pews in such Anglican churches as Immanuel in New Castle. Some natives of Scotland and Ireland could even be found in Anglican pulpits,[35] but they and a few Welsh were never enough to alter the overwhelmingly English make up of the Anglican Church on the Peninsula.

Anglicanism was the established faith in Maryland and Virginia but was not state supported in Delaware. In the first two colonies, the Anglican clergy was supported by taxes, usually paid in tobacco. By contrast, the clergy in Delaware was supported by lay donations and contributions from the Society for the Propagation of the Gospel in Foreign Parts (S.P.G.), based in London.

All Anglican clergy who served in America needed a license issued by the bishop of London. In Virginia the selection of licensed clergy to fill vacancies was made by the vestry, subject to the approval of the royal governor. The latter step was usually just a formality. In Maryland, Lord Baltimore made the selection and appointment of clergy, a proprietary right that he jealously guarded. In Delaware, where the Anglican Church was not tax supported, the individual vestries appealed to the S.P.G. for missionaries to fill vacancies. Thus, vestry control over the selection of clergy was considerably stronger on Virginia's Eastern Shore than in the rest of the Peninsula.[36]

Because most Anglicans were Arminians—that is, they believed that the individual had considerable responsibility for his or her own salvation—they opposed the Calvinist concept of predestination. The Church of England also taught respect for and obedience to the English throne, and accepted as right the deferential society of the eighteenth century. Anglican services on the Peninsula probably resembled Anglican services on the Western Shore of Virginia. The gentry used the occasion to demonstrate its social superiority by waiting outside until the last possible minute and then entering en masse past the seated "lesser sorts" to arrive in grand manner at the preferred pews up front.[37]

In general, Low Church attitudes were strongest from Pennsylvania south, and some Anglican services on the Peninsula, as elsewhere in the South, used such evangelical practices as extemporaneous prayer and preaching. For the most part, however, a sermon was read that "was intentionally quiet, prosaic and always genteel." The purpose: to buttress moral behavior and the performance of duty. Increasingly, Christianity was presented as both beneficial and reasonable. The traditional Christian concepts of sin and redemption were pushed aside in the attempt to focus on obedience, duty, goodness, and character. But to some, like Joseph Everett of Queen Anne's County, the message preached was "a parcel of dead morality."

Sunday services were sometimes conducted by clergymen considered objectionable by their parishioners and peers. Because salaries paid to Maryland's clergy were the highest in the colonies, there was often a waiting line for parish positions on Maryland's Eastern Shore. Since appointments were the prerogative of Lord Baltimore, his favorites were often forced on unwilling congregations. There were no bishops in America to discipline errant clergy, and, after 1764, the bishop of London no longer seemed interested in exercising responsibility over clergy on the other side of the Atlantic.[38] Given almost no restrictions, some of Maryland's Eastern Shore clergy strayed away from traditional Anglican theology. In 1752, for example, came the charge that during services, some of the younger clergy weren't even reading the Nicene Creed.

More upsetting was the evidence of immoral behavior. The Reverend Thomas B. Chandler toured the lower Eastern Shore of Maryland in 1767 and reported that "the general character of the clergy . . . is most wretchedly bad." One overview of the situation held that the Anglican clergy of Maryland was the best provided for and least restrained of any in America, but those same high incomes and lack of controls made individual clergymen "less respectable," and "less guarded in their morals."[39]

Charges of immorality were not restricted to Maryland. A case in point was S.P.G. missionary Thomas Bluett, who served the Kent County, Delaware, region from 1745–49. Only three years after Bluett accepted his position, the wardens of Christ Church, Dover, were labeling his "life and conversation a scandal to the Church." A month later Bluett was called "erroneous in his principles as well as immoral in his actions." Another cleric maintained that Bluett's immoralities had become so flagrant that he was becoming an "odium" upon the cause of the church in Dover. The Eastern Shore of Virginia had a similar experience with some of its Anglican clergy.[40]

Criticism of Anglican clergy was not new to the Peninsula, but it became more intense as violations of clerical propriety were increasingly noted. In 1740 Whitefield opened the attack by calling S.P.G. missionaries corrupt and immoral. This criticism would continue even after the Methodists were victorious in winning most former Anglicans from their ancestral church.

Understandably, many Anglican congregations were upset by the actions of their clergy, and this dissatisfaction expressed itself through the rise of anticlericalism, particularly in Maryland. From 1768 to the American Revolution, the Maryland Assembly unsuccessfully pressed for a visitorial board to check on clerical abuses. Unable to create this board, the Assembly turned to reducing tax support of clerical salaries through acts passed in 1771 and 1774. This legislative action caused clergymen on Maryland's Eastern Shore to lose between one-third and one-fourth of their incomes, bringing their livings in line with other Anglican clergy on the Peninsula.

Even without the onus of clerical immorality, Anglicanism was in for some tough sledding on the Peninsula. Typical of most of the residents of the region were Sussex Countians, who were described as

> a people without learning, which proceeds altogether from their extreme poverty. There is not a grammar school within the county and it is a thing extremely rare to meet with a man who can write a tolerable hand or spell with propriety the most common words in the English language.[41]

How could people like that respond to a church run by and

for the gentry, featuring a rector who was educated and somewhat refined? Dryly delivered sermons on the significance of moral responsibilities did little to address the needs of people whose lives were dictated by the realities of poverty, disease, deprivation, violence, and sudden death. Moreover, even if the populace of the Peninsula were interested in its message, with the exception of Maryland the Anglican Church lacked enough licensed ministers to fill all of the vacancies on the Peninsula. Part of the problem was the requirement that all clerical appointees be well educated and travel to England for consecration.

Despite the deficiencies of its clergy, the Anglican Church did have some impact on the Peninsula. Kent County, Delaware, offers a brief case study. In 1762, one estimate put the population of Kent County of about seven thousand, with about one-sixth considered Anglican Churchmen. There were a large number of dissenters in Kent—Presbyterians, Quakers, Nicholites, and even five or six Roman Catholic families—and together they slightly outnumbered Churchmen. By contrast, dissenters were far less numerous than Anglicans in most areas of Maryland's Eastern Shore and were almost nonexistent on Virginia's Eastern Shore.[42]

Most of those who considered themselves Anglicans had been baptized, but few took communion. In 1758, for example, the combined number of Christmas communicants for the three Anglican churches in Kent was forty-six, though it rose to seventy-three for Easter. Baptisms, by contrast, could number up to twenty-five at a single service. One Anglican divine baptized 756 children and 23 adults during his six years in Kent County. The low number taking communion was probably caused by restrictions found in the *Book of Common Prayer* that limited communicants to those confirmed by a bishop. There were no Anglican bishops in America, nor did any Anglican bishop travel to America during the colonial period. The fact that some Anglicans did take communion without official confirmation reflected the flexibility of colonial Anglicanism in the face of unique American conditions.

Probably two-thirds of the population of Kent County was unchurched during the late colonial period. Charles Inglis, the rector at Christ Church, Dover, understated the case in 1760 when he reported that there were "several hundreds of people" in Kent County who "perhaps have never heard a sermon and do not belong to any religious denomination of Christians." Inglis specifically referred to those living in the thinly populated forests near the Maryland line west of Dover and to the residents of the marshes east of Dover.[43]

Lambert Hopkins, a contemporary of Joseph Nichols, labeled the late colonial period on the Delmarva Peninsula as a time of "laxity of manners and insensibility of mind." From Dover, Charles Inglis laconically commented, "the people, in general, are very loose." Inglis blamed much of the immorality on the rivalry between political factions and candidates. Once a week, beginning two months before elections, political factions and candidates would invite the electorate to "publick meetings," where free liquor was provided. The results were outrageous. Amid scenes of "grossest debauchery and vice," the "people's morals were entirely" corrupted.

The Anglican Church tried to deal with such revelry. Inglis responded to the drunken political orgies by scheduling preaching at the dates and near the sites of the debaucheries. Indeed, Anglican vestries all over the Peninsula had long been responsible for morals in their respective parishes. Toward the end of the colonial period, however, there is little evidence that the vestries exercised this responsibility with vigor.[44]

Under strong criticism for the conduct of its clergy, unwilling for the most part to be energized by the "enthusiasm" of the Great Awakening, and incapable of meeting the needs of the vast majority of the populace, Peninsula Anglicanism depended for survival on legislative fiat, the overseas support of the S.P.G., and the fact that it was the ancestral church of most of the white populace. Wesley M. Gewehr, after examining the Anglican Church in colonial Virginia, observed that "if the Church meant little from the religious standpoint to the social group to which it catered, it was next to nothing in the lives of the common folk."[45] By the late colonial period, the same generalization was generally true for most of the Peninsula.

Evangelical Anglicans

Not all Anglican clergymen were content with a church that lacked religious fire. An evangelical wing of the Anglican clergy, with some original roots in Presbyterianism, had some sympathy for "enthusiasm." On the Western Shore of Virginia the best known was Devereaux Jarratt. On the Peninsula the three best examples were Hugh Neill, Samuel Magaw, and Sydenham Thorne.

Hugh Neill, originally a Presbyterian, was ordained an Anglican clergyman in 1749. From 1750 to 1757, Neill simultaneously served all of the Anglican congregations in Kent County, Delaware. (It is unclear whether there were three or four congregations at the time.) After serving a number of years in Pennsylvania, Neill returned to the Peninsula in 1765 as rector of St. Paul's Parish, Queen Anne's County, Maryland, until his death in 1781. Samuel Magaw, also a convert from Presbyterianism, was ordained in 1767. From 1767 to 1781 he served in Neill's former post in Kent County. In 1781 he moved to Philadelphia, where he subsequently held a number of distinguished posts until his death in 1812. Sydenham Thorne served two Anglican congregations along the Kent-Sussex boundary from 1774 to 1777. For at least two years after that date, his refusal to omit prayers for the royal family caused Delaware's revolutionary government to restrict Thorne's participation in church services. He died a wealthy landowner in Milford in 1793.[46]

During his early years as an Anglican convert, Neill had little use for "enthusiasm." From Dover in 1750, he harshly criticized "enthusiasts," but years later his attitude began to change. St. Paul's in Philadephia had been built by Anglican "enthusiasts,"unhappy with the lack of religious zeal in Philadelphia's other Anglican churches. Accordingly, St. Paul's evangelicals were very selective about whom they would allow in their pulpit. With a great deal of pride Neill reported he had preached at St. Paul's in 1766, much to the consternation of Philadelphia's clerical establishment and the disapproval of the archbishop of Canterbury. That same maverick Anglican church made Samuel Magaw its rector in 1781.[47] All three Anglican clerics would demonstrate their sympathy for "enthusiasm" by supporting the growth of Methodism on the Peninsula during the American Revolution.

Chapter Two

The Coming of Methodism

Because of his early affiliation with John Wesley, George Whitefield was branded a Methodist. But his Calvinist leanings really placed him in the camp of the New Side Presbyterians. Indeed, he was buried beneath the pulpit of a Presbyterian church in Newburyport, Massachusetts. A few other "enthusiasts" produced by the Great Awakening were also labeled Methodists, but only because they were Whitefieldites. Although the Great Awakening shared a spiritual kinship with later Methodist revival efforts, and its evangelists helped prepare the soil for Methodist seeds, the real roots of American Methodism are found in the Wesleyan practices and traditions of Great Britain and Ireland. American Methodism did not actually begin until unofficial and official representatives of John Wesley arrived in the thirteen colonies in the decade before the American Revolution.

The Wesleyan Heritage

John Wesley's small band of Oxford University students were so methodical in their religious devotions in the early 1730s that they were called Methodists, and the label stuck. But it wasn't until 1738–39 that Wesley, an ordained Anglican priest, underwent a series of personal religious experiences that caused him to launch a reform movement to revitalize the Church of England. Because most of the Anglican clergy were uncomfortable and unsympathetic with the Wesleyan movement and closed their churches to Methodist preaching, Wesley and his preachers had no choice but to speak in open fields, in graveyards, or anywhere else that people were willing to gather.

Despite criticism from most of the Anglican establishment,

John Wesley
(Courtesy, Methodist Collection, Drew University, Madison, NJ)

Wesley maintained that he was only leading a reform movement, not founding a new church. He encouraged Methodists to remain part of the Anglican Church community, to attend Anglican services, and to receive the sacraments only from ordained Anglican priests. To insure this end, Wesley forbade his lay preachers—they were, after all, unordained—to administer baptism and communion and insisted that Methodist meetings be scheduled so that they did not conflict with Anglican services. It was only after Wesley's death that British Methodists officially cut their ties with the Anglican Church.

Wesley's theological and political ideas differed mainly in emphasis rather than in substance from the Church of England. On the question of salvation Wesley was an Arminian; on matters political he was a Tory. In his strong emphasis on the significance of being reborn in Christ, however, Wesley did differ from most Anglican divines. The latter, attracted by the rational syllogisms popular during the eighteenth century, found Wesley's emphasis too emotional. Moreover, Wesley's Methodism was a preaching religion, while the Church of England held fast to the importance of ritual and tradition.

To some Englishmen, Wesley's Methodism, like the Great Awakening in America, smacked of "enthusiasm," which was not only repulsive but suspect as well. After all, it was self-evident to those who thought in a sequential pattern that the challenge to the religious establishment posed by "enthusiasm" could just as easily become a threat to the political and social status quo.

Wesley emphasized freedom of choice, Christ's saving grace, and the possibility of earthly perfection to those whom the Anglican Church, in its apathy and its preoccupation with the upper class, had chosen to ignore. The mill workers of the newly industrialized midlands, the miners of Cornwall and Wales, and the craftsmen of Bristol and London were drawn to a theology that emphasized not only the sinfulness of man but, more importantly, the spiritual possibilities available to all men.

Wesley's itinerating ministry organized Methodist classes which were, in turn, drawn together to form local societies. As Methodist societies increased geometrically, they were joined together on individual circuits. Short of Anglican priests who were sympathetic to his reform movement, Wesley was forced to assign commited laymen to preach on the circuits. Although portrayed by the Anglican clergy as theologically ignorant, Wesley's preachers spoke the patois of the "middling and lower sorts" and were very effective in making converts. By 1813 there were an estimated two hundred thousand Methodists in England[1], and their significance was undeniable.

In 1791 Joseph Priestly credited "the civilization, the industry and sobriety of great numbers of the labouring part of the [English] community" to Methodism. In 1906 historian Elie Halevy maintained that England avoided the violence and anarchy of the French Revolution because of the impact of Methodism. Contemporary historian Bernard Semmel suggests that the stability and liberalism that has characterized modern English society may owe a great deal to the Methodist influence.[2]

Wesley's Message Reaches America

To John Wesley, winning souls was the central issue, and all these other developments, so dear to the hearts of historians, were of peripheral interest. Because he was so busy broadcasting the Methodist message throughout Great Britain and Ireland, Wesley had little time to consider the needs of Anglo-Saxons across the Atlantic. Prior to his pivotal religious experiences in 1738–39, Wesley spent two years in Georgia as an Anglican missionary. It was a frustrating experience, leaving him discouraged and questioning his own religious convictions. Subsequently, news of religious stirrings in America and reports of the extraordinary crowds that gathered to hear his sometime friend George Whitefield brought America to mind again. But it wasn't until after he received a written request from Thomas Taylor of New York City, in 1768, that Wesley seriously considered sending Methodist missionaries to America.

By 1768 a few unofficial representatives of Wesleyan Methodism were already setting up Methodist societies on this side of the Atlantic. Probably the first was Robert Strawbridge, a maverick of sorts from Ireland where he had been a Methodist local preacher. The date of Strawbridge's arrival from Ireland and the date he first set up a Methodist society in Maryland are unknown, but Strawbridge did have an active society functioning in the Sam's Creek area of Frederick County, Maryland, by the spring of 1766. Strawbridge was not acting in an official capacity nor had he asked the Methodist connection across the Atlantic for permission when he set up that first society. Moreover, contrary to Wesley's instruction to all Methodist preachers, Strawbridge proceeded to administer the sacraments of baptism and communion. In administering the sacraments, Strawbridge made inevitable a great deal of tension between himself and official Methodist missionaries subsequently sent by John Wesley.

In the fall of 1766, Philip Embury, formerly a local preacher and class leader in Ireland, and his cousin Barbara Heck formed a Methodist society in New York City. In 1768 a chapel was erected. Among those attracted to the New York society was Capt. Thomas Webb, a retired British officer who had become a Methodist while in England in 1765. With a green patch covering an eye lost in the Quebec campaign and attired in a military uniform and sword that he would unbuckle and place, in dramatic fashion, on the desk or podium prior to announcing his text, Captain Webb was a colorful lay preacher. He helped spark the formation of the first Methodist society in Philadelphia in 1767. John Adams heard Captain Webb speak there in 1774, and called him

> one of the most fluent, eloquent men I have ever heard; he reaches the imagination and touches the passions very well, and expresses himself with great propriety.

John Wesley agreed that Captain Webb was a very effective preacher but added that Webb lacked depth.[3]

In 1769 Methodist preacher Robert Williams, whose most recent abode had been Ireland, arrived in New York City. Williams had arranged for passage on his own and, like Strawbridge, Embury, and Webb, was not an official Methodist emmissary. Williams became an important, if somewhat independent, evangelist and religious book publisher with a particular impact on Virginia.

Also in 1769, Richard Boardman and Joseph Pilmore arrived in Philadelphia as the first official missionaries appointed by Wesley in response to Thomas Taylor's letter. Boardman was thirty-one and periodically suffered from ill health. After landing in Philadelphia he moved on to New York, where he spent much of his time until returning to England with Pilmore in 1774.

Pilmore was a year younger than Boardman and more aggressive and effective. He spent much of his time in Philadelphia, although he did make an important trip through the colonial South in 1772. Pilmore and Boardman had their differences, but they were united in opposing extensive itinerating because they both preferred the urban amenities found in New York and Philadelphia. Interestingly enough, Pilmore was particularly adamant that the Methodist societies never separate from the Church of England. Two years after American Methodists declared their independence from the Anglican Church in 1784, Pilmore returned from England

Captain Thomas Webb
(Courtesy, Methodist Collection, Drew University, Madison, NJ)

Joseph Pilmore
(Courtesy, Methodist Collection, Drew University, Madison, NJ)

as an Anglican priest and became Samuel Magaw's assistant at St. Paul's Episcopal Church in Philadelphia.

John King, a physician and another unofficial representative of Wesleyan Methodism, arrived in Philadelphia in late 1769. He found Pilmore already in charge of the local Methodist society and applied to him for permission to preach. Pilmore refused King's request, but the latter preached anyway in Pottersfield (now Washington Square). So favorably impressed were some local Methodists who heard King that they convinced Pilmore to grant him the right to act as an itinerant Methodist preacher.

By 1770 there were at least seven Methodist preachers in America—Embury, Webb, Strawbridge, Williams, Boardman, Pilmore, and King—and all but Embury and Boardman would spend some time preaching on the Delmarva Peninsula.

Wesley continued to send official missionaries, with pairs arriving in 1771, 1773, and 1774. The most significant was Francis Asbury, who arrived in America in 1771 at the age of twenty-six.

Destined to become the indispensable giant of American Methodism, Asbury spent almost two and one-half years on the Peninsula during the American Revolution. In addition, he itinerated through the region on numerous other occasions, leaving behind a remarkable legacy.

First Methodist Preaching on Delmarva

In 1769 or 1770—the exact date is unclear—two Methodists from Robert Strawbridge's society on the Western Shore visited and prayed with John Randle, who lived near Worton in Kent County, Maryland. Soon after, Robert Strawbridge preached at Randle's home. Strawbridge was of medium height with a heavy build, dark hair and skin, and a good preaching and singing voice. Full of anecdotes, he resembled subsequent Methodist preachers because he prayed without a book and preached without a written sermon, practices that were uncommon among Anglican divines. There is no indication that Strawbridge preached anywhere else on the Peninsula before returning to the Western Shore, but his steps were soon followed by other itinerants, including Robert Williams.[4]

In 1769 Captain Webb itinerated through New Castle County and later on, perhaps in 1770, preached with success in northern Queen Anne's County. Webb was followed by the headstrong and stubborn John King, who didn't hesitate to "make the dust fly." In 1770 Joseph Pilmore sent King to Wilmington to preach to "a few people who were then earnestly seeking the Lord." Evidently King was quite successful in Wilmington and in other areas of New Castle County, before moving on to the Western Shore. The next year, when Pilmore made his first visit to Wilmington, he found "a fine congregation ready to receive the work of the Lord." Pilmore was also happy to observe that in the more rural areas of New Castle County, God had made King "an instrument of abundance of good among the country people." Pilmore's sweep through New Castle in the spring in 1771 included six preaching stops. Toward the end of 1771, Richard Wright, like Pilmore one of John Wesley's official emmissaries, arrived at Bohemia Manor in southern Cecil County and spent the winter laboring hard to spread the Methodist message.[5]

By the spring of 1772, parts of New Castle County, Delaware, and Cecil, Kent, and northern Queen Anne's counties, Maryland, had been exposed, in a haphazard fashion, to the Wesleyan message. To systematize the preaching, to set up societies, and to spread the Methodist message to the rest of the Peninsula became the next priorities. The two men who would be the driving force behind that, and more, were Francis Asbury and Freeborn Garrettson.

Francis Asbury

In 1772 a twenty-seven-year-old Francis Asbury was Wesley's General Assistant to the Methodist societies in America, and it was in that capacity that he first visited the Peninsula. He stood a slender 5'9", with piercing blue eyes, prominent nose, broad forehead, and flowing blond hair that turned silver in later life. A charismatic personality—some maintained that he was graced with natural wit, although it rarely comes through in his journals—he was not a particularly gifted preacher. Freeborn Garrettson later explained that because of his constant traveling—270,000 miles in the service of American Methodism—Asbury preached less often and, therefore, had less practice than those itinerants who served a specific circuit. Nevertheless, he was a commanding figure with inexhaustable energy. An astute administrator and judge of men, Asbury never married nor, it seems, gave much thought to anything else but the spread of Methodism in America. That single-mindedness combined with a certain austerity to make strangers uneasy in Asbury's presence. Under the leadership of this driven man, American Methodists grew from less than one thousand to well over two hundred thousand.[6]

On April 9, 1772, Asbury preached his first sermon on the Peninsula at Robert Furness's tavern in New Castle. He found the audience small and unreceptive. He had already been denied the right to speak at the nearby courthouse. A few days later Asbury preached at Solomon Hersey's, at the head of Bohemia River in Cecil County, Maryland. He also preached in Wilmington, finding there were "but few to hear." He met with mixed success in other preaching stops on the northern end of the Peninsula during 1772.[7]

Methodist Growth in Northern Delmarva

In the latter part of 1772, Richard Webster and Isaac Rollins assisted John King in a circuit that included Cecil and Kent counties, Maryland, as well as part of Maryland's Western Shore. Other

Methodist preachers who traveled the Philadelphia-Baltimore route halted just long enough to preach in New Castle, Cecil, and Kent counties. Seventeen seventy-three found Joseph Pilmore back preaching in New Castle County to "a vast congregation" at Christiana and to considerable crowds at New Castle and Wilmington. Asbury also was back in 1773, preaching from Wilmington to Bohemia Manor. By September 1773 there were five Methodist meeting places on the Eastern Shore of Maryland, all in Cecil and Kent counties. New Castle County probably had three Methodist meeting places, but the number is hard to pin down. All of the meeting places were in private homes. In 1774, on the road from Chestertown to Rock Hall, Kent County, Peninsula Methodists constructed their first meetinghouse, which they initially called Kent Chapel and subsequently Hynson's Chapel.[8]

The first Methodist society on the Peninsula—if the temporary societies set up by Whitefield are ignored—was organized in the town of New Castle, Delaware, about 1770, no doubt in response to the preaching of Captain Webb and John King. Like Whitefield's societies, however, the Wesleyan society in New Castle soon died out. On Maryland's Eastern Shore, societies had more staying power. Evidence indicates that Delmarva's first permanent Methodist society was organized in the home of Solomon Hersey, just below Bohemia Mills, Cecil County, in 1772. By the next year, two other Methodist societies had been organized in Kent County: one at John Randle's home near Worton and the other at Carvil Hynson's near Rock Hall.

Since 1772 Maryland's upper Eastern Shore had been included in the greater Baltimore circuit. By late 1773, itinerant preacher William Watters was serving the budding Methodist communities in the Cecil and Kent county areas. Watters met with success and, in response to requests, extended his preaching to Queen Anne's County. In 1774 the growth of Methodism in the upper Eastern Shore was recognized by the formation of a separate Kent Circuit to serve Cecil, Kent and northern Queen Anne's. That same year the Chester Circuit, which included Chester County, Pennsylvania, and New Castle County, Delaware, was organized. Despite the efforts of Webb, King, Pilmore, and Asbury, Methodism was far less successful in New Castle County than across the Maryland line. In 1774, for example, the Kent Circuit included 253 Methodists while the entire Chester Circuit counted only 74.[9]

The Methodist advance in the upper Eastern Shore was not without resistance. Philip Gatch, assigned to the Kent Circuit, reported verbal and physical confrontations in northern Queen

Key Place Names in the Methodist Advance Down the Peninsula

Anne's County. One Methodist preacher was attacked and tumbled down a stairwell with his assailant. At one point during an argument with a member of St. Luke's Parish, Gatch became so angry that he "felt disposed to hit him." On another occasion Gatch was attacked while praying at the end of a service. His assailant seized the posts of the chair at which Gatch knelt, intending to use the chair as a weapon. Gatch held on to the chair for dear life until members of the congregation came to his aid.

From Queen Anne's County, circuit riders made their way south into Caroline County and by 1775 were preaching at Greensboro. By 1777 Methodist preachers had entered Talbot County, Maryland, Kent County, Delaware, and the northern and western parts of Sussex County. By the end of 1777, the Kent Circuit extended south from the Elk River in Cecil County to Cedar Creek and the head waters of the Nanticoke River in Sussex County, Delaware.[10]

Freeborn Garrettson

As the Methodist drive continued southward, it was spearheaded by Freeborn Garrettson. He was born in 1752 into a slaveholding Anglican family of some means in Harford County, Maryland. In 1772 he pledged himself to God's service after narrowly escaping death in a riding accident. Prior to becoming a Methodist, Garrettson had heard Strawbridge and Asbury preach but found his father very critical of Wesleyans. His father assured Freeborn that he had no objection to his son's being religious, but why did he have to turn away from the Anglican Church? Freeborn replied that he had no intention of leaving the Anglican Church but wondered why "whenever persons become serious, they are called Methodists and their names are cast out as evil." Garrettson initially sympathized with American revolutionaries. On becoming a Methodist in 1775, however, he became a pacifist and determined "to have nothing to do with the unhappy war."[11]

In 1775 Garrettson first preached on the Peninsula, spending much of his time in Caroline County. At Tuckahoe Neck, he awakened to religion the thirteen-year-old Ezekiel Cooper, who was destined to become a very influential preacher and the head of the Methodist Book Concern. Garrettson returned to preach full-time on the Peninsula in May 1778 and remained until the spring of 1780. His two-year stay was interrupted only by two months of preaching in Philadelphia and a few weeks of preaching in New Jersey during the late summer and early fall of 1779. After a few

Freeborn Garrettson
(Courtesy: Methodist Collection, Drew University, Madison, NJ)

years away from the Peninsula, Garrettson returned to circuit appointments on Maryland's lower Eastern Shore in 1782–83, and he served as presiding elder for the Dorchester, Somerset, Annamessex, and Northampton circuits in 1787.[12]

No one worked harder than Garrettson. On July 5, 1779, for example, he spoke a little after sunrise in Dover, at 9:00 A.M. at a home south of Dover, at 1:00 P.M. at Frederica, and at 5:00 P.M. near Milford. His total preaching time was six hours, the distance traveled by horseback over poor roads was more than twenty miles, and he did it all while nourishing his body with only a little milk and water. Five years later Methodist Superintendent Thomas Coke met Garrettson in Dover, noting that Garrettson "seems to be all meekness and love, and yet all activity." Coke went on to admit that Garrettson made him ashamed because "he invariably rises at four in the morning . . . and now blushing I brought back my alarm to four o'clock."[13]

Garrettson had a strong, though harsh and high-pitched, voice which projected, on at least one occasion, a quarter of a mile. He brought home a simple message that focused on Christ, Heaven, and Hell. A convinced Arminian, Garrettson also believed strongly in the individual's ability to know that his sins had been forgiven through Christ's saving grace. Because of his genteel background, Garrettson was at ease with the gentry of the Peninsula as well as with "the middling and lower sorts."

His background may also explain Garrettson's equivocal attitude toward the emotionalism that he and other Methodist preachers on the Peninsula aroused. On the one hand he noted that

> to suppose a work of grace without the excitement of human passions, is as great an absurdity as it would be to expect a man to breathe without any movement of the lungs.

On the other hand, he found that on at least one occasion "a few noisy, jumping Methodists did more harm than good."[14]

With Garrettson leading the way, Methodism consolidated its push southward. In the spring and summer of 1778, Garrettson preached in Kent and Queen Anne's counties, Maryland, and in Kent County, Delaware. He often met violent opposition and was lucky on more than one occasion to escape with his life. Anti-Methodist feeling was common on the Peninsula because Methodism threatened certain established life-styles and institutions, and because Methodists were suspected of being Tories.

On June 24, 1778, Garrettson was riding near Church Hill,

northern Queen Anne's County, on his way north to Chestertown. Despite the threat of imprisonment, he had preached in Talbot and in parts of Queen Anne's, and while in Queen Anne's had become the first Methodist to preach on Kent Island. As he rode north he met John Brown, a former county judge. Garrettson asked the distance to Chestertown, only to have Brown insist that Garrettson must go to jail. Brown then seized Garrettson's horse's bridle and commenced striking the Methodist around the head and shoulders with a stick while yelling for assistance. Others came running with a rope and Garrettson, recognizing that his life was at stake, whipped his horse and galloped away. Brown pursued and renewed the attack, causing Garrettson to be thrown by his mount. The cumulative effects of the blows and the hard fall left the itinerant unconscious. Luckily for Garrettson, a woman happened by and brought him to a nearby house, where he was bled and recovered quickly enough to preach from his bed that evening.

On September 12, 1778, Garrettson was preaching in Dover to an unruly crowd. Some accused him of being a Tory and called for his hanging. Garrettson was rescued by the intercession of a group that included a Dover merchant by the name of Pryor who had formerly been awakened under Whitefield.[15]

In October 1778 a dream directed Garrettson to push southward to bring the Methodist message to Sussex County, Delaware, and Somerset County, Maryland. Although some itinerants, such as John Cooper, had already preached in some sections of Sussex and Somerset, most of the two counties remained virgin territory for the gospel. When Garrettson first preached in southwest Sussex near Laurel, the residents were "so far from the power of godliness that they had not even the form of it—they were swearers, fighters, drunkards, horse racers, gamblers, and dancers." How unchurched some were was exemplified months later when Garrettson asked a resident of Cypress Swamp, in southern Sussex, if he was acquainted with Jesus Christ. The swamp resident said that he neither knew the man nor where he lived.

In this land of the unchurched, Garrettson's life was threatened by gun-wielding antagonists on at least four different occasions. In three of the cases his followers acted quickly in disarming the assailants, with women doing the honors in one instance.[16]

Perhaps the most bizarre gun threat took place in early July 1779. Garrettson decided to travel from Milford to Lewes to make inroads in an area not yet touched by Methodism. Farmers along the way, having never seen a Methodist, turned out to stare at him.

Some of the onlookers remarked, in rather surprised tones, that this Methodist preacher was not unlike other men.

Arriving in Lewes on Monday, July 6, Garrettson began to preach, only to find that

> J. Wolf, brother to the man in whose house I was to preach, came to the door with a gun and a drum, and several other utensils, and after beating his drum for a while, he took the gun, and was dodging about as though he was taking aim to shoot me.

The women in the audience were particularly terrified, and confusion followed, forcing Garrettson to stop preaching and to retreat into another room. The town squire arrived on the scene and told Wolf to leave immediately or he would be thrown in jail. Garrettson then finished his sermon.

On Wednesday, Garrettson was preaching in the county courthouse at Lewes when "my old enemy Wolf, by nature and name," arrived and, though it was a hot summer day, built a roaring fire in the fireplace. Finding that a fire didn't disturb the preacher, he brought in a bell and began to ring it loudly. Garrettson had no choice but to finish his sermon at a private home "of a kind widow woman."

On Sunday Garrettson scheduled his preaching at 9:00 A.M. and 3:00 P.M., to avoid conflict with local Anglican services. Like other Methodist preachers, he considered himself an Anglican and did not wish to upset the local rector. After speaking to a crowded courthouse, Garrettson and his listeners moved to nearby St. Peter's for the regular service, only to hear the Reverend Samuel Tingley preach against the Methodist itinerant and all "such runabout fellows." From the local Presbyterian pulpit, the Reverend Matthew Wilson, a long-time enemy of "enthusiasm," echoed Tingley's words.

On leaving Lewes, Garrettson had an appointment to preach at a nearby stream. He had been forewarned that if he showed up he might be drowned by his opponents. He preached anyway to a large congregation without incident, and then rode on to another appointment five miles distant. But along the way he noticed behind him "a man dressed like a soldier, riding full speed, with a great club or stick in his hand." An obviously tense Garrettson was much relieved when the mysterious rider pulled up and offered his hand. He said that he had listened to Garrettson preach in Lewes and agreed with his theology. The rider had heard that Garrettson was to be attacked, and had ridden to defend the Methodist missionary.

According to Garrettson, opposition in the Lewes area eventually backfired against his opponents: "The more they preached and spoke against me, the more earnestly did the people search their Bibles to know whether these things were so." As for J. Wolf, eighteen years later he was still bitterly complaining about Garrettson.[17]

Threats and physical attacks did not stop Garrettson. He led the Methodist thrust into northern Somerset County (Wicomico County today), and by the end of 1778 there were Methodist societies in Quantico and Salisbury. A few weeks prior to going to Lewes, he was threatened by a mob in Salisbury but preached anyway, winning over an influential member of the opposition.

Persecution on Maryland's Eastern Shore

While Methodist preachers, led by Garrettson, pushed down the spine of the Peninsula to Salisbury, much of the lower Eastern Shore adjoining the Chesapeake had been bypassed. On August 2, 1779, for example, six or seven hundred gathered at a Methodist Quarterly Meeting in the Dover area. People came from as far away as Somerset and New Castle counties and Philadelphia. Conspicuously, Dorchester and Talbot counties were not represented.

This was for good reason. Along with Queen Anne's, Dorchester and Talbot counties were particularly strong in anti-Methodist sentiment during the American Revolution. Moreover, since Garrettson and some other Methodist preachers had refused to take the Maryland loyalty oath, they were barred by Maryland law from preaching on the Eastern Shore. Garrettson's threatened arrest and physical beating in Queen Anne's in 1778 did not stop his return the next year. This time he had to ride the best part of one night to escape a mob.

Itinerant Joseph Hartley, who also refused to take the Maryland oath, preceded Garrettson into Queen Anne's County in 1778, only to be arrested and held for a brief period. One of the conditions for his release was that he could pray but not preach. Since praying was done on one's knees, Hartley subsequently exhorted his listeners while kneeling. Persistence paid off. Hartley's enemies finally declared that he might as well preach on his feet as on his knees.[18]

During the summer of 1779, Hartley found himself again in jail, this time in Easton, the seat of Talbot County. Hartley proceeded to preach through the bars on his window, and after almost three months his enemies, "fearing he would convert the whole town and county, took bail on him and discharged him." After being released Hartley moved on to Delaware, "where the rules were more favorable to Methodist preachers." Evidently, Hartley left behind some newly formed societies. In October 1779 Asbury noted that Methodism was spreading into Talbot. As for Hartley, after preaching for a short time in Delaware and then Dorchester, he married into modest wealth and, in 1781, settled permanently in Talbot County.

A third itinerant arrested for preaching without taking the Maryland oath was Thomas Chew. In 1780 Chew was appointed to the Kent Circuit, which extended south into Queen Anne's and Caroline counties. Chew was arrested in Caroline County and was tried and found guilty. The presiding officer of the court was Squire Henry Downes, who didn't wish to send a preacher to the county jail. Rather, he ordered Chew to serve out the sentence in Downes's home. In less than three weeks, Downes and his entire family were converted to Methodism by their unique guest.[19]

By the fall of 1779, Dorchester County was surrounded by Methodism. Henry Airey, a magistrate and a wealthy Dorchester planter, had already converted. In early 1780, after visiting at Judge Thomas White's, southwest of Dover, and meeting Garrettson and Asbury there, Airey wrote to Asbury requesting that Garrettson be sent to Dorchester. At Asbury's urging, Freeborn Garrettson set out from Judge White's.[20]

This wouldn't be Garrettson's first venture into Dorchester. One morning in the summer of 1779, just after his bizarre visit to Lewes, Garrettson rode to the edge of Dorchester County and preached to an overflow crowd in a private home. Soon after he was threatened with jail by a magistrate because he hadn't signed the loyalty oath. Garrettson said he wasn't afraid of jail and the magistrate left. That afternoon a sheriff threatened to arrest Garrettson but backed off when Garrettson warned that God would be displeased by such an act. Garrettson then left Dorchester for his two-month stay in Philadelphia.

Because he expected serious trouble, Garrettson was very apprehensive as he rode into Dorchester County in early February 1780. He stopped first at Airey's plantation, located about five miles southeast of Cambridge, and spent three days preaching to large congregations. When he left Airey's for another part of Dorchester, word reached Garrettson that the county court had charged him with Toryism and gave "a very wicked man liberty" to kill him. Hearing that the murder attempt was to take place the next day, the Methodist itinerant made a hasty retreat to Henry Airey's. But after remaining for two days, a restless Garrettson set out again to preach in another part of Dorchester.

Returning to Airey's that evening, Garrettson's party was intercepted by a body of men. They beat Garrettson's horse and brought the Methodist preacher before a magistrate who ordered Garrettson locked up in the Dorchester County jail in Cambridge. Garrettson reminded the magistrate of Joseph Hartley's success in making converts through the window bars of the Talbot County jail in Easton, and then set off for Cambridge in the company of his enemies. It was a particularly dark winter night, but suddenly everything was illuminated by "a very uncommon flash of lightning." Convinced that the lightning may have been a sign of divine displeasure, Garrettson's enemies dispersed and Garrettson was free to return to Airey's home.

The next day, while Garrettson was leading worship at Airey's, about twenty horsemen arrived led by an old man brandishing a gun, who immediately grabbed Garrettson. Some of the worshippers had expected trouble and concealed clubs under their coats. To avoid bloodshed, Garrettson commanded his supporters to remain peaceful and said that he was willing to go to jail. After exhorting for a time and leaving his audience in tears, Garrettson allowed himself to be escorted five miles into Cambridge where he was kept in a tavern from noon until almost sunset.

His captors were delighted with themselves and drank away the entire afternoon in celebration. A young soldier friend, who had accompanied Garrettson to Cambridge, remained with him in the tavern. Resentment against Garrettson soon spread to his young companion. A heavy-set reveler struck at the soldier with a large whip "and in all probability would have killed him had not the whip struck the top of the door." Garrettson's friend sprang to the offensive, dropping his attacker with a fist to the temple. The other revelers roared in laughter and some called out, "The Methodists will fight." Upset by the violence, the pacifist Garrettson chastised his young companion, although he had to admit that his enemies at the tavern "behaved rather better afterward."

That night Garrettson began a two-week stay in a dirt-floor cell in Cambridge. The charge, according to Garrettson, was preaching the Gospel without signing the Maryland loyalty oath. According to Asbury, Garrettson was charged with being a fugitive, although from what or whom is never spelled out. People of status and political power came to Garrettson's aid. In addition to the attentions of his Dorchester County friend Henry Airey, Judge White from Delaware wrote to "Mr. Harrison, a gentleman of note," who was Garrettson's greatest enemy in Cambridge.[21] Harrison then became more friendly.

Francis Asbury soon persuaded Governor Thomas S. Lee of Maryland and Delaware President Caesar Rodney to work together to release Garrettson on technical grounds. The two agreed that Garrettson could claim to be a resident of Delaware as well as Maryland. Since Delaware "was more favorable" to Methodists, his case would get a more favorable hearing in Dover. Henry Airey put up security and Garrettson appeared before the executive council of Delaware. He brought back to Dorchester a letter of support from Delaware President Caesar Rodney and was released.[22]

Ironically, once hostile Dorchester County soon became a hotbed of Methodism. Even as Garrettson slept on the dirt floor of the county jail in Cambridge, Asbury was sending itinerants Joshua Dudley and Caleb Petticord to Dorchester. Although Petticord "was beaten until blood ran down his face," by the late spring of 1780 a Methodist circuit was serving Dorchester with Joseph Hartley its first assigned itinerant. The Philadelphia Annual Conference of 1782 reported that the greatest increase in American Methodists during the previous year took place on the Dorchester Circuit. By the turn of the century, Dorchester had the largest membership of any of the circuits on the Peninsula.[23]

Virginia's Eastern Shore

The last area of the Peninsula to develop verifiable Methodist societies was the Eastern Shore of Virginia. One unsubstantiated source maintains that an unnamed Methodist itinerant, on his way to and from Norfolk in 1772, traveled through Accomack and Northampton counties and made some converts. A second source talks vaguely of two itinerant Methodists who arrived prior to 1778, labored for three months and then, after visiting "almost every section of [Virginia's] Eastern Shore, departed as quietly and mysteriously as they had come."

The first Methodist missionary of record to push south of the lower Pocomoke into Virginia was Freeborn Garrettson. In late 1778, while itinerating through Sussex, Somerset, and Worcester counties, Garrettson also preached on the Eastern Shore of Virginia. By early January 1779 Francis Asbury reported, "Already I am informed that there is gracious work going on in . . . Accomack and Northampton counties in Virginia."

During the next two years a few other itinerants probably

pushed south into Virginia's Eastern Shore. In late December 1780 Samuel Roe was sent into the area and preached for a few weeks before returning north to Maryland and Delaware. More permanent was the work of Henry Willis, who followed Roe into the area. In 1784, when a circuit was finally established to serve Virginia's Eastern Shore, Willis became its first itinerant. By that time Accomack and Northampton counties together contained one hundred Methodists, including some local gentry. Now there were Methodists in every county on the Peninsula.[24]

The American Revolution

As they itinerated through the Peninsula, Methodist preachers spoke primarily of God's Kingdom. But they couldn't completely ignore the attitudes and emotions unleashed in the secular world by the American Revolution. Methodism was the evangelizing wing—officially unrecognized and unappreciated to be sure—of the Anglican Church. Because the Anglican Church was the state Church of England and headed by King George III, it was looked upon by many Americans as just another British institution and a reminder of British colonialism. Moreover, most colonial Anglican clergy were regarded as agents of the British crown.

True independence from Great Britain couldn't be won as long as the Church of England remained the established church in such colonies as Virginia and Maryland. Disestablishment of the Church of England, however, was initially opposed by Methodists. In 1776, for example, most of Virginia's dissenting faiths supported a petition to disestablish the Anglican Church. But Virginia's Methodists opposed this, pointing out that they were, after all, a religious society in communion with the Church of England. It is no wonder that American revolutionaries regarded Methodists with the same suspicion that they held for many devout Anglicans and their clergy.

Often judged guilty by association, American Methodists made matters worse by being so dependent on British preachers. In 1775, for example, almost half of the itinerating preachers in America were Englishmen. On top of that came the pro-British statements and actions by Methodists on both sides of the Atlantic.

The Charge of Toryism

John Wesley started it all in 1775 by taking a strong Tory position in his *Calm Address to the American Colonies*. A second problem for the Methodists was a commonly held view on the Peninsula that the secretary of state for the colonies, Lord Dartmouth, had been appointed because of his Methodist contacts. Dartmouth, it was said, sent Methodist missionaries to the colonies "to preach nonresistance."

Matters were further inflamed by the actions of British itinerant Martin Rodda. Assigned to the Peninsula in the spring of 1777, Rodda proceeded to get himself arrested by August for fomenting a Tory insurrection along the Queen Anne's–Caroline border. Released after a few weeks, Rodda circulated a British proclamation to the effect that all rebels would be pardoned if they renewed their allegiance to the crown. In the fall of 1777, the British army occupied Wilmington and New Castle. On October 18 a Methodist preacher—probably Rodda—entered the pulpit of Immanuel Anglican Church in New Castle and gave "a long and full prayer for the King and a blessing on his arms." Evidently, to avoid arrest, Rodda had fled to British-controlled New Castle. He subsequently made his way to Philadelphia and, finally, back to England. In 1778 itinerant John Littlejohn made ready to cross the Chesapeake to visit Asbury on the Peninsula. Littlejohn's friends objected, warning that "such was the rage of the people" against Methodists "on account of Rodda's conduct on the Peninsula" that Littlejohn might be killed.

In all probability, the actions of a few other itinerants on the Peninsula supported rebel suspicions. In addition to Rodda, other Methodist preachers were allegedly involved in the Tory insurrection along the Queen Anne's-Caroline border. All of this convinced Caesar Rodney of Delaware that Methodist preachers were recruiting a Tory unit along the Maryland border in 1777.[25]

Just as damaging to the Methodist reputation were the actions of Chaney Clow. In 1778 the English-born Clow, once of some importance in his local Methodist society but now "a backslidden Methodist," raised a force of a few hundred Tories near his home in Kent County, Delaware, very close to the Maryland line, and erected a fort. Clow's force created a stir in Maryland, but it generally fled at the approach of the Maryland militia. A unit of the Delaware militia finally routed Clow's force and burned the fort. Although Clow and his followers continued activities in Maryland for the rest of 1778, they were more of a nuisance than a real threat. Clow was captured four years later and executed for murder in 1787.

Many of the facts of the Clow insurrection are still unclear, but Clow's actions clearly spelled trouble for the Methodists, because some Delawareans cited his Methodist connection as proof that

John Wesley's followers were Tories. A mob in Dover almost lynched Freeborn Garrettson after accusing him of being one of Clow's men. Luckily for the Methodists, Delaware President Caesar Rodney refused to be stampeded by demands that he crush the Methodists. Instead, he insisted on a count of the denominational affiliations of Clow's men. When only two turned out to be Methodists, Rodney saw no reason for action.[26]

Pacifism

Some of the charges of Toryism on Maryland's Eastern Shore could have been avoided if Methodist itinerants had been willing to take the oath of allegiance to Maryland. In October of 1777, the Maryland legislature passed an act requiring that every free male over eighteen sign a loyalty oath by March 1, 1778. Nonjurors—those refusing to sign—faced a number of restrictions on traditional rights, including the right to preach and travel. In Delaware, by contrast, clergymen were not required to take an oath.

Despite reservations by Garrettson and, to a lesser extent, Asbury, most Methodists would take oaths. The Maryland oath, however, created a particular problem. Unlike the loyalty oaths of such states as Virginia, Delaware, Pennsylvania, and New Jersey, which did not involve a pledge to fight, the Maryland oath implied that the signers must be willing to bear arms. This obligation was particularly upsetting to most Methodist preachers and many laymen because they were pacifists.

In the spring of 1776, the Methodist position on bearing arms was clearly stated by Thomas Rankin, Wesley's General Assistant in America. Speaking before a large gathering at the home of Carvil Hynson in Kent County, Maryland, Rankin pointed out that

> it was a principle of conscience alone that the people called Methodists do not take up arms as others had done; and therefore, if we are called to suffer on this account we will suffer for conscience sake.

A pacifist conscience prevented most Methodists from taking the Maryland oath, but not the Delaware oath. Although itinerant Joseph Hartley was exempted from signing the less objectionable Delaware oath, he signed it anyway. But not all itinerants had problems with the Maryland oath. Joseph Everett and possibly Joshua Dudley signed their allegiance to the government in Annapolis. It was probably for this reason that Asbury sent the two into

Thomas Rankin
(Courtesy: Methodist Collection, Drew University, Madison, NJ)

Dorchester County in 1780, after Garrettson had been locked up in the county jail.[27]

The American Revolution and the Methodist Position

In retrospect, the actions and attitudes of Delmarva's Methodists concerning the American Revolution were understandable. Attachment to the Church of England made many reluctant to cut their ties with the mother country. Moreover, the Toryism of John Wesley and British preachers such as Martin Rodda reinforced that reluctance.

By 1777, however, most of the British preachers had left for England, and the American Methodists left behind seemed willing to accept the inevitable. In 1777 Asbury bemoaned Wesley's Tory stand, regretting "that the venerable man ever dipped into the politics of America." He wrote Thomas Rankin that same year that he expected and willingly accepted American independence.

Military participation on either side by Delmarva's Methodists—by 1781 they numbered approximately 3 or 4 percent of the Peninsula's adult population—was restricted, of course, by their commitment to pacifism. Militia recruiters reported hard going in areas where Methodism was strong. One disgusted militia commander in Caroline County said that when military prospects "embrace the Methodist faith, they change their attitude toward war." Evidently, some frustrated mustering officers dealt harshly with Methodists. Thomas Rankin heard that on Maryland's Eastern Shore some Methodists "were dragged by horses over stones and stumps of trees till death put a period to their suffering."

Also discouraging participation on either side during the American Revolution were the priorities of these early Methodists. The Kingdom of God was of critical significance, while the political affectations of men were of secondary import. In his study of Delaware during the American Revolution, John Munroe notes that "the Methodists were more interested in freeing themselves from sin than freeing their land from the British." That generalization is applicable to the entire Peninsula.[28]

Military Developments and the Methodist Image

After 1778 the persecution of Methodists abated considerably. In part, this reflected a decrease in Tory activity on the Peninsula. Delmarva's exposed geographic position and its numerous tidewater rivers and creeks, which gave some access to the interior, made it vulnerable to attack by sea. The almost continuous presence of British ships in nearby waters, numerous raiding incursions, the rumors of imminent invasion, and a large Tory population made Delmarva Whigs particularly paranoid. Presbyterian New Castle County was fairly firm in its support of independence, but much of the rest of the Peninsula seemed, at times, to be Tory country. Loyalist insurrections broke out in Sussex, Somerset, Worcester, and elsewhere during the early years of the Revolution.

On August 25, 1777, General Howe's army landed in Cecil County and began a cross-country march through New Castle County and southeastern Pennsylvania, which ended in the capture of Philadelphia. News of the British landing spread shock waves up and down the Peninsula, and Whigs adopted strong measures to suppress dissent.

With the British evacuation of Philadelphia in June 1778 and the British army's subsequent overland march through New Jersey to New York, Tory activities on the Peninsula subsided. Although occasional British raids by sea or Tory forays on land continued, Delmarva's Whigs became less paranoid during the last years of the war. Consequently, they tended to act more judiciously in their attempts to ferret out and punish loyalists. A case in point was Whig Caesar Rodney's refusal to "crush the Methodists" without conclusive proof of their complicity in Chaney Clow's rebellion. As late as 1780 Asbury continued to exhibit a persecution complex, but after that date the Tory label was rarely applied to Methodists on the Peninsula.[29]

As the ebb and flow of military events became more favorable to the revolutionary cause, another source of paranoia concerning Methodism also diminished. In Philadelphia, Methodist Thomas Rankin did not hesitate to point out to several members of the Second Continental Congress that it was a "farce" for them to fight for liberty while simultaneously keeping "hundreds of thousands of blacks in cruel bondage." On the Peninsula, itinerants such as Garrettson, Asbury, William Watters, and others called for the emancipation of blacks. Understandably, when there was unrest among the Peninsula's black population, some whites were quick to blame the Methodists. The specter of a slave insurrection was a terrifying vision to contemplate, particularly while British troops were occupying sections of the Peninsula or when British landing parties could plunder and pillage at will. The withdrawal of British forces from Philadelphia, in the summer of 1778, considerably diminished the fear of slave insurrection.

By 1782 the Maryland legislature was so confident that the American Revolution had nothing to fear from Methodists that it allowed the followers of John Wesley to preach without taking the loyalty oath.[30]

Asbury and the Methodist Image

Part of the improved Methodist image was due to Francis Asbury. Designated John Wesley's General Assistant in charge of the Methodist societies in America in 1772, Asbury became just another itinerant the following year when his position was taken by the newly arrived Thomas Rankin. Rankin shared Wesley's views on the American Revolution and became increasingly distrusted by American authorities. While discrete on some occasions, Rankin declared from the pulpit of St. George's in Philadelphia that God's work would not revive until the people submitted to the

Francis Asbury
(Courtesy, Methodist Collection, Drew University, Madison, NJ)

king. In August 1775 Rankin informed Asbury that he intended to return to England. Asbury responded that the work in America was so important that he certainly wouldn't leave. Two years later Rankin sailed for England leaving the American Methodists leaderless. By the end of 1778, of the eight missionaries sent over by Wesley, five had returned to Great Britain, one had left the ministry, one had become a Presbyterian minister, and one, Francis Asbury, had dropped out of sight.

There was good reason for Asbury's disappearance. While Howe's army was invading the Peninsula, Asbury was preaching on Maryland's Western Shore. Much on his mind was the deadline of March 1, 1778, for signing the state oath. On December 1, 1777, Asbury set out for the Peninsula, not quite sure of his specific destination. In other years he had preached at the northern end of the Peninsula and had been generally well received. His mind, however, was uneasy because of the unsettled times. Methodists already were in ill repute with Peninsula Whigs, thanks to Martin Rodda's actions. Asbury roamed unmolested through the upper Eastern Shore and adjacent parts of Delaware for a few months, but increasingly his journal projected dark forbodings. One of the few bright notes was that "the martial threatening aspect of the times had a great tendency to keep me close to God."[31]

In mid-February 1778, searching for security, Asbury arrived in Delaware at the home of Judge Thomas White, a minor Tory magistrate. White lived approximately fifteen miles southwest of Dover, close to the Maryland line, in a heavily forested area near Whiteleysburg. As in a number of cases on the Peninsula, Judge White's wife, Mary, was first converted and then led her husband to the Methodist persuasion. Martin Rodda, in 1777, had been the first Methodist itinerant to visit Thomas White's. In December 1777 Asbury had preached there.

In addition to his Methodist friends, Thomas White was also well connected with the conservative faction that controlled the Delaware government from 1776 to early 1778. Unfortunately for White and Asbury, the power of the conservative faction was now on the wane and the Whigs were taking control. To make matters worse for White, the Whigs remembered that he had taken part in a Tory insurrection in Kent County in 1776.

From mid-February to April 1778, Asbury remained in partial concealment at White's, making only a few short ventures into southern Delaware and nearby Maryland. Much of the time Asbury lived out back, in a building screened from the main house by a stand of trees. During February and March, Methodist preachers visited Asbury, and he conducted religious services and a quarterly meeting at White's or at nearby locations. Asbury's effectiveness at these services is attested to by Joseph Everett of Queen Anne's County. A member of the Maryland militia and a persecutor of Methodists, Everett's curiosity brought him to an evening meeting at White's on March 14. Asbury's message marked a turning point in Everett's life, starting him down a new road that led, two years later, to the Methodist ministry.

Now that Thomas Rankin had left for England, the native-born itinerants increasingly regarded Asbury as their leader. After all, he had preceded Rankin as General Assistant and he did represent the only available direct link with John Wesley.

On April 2, Thomas White was arrested by order of the Continental Congress. Asbury felt in real danger. He remained at White's for four days and then crossed into Maryland. Fearful of arrest, Asbury spent one day hiding out in a swamp and then made his way to Methodist John Fogwell's near Sudlersville, Queen Anne's County. Fogwell, a reformed drunkard, provided a private room and here Asbury remained in hiding for three weeks. But even at Fogwell's he didn't feel secure. The general area was the scene of Tory activity countered by rebel militia forays. Still very concerned over his own safety—he was, after all, an Englishman and a Methodist to boot—Asbury returned to Delaware and Thomas White's on April 29.

In the meantime, favorable events nationally and in Delaware led that state's Whigs to establish a more moderate position toward Tories. Also contributing to an improvement in White's situation was the inevitable tension between state and national governments. Congress had ordered White's arrest, but Delaware balked at having him removed from the state without specific charges being filed against him. On May 9, 1778, Thomas White rejoined his family. He was subsequently put on parole, and on August 3, 1779, his name was cleared by act of Congress at the insistence of the Delaware delegation.[32]

Asbury remained on the Peninsula until April 21, 1780, spending much of that time at White's. During Asbury's stay, most Peninsula Whigs ceased assuming that Asbury and his fellow Methodists were automatically Tories. Pivotal in this change of attitude was the interception of a letter written by Asbury.

While waiting passage to England from British-occupied Philadelphia in 1777, Thomas Rankin wrote Asbury that Americans should "submit to their rightful sovereign, the English King." Asbury replied from the Peninsula that he was so strongly attached to many of the Americans that he couldn't tear himself away. Moreover, he was convinced that the Americans would not give up the struggle until they achieved independence, and he was confident that they would be successful in creating a new and independent nation. The letter was intercepted and read by American officers. Apparently Asbury wasn't aware of the interception until the spring of 1779, when he referred to the event as "agreeable news." Itinerant Thomas Ware was told, some years later, that the intercepted letter changed attitudes toward Asbury "so that he was afterward treated with more favor than he had been before."[33]

Asbury Assumes Leadership

Feeling more at liberty to itinerate, Asbury increasingly ventured forth from White's during the remainder of 1778 and the spring of 1779. For the most part, Asbury continued to be apprehensive about traveling, but his courage and character were being challenged by the examples of Freeborn Garrettson and Joseph Hartley. While the latter was braving jail sentences or physical assaults, Asbury was in hiding at Thomas White's or at John Fogwell's. In September 1778, after he had preached to a threatening mob in Dover, Garrettson wrote that Asbury's way "was open into any part of the state." That same month, Asbury screwed up his courage and visited Joseph Hartley, who was in the Talbot County jail at Easton. In November Asbury followed Garrettson's trail into Somerset County. He was surprised and relieved that, "not withstanding all apprehension of my mind, no person offered me the smallest insult."

It bothered Asbury that brother Garrettson could summon up such courage while he could only shudder at the prospect of trouble. In late December he voiced his frustrations:

> It is my deliberate opinion, that I do the least good, in the Church of Christ, of any that I know, and believe to be divinely moved to preach the Gospel. How am I displeased with myself! Lord in mercy help or I am undone indeed.

In later years Asbury felt obliged to defend his hiding out in Delaware during 1778–80. In 1810 he wrote that his "compelled seclusion in the beginning of the war, in the state of Delaware. . . , was the most active, the most useful and the most afflictive part of my life."[34]

Asbury's days in hiding and semiseclusion were particularly important for the long-term development of Methodism. Left to himself, he studied and thought a great deal about the future of Wesley's societies in America. He corresponded with or met most of the key Methodist preachers and was encouraged by much of what he heard. Garrettson and others might be on the cutting edge of the Methodist offensive, but the plans for the organizational machinery that would propel Methodism into every state in the Union were slowly taking shape in Asbury's mind while he waited in Delaware for the storm to pass.

While Asbury pondered the future of Methodism, societies continued to grow in number and in membership. In 1775 there were 3,148 Methodists and 19 preachers in America. By 1779 there were 8,577 Methodists and 49 preachers. Approximately 35 percent of the laity and 40 percent of the itinerants were located north of the Potomac, most heavily concentrated in the Western and Eastern Shores of Maryland and in Delaware.

By early 1779 Asbury had assumed supervision of the seventeen itinerants serving circuits north of the Potomac. In April 1779 Asbury used his influence to organize a Preparatory Conference at Thomas White's, one month prior to the Annual Conference of Methodist preachers which was to be held in Fluvanna County, Virginia.[35] To understand Asbury's reason for calling the Preparatory Conference, it is necessary to look at some significant developments.

"Old Methodism"

Francis Asbury was a loyal disciple of John Wesley. He regarded Wesleyan theology and practices, brought to America by official missionaries like himself, as a precious inheritance that must be preserved as the very essence of American Methodism. Asbury called this Wesleyan inheritance "old Methodism."

"Old Methodism" insisted on an itinerating clergy because a situated clergy would fall prey to the same snares that bedeviled many in the Anglican priesthood. "Old Methodism" held that the Wesleyan movement was a reform movement within the broad Anglican community and must remain part of that community. "Old Methodism" believed that the sacraments of baptism and communion should be administered only by ordained Anglican priests and not by unordained Methodist preachers. "Old Methodism" affirmed that Methodist societies must be bound together in a connectional way, governed in a centralized, autocratic fashion.

"Old Methodism" was challenged at the outset when Robert Strawbridge administered the sacraments to Methodists on the Western Shore of Maryland. A second challenge came from Boardman and Pilmore, who let it be known, shortly after their arrival in 1769, that they were against extensive itinerating and wished to situate in the comfortable surroundings of New York and Philadelphia.

The first two annual conferences of Methodist preachers took a clear stand in favor of "old Methodism." In 1773 the preachers affirmed John Wesley's authority over American Methodism. In an obvious slap at Strawbridge, preachers were barred from administering baptism and the Lord's Supper, and directed to exhort Methodists to attend Anglican services and to receive the sacraments there. In 1774, thanks to a motion by Asbury, the Annual Conference decided to enforce itinerancy.[36]

The Decline of the Mother Church

During the American Revolution the Anglican Church, the anchor of "old Methodism," suffered almost irreparable damage because of its ties with the English crown and the suspect political allegiances of some of its clergy and laity. On the Peninsula, activities of some Anglican clergy and laity supported these suspicions. Of the twenty-one clergy on Maryland's Eastern Shore in 1774, only eight took the Maryland loyalty oath. Unlike the situation with the Methodists, pacifism was not a significant contributing factor to Anglican reluctance. So strong was Anglican Toryism in Accomack County, Virginia, that, according to one recent account, a mock funeral for George Washington was held at St. James Church in 1779, complete with ritual, pall bearers, and coffin.

Anti-Anglican feeling wasn't long in surfacing, expressing itself in disestablishment in Maryland in 1776 and in Virginia in 1779. In Delaware, of course, there had never been an established church.

The dismal state of Delmarva Anglicanism was reflected by the numerical drop in Anglican clergy from more than thirty just prior to the American Revolution to less than fifteen by 1780. Moreover, some of those remaining, like Sydenham Thorne of Milford, were restricted in their clerical activities. So grave had the situation become by 1784 that a frustrated Anglican (Episcopal) layman, with some exaggeration, lamented that there were but two Anglican clergymen "on this whole Peninsula, and one of these is a drunkard."[37]

Loyalty to the Mother Church

In Great Britain, Anglicans were long embarrassed by the Methodist connection. In America during the Revolution, however, this embarrassment could have been reversed. "Old Methodism," nevertheless, demanded an affirmation of and good relations with the Anglican Church. On the Peninsula, Asbury and his itinerants set out to strengthen their Anglican ties and were aided by the willingness of three evangelical Anglican clergymen—Syndenham Thorne, Hugh Neill, and Samuel Magaw—to work with the Methodists.

Relations had not been good on the Peninsula between Methodists and Anglicans in earlier years. In 1773 and 1774, for example, itinerants William Watters, Abraham Whitworth, and Philip Gatch found themselves under verbal attack by Samuel Keene of St. Luke's Parish in northern Queen Anne's County. Even Asbury had problems with Anglican clerics. About to preach in Kent County in 1772, he was confronted by the Reverend Robert Read, who claimed that he, not Asbury, had sole responsibility for people's souls. When Asbury ignored Read's claims and preached anyway, Read fell into a rage and charged that Asbury "spoke against learning."[38]

In subsequent years, however, it became evident to Anglicans that Methodist leadership was determined that its preachers not administer the sacraments and that Methodist preaching hours not conflict with regular Church of England services. While itinerating on the northern Eastern Shore in early July 1775, Methodists Thomas Rankin and Captain Webb struck up a friendly relationship with the formerly hostile Samuel Keene. But Rankin and Webb soon returned to England, leaving responsibility for Methodist-Anglican relationships in the hands of Francis Asbury and the American-born preachers.

Whenever possible, Asbury attended Anglican services. One Sunday in 1779, for example, Asbury "preached at 9:00 o'clock at Boyer's, then went to the Church [Christ Church] at Dover; and preached in the woods at 3:00 o'clock." Because of Asbury's insistence that Methodists support the Anglican Church, the three evangelical priests—Magaw of Dover, Neill of St. Paul's Parish, Queen Anne's, and Thorne of Milford—began to warm to Asbury and his movement. Moreover, the Methodist impact was clearly desirable: the Methodists awakened the populace, and then the awakened sought out Anglican churches, in numbers that "increase daily," for the Lord's Supper. By April 16, 1779, Magaw had so warmed to Asbury's presence in the Dover area that Asbury thought it the time to present "his view on the whole plan of Methodism." Magaw liked "old Methodism" and, joined by Thorne and Neill, began participating in Methodist services.

On October 31, 1779, for example, Asbury and other Methodists attended an Anglican service in the presence of Magaw, Neill, and Thorne. By this time Neill, a nonjuring Maryland clergyman, was probably residing in the more tolerant boundaries of Delaware. The Methodists received the sacraments and then heard Neill and Magaw preach. A Methodist Quarterly Meeting followed the next day and the three Anglican priests "attended with great friendship," while they listened to Asbury, Garrettson, and another itinerant preach. The following day the three Anglican priests were presented with the rules and other information concerning Methodism and "were willing to give . . . all the assistance they could by word and deed."[39]

Magaw was of particular help to the Methodists by offering lodging to Asbury and by participating in Methodist services. Moreover, his presence at Methodist gatherings reduced local prejudice against the Wesleyan preachers. One disputed claim has Magaw, in 1779, giving the Methodists Thomas's Chapel, their first home of worship in Delaware. In all probability, Magaw simply officiated at the initial service at the chapel after Methodists had constructed it. Of particular significance was Magaw's help in introducing Asbury and other itinerants to some of the wealthier and more influential families in the Dover area. Finally, the two worked together to found a short-lived school for boys in Dover.

Magaw's friendship with Asbury and the Methodists continued long after the two left the Peninsula. After Magaw moved on to the rectorship of St. Paul's, Philadelphia, in 1781, he invited at least one Methodist into the pulpit and had former Methodist itinerant Joseph Pilmore serve as his assistant for a number of years. As late as 1783, Magaw was attending Methodist Quarterly Meetings in the Philadelphia area. Moreover, when Asbury spoke in Philadelphia, Magaw was often in the audience.

Just how well the Anglicans and the Methodists worked together on the Peninsula was exemplified in the funeral of an elderly couple in Judge White's barn in March 1780. Magaw preached the funeral sermon, itinerant Joseph Cromwell gave "a pretty long and rough" exhortation, followed by a second exhortation by Hugh Neill. During that day, Asbury seems to have assisted Magaw in baptizing children.[40]

There continued to be friction between some Anglican priests and Methodist itinerants. Certainly, Samuel Tingley's attack on

Freeborn Garrettson in Lewes in 1779 is a case in point. But in the heart of the Peninsula, where Francis Asbury planted firmly the banner of "old Methodism," the Methodists and Anglicans worked together in bringing the Christian message to the area's inhabitants.

The Virginia Challenge

Virginia was another story. In November 1779, Asbury received an alarming note from Devereaux Jarratt, rector of Bath Parish, Dinwiddie County, Virginia. Jarratt had long been a friend of Methodists in the manner of Magaw, Neill, and Thorne. In 1773 pioneer Methodist itinerant Robert Williams stayed for a week with Jarratt in Virginia. While there, Williams assured the Anglican rector that Methodists were true members of the Church of England, and that their purpose was to build up rather than divide the Church. Jarratt took Williams at his word and became a Methodist in everything but name. It was a disturbed Jarratt who wrote to Asbury that Methodists in his area now wanted to serve the sacraments. Asbury unhappily noted the growing separation betwen Methodists and Anglicans in Virginia and North Carolina. He realized that despite all of his "labour to unite the [Anglican] ministry to us," the Methodists south of the Potomac were creating division.[41]

Jarratt's note may have been alarming, but it certainly wasn't unexpected. During the American Revolution, the flight of so many Anglican priests and the restrictions imposed on many who remained behind left large areas of the American South without ordained clergy. With no ordained Anglicans to administer the sacraments, many Methodist preachers were tempted to give in to public pressure and provide baptism and the Lord's Supper.

At the Annual Conference of 1777, held in Harford County, Maryland, it was affirmed that "the old plan" concerning the administration of the sacraments would be followed for another year. However, the issue of sacraments was hotly debated and it was unanimously agreed to take it up again the next year. At the Annual Conference at Leesburg, Virginia, in 1778, no decisive action was taken, but the divisive nature of the issue was increasingly recognized, and the next Annual Conference at Broken Back Church, Fluvanna County, Virginia, would be crucial.

From Judge White's home in Delaware, Asbury exercised control over Methodism north of the Potomac, but he had little influence in Virginia and North Carolina where the majority of Methodists lived. In those two states a young, native-born ministry had taken command, and it had little reverence for the Church of England. Predictably, Virginia Methodists reversed an earlier position by joining the Baptists in 1779 in supporting the disestablishment of Anglicanism.[42]

The Preparatory Conference of 1779

In the early spring of 1779, a very concerned Francis Asbury pondered the decisions that would be made at the Annual Conference to be held in Virginia in May. The military focus of the American Revolution had shifted to the South, and travel for Methodist preachers in that direction—particularly for those suspected of Tory sympathies—was difficult and dangerous. But without some representation of the views of the northern preachers, the Annual Conference would reflect only the interests and sentiments of the southern itinerants and would certainly sanction administration of the sacraments by Methodist preachers. Surely this action would rupture the strong ties with Anglicanism insisted on by Wesley and Asbury.

Intent on heading off this challenge to "old Methodism," Asbury called for a preparatory conference of the northern itinerants at Judge White's in April 1779. Because the conference at White's was deliberately regional, it was the first sectional annual conference of American Methodism. The site was within easy traveling distance for most of the northern brethren, and its forested surroundings and isolated location in southwestern Kent County, Delaware, offered the privacy that the participants wanted. Sixteen northern preachers and William Watters of Fairfax Circuit, Virginia, attended.

The Preparatory Conference took a predictably strong stand against any action by Methodists that would lead to separation from the Church of England. It also chose Asbury as Wesley's General Assistant in America, a position previously held by Asbury in 1772. Asbury was elected General Assistant because of his age— at thirty-three he was older than the other itinerants—his previous experience, and his link with John Wesley. For the first time the General Assistant's powers were spelled out in the Conference minutes. He was responsible for assigning itinerants to circuits and, after listening to debate, for making final decisions on issues concerning Methodism in America—awesome powers indeed!

Asbury Stands Firm

One month after the Preparatory Conference at Judge White's, the Annual Conference was held in Fluvanna County, Virginia, with only southern preachers in attendance. William Watters returned from the Preparatory Conference with the sentiments of the northern preachers and letters from Asbury. The southern preachers, choosing to ignore the views of their northern brethren, voted to ordain themselves and then administer the sacraments. The southern itinerants were now on the brink of creating a schismatic church.[43]

Asbury received the minutes of the Fluvanna Conference and lamented the action of the southern brethren. He was unwilling, however, to accept the decision at Fluvanna. He decided that firmness combined with a conciliatory tone would bring the southern preachers back into "old Methodism." By July he was writing "to our dissenting brethren in Virginia."[44] But Jarratt's note, that November, was not reassuring.

In 1780 the northern itinerants again had their own Annual Conference, this time in Baltimore. On April 20, Asbury left Delaware for the conference. Three weeks earlier he had received a conciliatory note from southern itinerant William Moore, intimating that reconciliation was possible if healing measures were adopted. Now, leaving behind the Peninsula where he had built Methodism on John Wesley's model, Asbury wrote, "If I cannot keep up old Methodism in any other place, I can in the peninsula: that must be my last retreat."

At Baltimore, Asbury's leadership was reaffirmed and the dissenting southern preachers were declared out of the Methodist connection. Asbury, Garrettson, and Watters were then sent to the annual meeting of the southern itinerants in Virginia and a last-minute compromise was worked out. The southern preachers promised to hold off on administering sacraments for one year so that Wesley might be consulted on the issue. Wesley responded with strong support for Asbury's position. That, along with a fence-mending trip by Asbury through the South in 1780, calmed the waters and kept American Methodism temporarily united with the Anglican Church under the old Wesleyan plan. Only a few local preachers in the South continued the administration of the sacraments.[45]

The Peninsula: A Strong Support Base

The victory of "old Methodism" was possible because Asbury, during his almost two and a half years of semiseclusion on the Peninsula, built up a broad base of popular support. Restricted as his traveling was during those years, he still managed to preach often, particularly in central and southern Delaware. In addition, Asbury's presence seemed to inspire the other itinerants to work harder and longer, and their diligence bore fruit. In the spring of 1777, approximately seven months prior to Asbury crossing over from the Western Shore of Maryland, only about 13 percent of American Methodists lived on the Peninsula. In 1781, a year after Asbury ended his Peninsula stay, Delmarva's Methodists represented 27 percent of the national total. Moreover, one of Methodism's most famous itinerants, Jesse Lee, singled out the Peninsula as the place, in 1781, "experiencing the greatest revival of religion among us."

Although he had been much frustrated by his confinement on the Peninsula, Asbury sensed that it had provided him with time to reflect and the popular support he needed in order to stand firm on the issue of the sacraments and on the larger issue of the preservation of "old Methodism." As Asbury left the Peninsula on April 21, 1780, he noted his "tender feelings for the people I left behind; this makes me think I must return." The next day Asbury admitted that he could not pray for the friends that he left behind "without weeping."[46]

Chapter Three

Methodism Victorious, 1781–1820

When Garrettson, Asbury, and other itinerants pushed down the Peninsula during the American Revolution, they were met by curious farmers who had never seen a Methodist (in at least one case by someone who hadn't even heard of Jesus Christ), by threatening mobs, physical violence, arrest, and imprisonment. These were hard times, and for a while it was questionable whether the small, newly founded Methodist societies could survive.

In 1809, thirty-four years after first preaching on the Peninsula, Freeborn Garrettson made his final visit to Delmarva. He intended to spend three or four weeks traveling down the Chesapeake side and then back north along the east side. He wanted to preach to as many people as possible and to see some of his old friends. As Garrettson began his journey, he found camp-meeting notices everywhere. Persuaded by Richard Bassett and other leading laymen to attend as many as possible, he curtailed his preaching tour to visit camp meetings at Smyrna and Milford, Delaware.

Garrettson was astonished at what he saw. At Smyrna he proclaimed that "the people in this country must be either Methodists or nothing, for there is scarcely a minister of any other name." After the camp meeting at Milford, he made an almost identical observation.[1]

Asbury, on return trips to the Peninsula, was equally euphoric about Methodist progress. In 1803 it seemed "as if the whole Peninsula must be Methodized." He proclaimed in 1806 that "in Delaware the millenium has certainly begun." That same year he wrote Thomas Coke that in the spread of Methodism, "the Eastern Shore excells all." Indeed, so extraordinary were developments on the Peninsula that Asbury assured the English Methodist that it "will stretch the credibility of your British brethren."[2] The road to Methodist success on the Peninsula was not, however, without its bumps, potholes, and detours.

Part of "Old Methodism" Rendered Obsolete

By the spring of 1781, Asbury was back on the Peninsula. After preaching at several places, he met with about twenty itinerants at Judge White's to prepare for the Annual Conference scheduled for Baltimore on April 24.[3] Thanks to developments of the previous year, tension between northern and southern itinerants had considerably abated, with both groups recognizing Asbury's leadership. Asbury wished to finalize the ascendancy of "old Methodism" at the Baltimore conference and probably used the preparatory meeting to plan strategy and line up support. Two weeks later the Annual Conference in Baltimore declared "old Methodism" victorious when it defined Methodist preachers as those "determined . . . to preach the old Methodist doctrine."[4]

But at that very moment, events were unfolding a few hundred miles to the south of Baltimore that would render part of "old Methodism" obsolete. General Cornwallis was leading his British army northward toward its rendezvous with destiny at Yorktown. On October 19 Cornwallis surrendered his entire force to George Washington, assuring American ecclesiastical as well as political independence. Although American Methodists would continue "old Methodism's" emphasis on an itinerating clergy and a connectional, autocratic polity, the insistence on close ties to the Anglican Church would be abandoned.

Even before the battle of Yorktown, Peninsula Anglicans recognized that political realities made continued ties with the Church of England impossible. In 1780 Peninsula Anglicans took the first step in organizing the American Protestant Episcopal Church, but as this church eventually emerged it was so weakened by the American Revolution that it couldn't possibly meet the needs of the rapidly growing Methodist societies.

Growth During the Revolution

In 1775 there were only 3,148 Methodists in the thirteen colonies; by 1784 there were five times that number. Even more dramatic was the spectacular increase in Delmarva Methodists from 253 in 1775 to 4,604 in 1784. In 1775 Methodists represented considerably less than 1 percent of the Peninsula's adult (sixteen years and over) population; by 1784 they comprised approximately 6 percent. Since only a small minority of Americans—probably no more than 5 to 10 percent—belonged to any church during the late eighteenth century, by the end of 1784 Methodists considerably outnumbered any other single faith on the Peninsula and probably outnumbered the combined membership of Delmarva's other churches. Only in the Scotch-Irish country of the extreme north, where the Presbyterian influence was so strong, and on the Eastern Shore of Virginia, which had yet to feel the full force of the Methodist offensive, were Wesleyans outnumbered by other denominations.

The spectacular growth of Peninsula Methodism was reflected in national statistics. In 1775 about 9 percent of American Methodists lived on Delmarva; by 1784 the figure rose to 31 percent.[5]

On the Peninsula, first-generation Methodists didn't tolerate deadwood in their societies. Every Wesleyan went through a similar rite of passage that demanded a strong commitment and a personal confession of faith, carefully scrutinized by an itinerant. Sometimes even a strong commitment wasn't enough. In 1777, for example, Freeborn Garrettson was in southeastern Sussex examining prospective members. Evidently the procedure was exhausting for the examiner as well as the examinees. After admitting thirty new members, Garrettson was too tired to go on, forcing anxious applicants to wait for the itinerant's return at some future date.

Once accepted as a Methodist, the convert was assigned to a class meeting of approximately ten to fifteen members, where his or her spiritual progress was monitored by the class leader and other class members during weekly meetings. One can sense the anxiety and expectation that rippled through those class meetings when the leader turned to a member and said, "Sister, does your soul prosper?"

If the soul wasn't prospering and the brother or sister was guilty of "backsliding," he or she would be expelled from society. Even lay leaders were expelled for not measuring up to Methodist standards. Cases in point were the expulsions at Barratt's Chapel, north of Frederica, Kent County, Delaware. Fifteen trustees served the chapel during the late eighteenth century and, by 1804, three had been expelled from society.[6]

The Methodist message reached beyond the very selective membership of local societies to thousands of nonmembers who attended Methodist preaching. Robert Ayres best summarized the situation while itinerating through the central section of the Peninsula in 1785. He found that the large crowds that came to listen to the Wesleyan message were of two parts: the Methodist core who were the minority, and the non-Methodists who were the majority.[7]

Methodist success on Delmarva from 1775 to 1784 was reflected in the increase in circuits from one to seven and in the increase in itinerants from two to seventeen. The revolutionary era was also marked by the construction of a number of Methodist chapels. Prior to the American Revolution, Kent [Hynson's] Chapel in Kent County, Maryland, was the only Methodist house of worship on the Peninsula. In 1773 a chapel was built by Anglicans near the Caroline-Queen Anne's boundary. Subsequently the brick structure was confiscated by the Maryland government, turned over to a small Presbyterian congregation, and then passed on to the Methodists in 1778. The original Methodist Bridgetown Chapel continues today as a church on the Ridgely Charge and is probably the second-oldest Methodist church building still in use in the United States. During the last years of the American Revolution, Peninsula Methodists built a number of other chapels. By 1784 there were at least twenty Wesleyan houses of worship on the Peninsula with only Virginia's Eastern Shore without a Methodist chapel.[8]

Strained Relations

As Peninsula Methodism grew stronger, relations with the Anglican Church and its direct descendent, the American Protestant Episcopal Church, became less friendly. In part, the growing tension reflected the absence of Asbury, Samuel Magaw, and Hugh Neill, and the growing estrangement of Sydenham Thorne. By 1784 Neill was dead, Magaw was in Philadelphia, and Asbury was usually on the road directing the Methodist offensive elsewhere. Thorne, the only remaining member of the quartet that had worked hard to preserve Anglican-Methodist unity, had become critical of the Methodists in his sermons by 1786.

Signs of strain began to appear during the final years of the war. By 1782, a clerk of Christ Church, Dover, was making ready a verbal attack on a circuit rider in his area. That same year, further south in Worcester County, an Anglican vestryman strongly criticized Methodist preachers.[9]

In 1783 itinerant Thomas Ware was invited to preach at the Anglican church in Smyrna, Delaware. In the middle of the service, three men marched in Indian file down the aisle. The lead one announced that he was a vestryman and ordered Ware to leave. When the Methodist preacher refused, the vestryman grabbed Ware by the collar and commenced dragging him out of the church. "A giant of a man" named Skillington seized the vestryman and, cocking a huge fist, demanded that Ware be released. Skillington's fist and the threat of incarceration voiced by a judge in the congregation forced Ware's assailant to release the Methodist preacher and join his two companions in a hasty exit.

In 1784 Dr. William Smith, rector at Chestertown and one of the architects of the Protestant Episcopal Church, preached against the Methodists, calling them "enthusiasts." He was rebuked by a woman in the congregation who cried out, "Glory to God! If what I now feel be enthusiasm, let me always be an enthusiast."

That same year, English Methodist Thomas Coke, who had recently arrived from England and had been invited into the pulpit at St. Paul's in Philadelphia, was denied a similar opportunity in Cambridge, Maryland. The Anglican church in Cambridge hadn't been used for services for several years and had been frequently left open "for cows, and dogs, and pigs." In a decision that found the church divided along sex lines, the men prevailed over the women in the congregation, and Coke was denied access previously granted to domestic animals.[10]

Wesley Takes Action

Thomas Coke had been sent to America in 1784 by John Wesley with a specific purpose in mind. Wesley recognized that the tottering Anglican Church wasn't capable of providing enough ordained clergy to meet the sacramental needs of the growing number of American Methodists. He also knew that if immediate steps weren't taken, restive American Methodists would challenge Asbury's leadership and, ultimately, his own. Thanks to Asbury's determination, "old Methodism" was temporarily ascendant in America. But the fundamental problem that had already divided Methodists in 1779 remained. How much longer could Asbury restrain the Methodist societies, particularly those south of the Potomac? Back in 1770, Joseph Pilmore had anticipated this difficulty when he wrote, "The chief problem we labor under is the want of ordination."[11]

As a professed supporter and ordained clergyman of the Church of England, Wesley didn't relish the creation of an independent Methodist Church. He certainly didn't want to create a Methodist Church independent of his own authority. But he was a realist. When he asked the bishop of London to ordain Methodist missionaries to America, the bishop refused and Wesley couldn't wait any longer.

Early in 1784, he approached Methodist Thomas Coke who, like Wesley, was an ordained Anglican cleric. Wesley explained that he wanted Coke to provide American Methodists with strong leadership as well as the sacraments. After some thought, Coke agreed to go to America along with two unordained Methodist preachers, Richard Whatcoat and Thomas Veasey.

Wesley then ordained Whatcoat and Veasey as elders and Coke as Superintendent. His actions were contrary to Anglican practice, which insisted that only a bishop could ordain, and Wesley certainly wasn't an Anglican bishop. But he maintained that the ordinations were valid because they were based on practices followed in the early Church.

Coke's powers as Superintendent were basically those of a bishop. Once in America, Coke was to administer the sacraments and ordain itinerant preachers with the assistance of Whatcoat and Veasey. Of particular importance was Wesley's directive that Coke ordain Asbury as joint Superintendent.

Wesley's action not only met the sacramental needs of the American brethren but also provided for a hierarchy, headed by Asbury and Coke, answerable to himself. In the instructions that he sent with Coke, Wesley did acknowledge the ecclesiastical independence of the American brethren, but his words implied an anticipation that the American societies, although no longer part of the Anglican Church, would continue in connection with him.

Coke, Veasey, and Whatcoat landed in New York on November 3, 1784. Word of their mission had gone ahead, although details of Wesley's instructions would have to be subsequently spelled out. Once in America, Coke was willing to confide in Methodists but kept his silence in the presence of Anglican rectors.

Heading south to Philadelphia, Coke preached twice the same day at St. Paul's at the request of Samuel Magaw. No doubt he revealed little to that Anglican friend of "old Methodism." In the evening, Coke spoke at St. George's Methodist Chapel and then "opened to the society our new plan of church government." He had "reason to believe that they all rejoice in it."[12]

Coke and Whatcoat continued south into the Peninsula and by Friday, November 12, reached Smyrna, Delaware, where Whatcoat preached in the morning and Coke in the evening. The next day the two Englishmen reached Dover and were entertained by Richard Bassett. Although not yet a member of a Methodist society, Bassett had contributed a considerable amount of money for the building of Wesley Chapel in Dover. At Bassett's home, Coke met Freeborn Garrettson and was very impressed. Coke was taken by

Thomas Coke
(Courtesy, Methodist Collection, Drew University, Madison, NJ)

the fact that, although just beginning as an itinerant, Garrettson had put all of his energies at the disposal of Asbury "during the dreadful dispute concerning the ordinances [sacraments], and bore down all before him."[13]

Barratt's Chapel

Sunday, November 14, 1784, was an extraordinary day in the history of American Methodism. Announcements of circuit assignments were usually made by Asbury at the Annual Conference in May and again at the last Quarterly Conference of the year, usually held in November. The Quarterly Conference for the central Peninsula area was scheduled for November 14 at Barratt's Chapel, a plain but handsome two-story brick structure located in the midst of a forest about ten miles southeast of Dover. It was primarily through the generosity of Philip Barratt, Kent County sheriff and member of the landed gentry, that the chapel was built in 1780. It was considered, for a number of years, to be the "grandest" rural Methodist meeting house in the nation. It wasn't the largest in the United States, or even on the Peninsula—Blackiston Chapel southwest of Smyrna had a larger floor plan—but events of November 14 were about to make Barratt's Chapel the most important of the rural Methodist meeting houses. (Today it is the oldest house of worship built by American Methodists that is still in use.)

Interestingly enough, along with White's Chapel near Whitleysburg, Kent County, and Dudley's Chapel near Sudlersville, Queen Anne's County, Barratt's Chapel had a vestry room. The presence of the vestry room is further testimony to Peninsula Methodism's close ties with Anglicanism. On Sunday, November 14, however, this architectural symbol of ecclesiastical unity was ignored as Coke, Whatcoat, Asbury, and eleven itinerants initiated the creation of an independent Methodist church.[14]

Sunday started off normally enough for Coke and Whatcoat. At 6:00 A.M. a "very good congregation" gathered at the courthouse in Dover to hear Whatcoat give the message. Then, accompanied by Garrettson, it was on to the Quarterly Conference at Barratt's Chapel. The two English Methodists arrived at 10:00 A.M. and Coke preached on "Christ our wisdom, righteousness, sanctification and redemption."

As General Assistant, Francis Asbury had been touring the Peninsula since October 2. While Coke was preaching in Philadelphia at St. Paul's and St. George's, Asbury was getting acquainted

Barratt's Chapel, as sketched by Helen Lucia
(Courtesy, Helen Lucia)

White's Chapel
(Courtesy, Methodist Collection, Drew University, Madison, NJ)

with Methodists in Accomack County, Virginia. Asbury steadily made his way north, stopping to preach and to confer with circuit riders along the way. He had "some intimations" of Coke's arrival in America and thought that Coke might meet him at the Quarterly Meeting at Barratt's Chapel.

As Coke spoke from the pulpit to a packed house, Asbury entered the Chapel. Although he had never met Coke, Asbury must have instantly recognized the speaker. Coke tells us that after the sermon, "a plain, robust man came up to me in the pulpit, and kissed me. I thought it could be no other than Mr. Asbury, and I was not deceived." They must have made an incongruous pair, all 5′2″ of the corpulent, cherubic Coke in the arms of the tall, lean, ascetic Asbury. To the assembly looking on, however, it was an electric moment charged with emotion.

Then came the administration of the Lord's Supper, a great watershed in Methodist history. Assisted by Richard Whatcoat, Coke delivered the bread and wine to an estimated five or six hundred communicants. Asbury was surprised at Whatcoat's participation. Evidently, he knew that Coke was an ordained Anglican priest, but he didn't realize that Whatcoat had been recently ordained by Wesley.

Asbury was even more surprised—"shocked" was his word for it—when, later that day, Coke spelled out the details of his mission. Asbury, Coke, Whatcoat, and eleven other itinerants had gathered to dine at Widow Barratt's (Philip Barratt had died two weeks earlier) about a mile east of the chapel.

There, in privacy, Coke presented Asbury with the plan for Methodist independence. In retrospect, Coke's presentation seems almost academic. After all, with Whatcoat's participation in administering the Lord's Supper a few hours earlier, American Methodism had already made a symbolic declaration that it no longer needed the Anglican connection. In a rural chapel a precedent had been set: Methodists would henceforth take care of their own sacramental needs. Of course, Robert Strawbridge and itinerants south of the Potomac had administered baptism and the Lord's Supper prior to the victory of "old Methodism" in 1780. But the communion at Barratt's Chapel was different. It was sanctioned by Wesley and administered in the heartland of "old Methodism" by ordained Methodist preachers in the presence of Francis Asbury. The dye was cast! Although six more weeks would pass before an official declaration of independence for American Methodists would be drafted, that was little more than a formality. With considerable justification, Barratt's Chapel can call itself the Independence Hall of American Methodism.

As Coke went into details at Widow Barratt's, Asbury "expressed considerable doubts." On hearing that Wesley directed him to give up the position of General Assistant in order to serve as joint Superintendent with powers of a bishop, Asbury balked. In a response shaped by years of experience in America and, one suspects, by a newly developed desire to be independent of John Wesley, Asbury agreed to accept the joint Superintendency only if the preachers "unanimously" elected him.[15]

Asbury realized that American itinerants would more willingly take direction from a Superintendent they elected than from one whose only claim to power was by appointment from England. And he was taking no great gamble in calling for election; he was, after all, the recognized leader of the American preachers and could expect their strong support. Hadn't they already elected him General Assistant even before Wesley gave his official stamp of approval?

In demanding election, Asbury was also sending a message to Wesley and all other interested parties. Years of leadership experience had left Asbury with considerable self-confidence and the realization that American independence had extraordinary implications for every aspect of American life. In 1779 Asbury considered close ties to the Church of England and Wesley a necessity. By 1784, however, new conditions dictated new relationships. Asbury was putting Wesley on notice that, henceforth, Wesley's authority over American Methodism would be limited. Wesley's theology would continue to be central, his character and writings revered, but his directives would no longer carry the force of law.[16]

What Were Wesley's Intentions?

But wasn't that exactly what Wesley wanted when he wrote to his American brethren, in 1784, that they were "now at full liberty simply to follow the scriptures and the Primitive Church"? Other evidence indicates that Wesley may have had some other possibility in mind. One view has Wesley really attempting to give American Methodists just enough autonomy so that they could survive in a holding pattern until an American Protestant Episcopal Church would arise, phoenixlike, from the ashes of the colonial Anglican Church. Then the Methodist societies would "dovetail" nicely into that new, but still very English, church.[17]

Freeborn Garrettson's personal copy of his published journal throws some new light on Wesley's intentions. Perhaps preparing for a future reissue of his journal (originally published in 1791), Garrettson penned in corrections. Most did little to alter the substance of his story, but when he dealt with Wesley's intent in sending Coke to America, Garrettson made a significant alteration. His published journal stated that Wesley made American Methodists very happy "in sending a power of ordination and giving his consent to our becoming a separate church." In editing, Garrettson struck out the phrase, "and giving his consent." New information and mature reflection on events at Barratt's Chapel, Widow Barratt's home, and the subsequent conferences in Baltimore and elsewhere must have convinced Garrettson that Coke, Asbury, and company had gone a bit further than Wesley had intended.[18]

After Coke and Asbury privately discussed Wesley's plan, they opened the question of an independent Methodist Episcopal Church to the other preachers gathered at Widow Barratt's. After some debate, the assembled Methodist itinerants unanimously decided to call all of the preachers in America to the now famous Christmas Conference in Baltimore. Freeborn Garrettson was "sent off . . . like an arrow" to the south as far as Methodist itinerants could be found, sending off messengers along the way "right and left," to summon all the preachers to Baltimore.

Nearly sixty preachers gathered for the ten-day conference that started on Christmas Eve, 1784, in Lovely Lane Chapel. The assembled itinerants declared themselves members of the independent Methodist Episcopal Church. They also hammered out the organizational details and unanimously elected Asbury joint Superintendent. Thus was created, according to Methodist historian Abel Stevens, "by its precedent organization and its subsequent numerical importance, the real successor to the Anglican Church in America."[19]

Coke's Itinerancy

Thomas Coke presided over the Christmas Conference. In the interim between the Barratt's Chapel meeting and the Christmas Conference, Coke had found out something of Francis Asbury's priorities. While at Widow Barratt's, Asbury presented Coke with a preaching schedule that would cover an estimated eight hundred to a thousand miles, primarily on the Peninsula, in less than five weeks. The rotund little Englishman must have been taken aback by such vast distances to be covered in this raw, new land in such a short time span. But Coke suppressed his dismay, and Asbury provided him with a horse and black preacher Harry Hosier as a companion.

English Methodism had been most successful in serving the populations of the towns and cities of Great Britain. Because of where they lived, English Methodists could gather for preaching in large groups at almost any hour. Early morning, midday, and evening services were equally common. By contrast, American Methodism had its greatest success in the countryside where farmers lived considerable distances from each other. The implications were clear to Coke after only a few days of itinerating on the Peninsula. Except in large towns, the best time for preaching in America was in the middle of the day.[20]

Coke's route, mapped by Asbury, brought him as far south as the heart of Virginia's Eastern Shore and then, in a zig-zag path, back north to Kent County, Maryland. Certainly the unsophisticated, overwhelmingly rural population of the Peninsula represented quite a challenge to the sophisticated, Oxford-educated Dr. Coke. To the rough, uneducated farmers and watermen, Coke's urbane appearance, mannerisms, and particularly his voice which, when raised to a very high pitch, could be "harsh, discordant, and squeaking," seemed foreign. What a contrast to the rugged, earthy types who usually rode the circuits of Delmarva. And yet Coke was generally well received—after all, he was providing the sacraments of baptism and the Lord's Supper to people who hadn't partaken in years—and his journey, though covering less mileage than initially estimated, had considerable impact on the Peninsula.

Even before he left Barratt's Chapel, Coke was impressed by what he had seen. In Dover there had been a good congregation to hear Whatcoat, and at Barratt's Chapel "it was the best season" he ever knew, "except at Charlemount, in Ireland." The service at the chapel must have been an extraordinary experience for all. Freeborn Garrettson, writing in 1791, said he "never saw a greater meeting than we had at Barratt's Chapel."[21]

From Barratt's Chapel, Coke's first stop was at White's Chapel on the farm of Judge White, near Whitleysburg, in southwest Kent County, Delaware. The judge was now the general steward of the local Methodist circuit. Here Coke preached to a "moderate congregation and baptized many children." He rode into western Sussex County, stopping southwest of Bridgeville at Brown's Chapel (named for Judge White's nephew, White Brown, who donated the land for the meetinghouse). From there it was south to Moore's

Thomas Coke's Journey through the Delmarva Peninsula in 1784

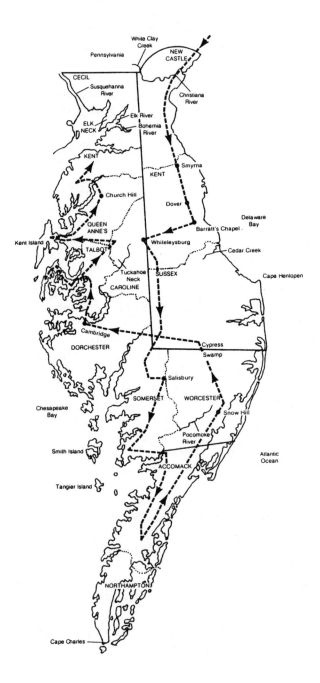

White Clay Creek

Pennsylvania

NEW CASTLE

CECIL

Susquehanna River

Christiana River

Elk River

ELK NECK

Bohemia River

KENT

Smyrna

KENT

Church Hill

Dover

Delaware Bay

QUEEN ANNE'S

Barratt's Chapel

Kent Island

Whiteleysburg

Cedar Creek

TALBOT

Cape Henlopen

Tuckahoe Neck

SUSSEX

CAROLINE

Cambridge

Cypress Swamp

DORCHESTER

Salisbury

SOMERSET

WORCESTER

Chesapeake Bay

Snow Hill

Pocomoke River

Smith Island

Atlantic Ocean

ACCOMACK

Tangier Island

NORTHAMPTON

Cape Charles

Chapel, west of Laurel (named for the many people of this surname in that society).

Saturday and Sunday, November 21 and 22, found Coke in Maryland at Quantico Chapel, about ten miles west of Salisbury, where the Sunday congregation overflowed the meetinghouse. Throughout his journey, Coke was impressed by the forest settings of most of the chapels he encountered. On Monday, he preached at Annamessex Chapel, near Crisfield, and noted, "It is quite romantic to see such numbers of horses fastened to trees."

Along the Virginia border, Coke encountered his first inattentive congregation. By November 24, he had crossed into Accomack County and discovered that Virginia's Eastern Shore had yet to build its first Methodist chapel. But, he was happy to note, "they talk of building and I encourage them."

Despite his hopes for the future, Coke found Virginia's Accomack County and Maryland's Worcester County "barren country." It was with relief that he crossed from Worcester into Delaware on December 1 to preach at Line Chapel, about twelve miles west of Selbyville. He praised God that his travels had brought him again "into the heart of Methodism."[22]

From lower Delaware, Coke rode thirty miles to Henry Airey's plantation southeast of Cambridge. He found that staunch Methodist the leader of a class meeting of thirty members. Coke preached to a very lively crowd and then headed for Cambridge where, as previously reported, he was locked out of the Anglican church. Coke then crossed to the north bank of the Choptank on December 6, in the face of high winds that made the ferry crossing unusually dangerous.

Coke rode seven miles north of the ferry landing to Bolingbrook Chapel. Here, in one day, he probably baptized more children and adults than he would have in a lifetime as a rector of an English parish. The next day Coke preached on the shore of the Chesapeake at Wittman to a very large congregation.

Then it was northeast to Tuckahoe Chapel along Tuckahoe Creek near Hillsboro in Caroline County. Here Coke heard "the best singers I have met with in America." Turning due west, he stopped at Kent Island. As at Cambridge, the doors of the Anglican church were closed to him, angering many who weren't even Methodist. Coke preached outside instead, and after a successful day, pushed northeast to Church Hill, where the local vestry requested him to speak at St. Luke's. The official Methodist declaration of independence from the Anglican Church was still a few weeks away.

On December 12, Coke was in Chestertown where he spoke

three times to large gatherings. The Methodist chapel ·could hold but half of the afternoon crowd and Coke was forced to preach standing at the chapel's door. Leaving Chestertown, Coke preached and administered the sacraments at Kent and Worton chapels to large audiences. On December 14 he crossed the Chesapeake on his way to the Christmas Conference.[23] Coke's itinerancy fell short of the eight hundred to a thousand miles projected, but he did get to see and to be seen by a considerable part of the Peninsula populace. Many who came to see Coke were thinking of moving west.

Westward Migration

As the end of the eighteenth century approached, much of the Peninsula had been under cultivation for well over a century. Much of the soil was exhausted from years of single-crop agriculture. Some crop changes, such as the substitution of wheat for tobacco, helped put off the day of reckoning, but the remarkable revolution in farming techniques and fertilizer use that marked the antebellum period in the Chesapeake region was still a development of the future.[24]

Riding through Maryland's upper Eastern Shore in 1799, Nathaniel Luff was unimpressed with the region's winter wheat crop. Luff mentioned the Hessian fly as one factor but felt that the greatest problem was the "excessive tillage and want of manure." He also noted a concomitant decline in houses and industry. As Eastern Shoremen became increasingly aware of their region's decline in economic vitality, they went so far as to propose breaking away from the more successful Western Shore to join with Delaware in setting up a new state formed by the Peninsula.

Combined with the natural population increase, the exhausted soil led many to move westward beyond the Appalachians to the Ohio country. A precise quantitative estimate is impossible, but out-migration from the Peninsula during the late eighteenth and early nineteenth centuries must have been considerable. The impact of this out-migration is reflected in comparative census statistics. From 1790 to 1820 the Peninsula's population increased by only 16 percent while the nation as a whole increased 144 percent.

Methodists were particularly tempted to join the westward migration. Those Methodists who were land-poor, like some at Brown's Chapel in western Sussex, were encouraged by Asbury to go west where "the means of rearing a family and advancing in the world were in the reach of the inhabitants." Ohio was a good place for them to live in a slave-free economy. Some Peninsula Methodists who weren't poor but had manumitted their slaves also preferred living in slave-free Ohio. For some reason many of the latter group, led by White Brown of western Sussex, were particularly drawn about 1800 to Ross County in south central Ohio.[25]

Growth/Stagnation, 1784–1800

The out-migration to the West seemed to drain the Peninsula of religious vitality as well as population. Delmarva Methodists, numbering 4,604 in 1784, more than doubled to 9,911 by 1792. But then, after maintaining that level for a few years, the number declined. By 1800, there were 8,705 Methodists on the Peninsula, almost double the 1784 figure but 1,206 less than the high point reached in 1792.

In 1784, almost one out of three American Methodists lived on Delmarva. Over the next sixteen years, the national Methodist total quadrupled, while on the Peninsula, Methodists did not quite double their number. As a result, by 1800 only 13 percent of the nation's Methodists lived on Delmarva.[26]

Methodist momentum, built up over the war years, explains the upward membership surge into the early 1790s. The newly established Protestant Episcopal Church, despite its claim to be successor to the Anglican Church, lacked both the manpower and the appeal to bring large numbers of nominal Anglicans back into

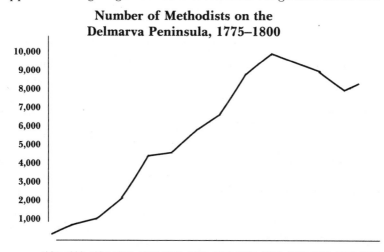

Number of Methodists on the Delmarva Peninsula, 1775–1800

the fold. Those former Anglicans who chose to continue a religious affiliation were drawn increasingly to Peninsula Methodism.

Peninsula Methodism even infiltrated the ranks of the "better sort," the wealthy planters, attorneys, physicians, merchants, and others who represented Delmarva's elite. Landed gentry of Maryland's Eastern Shore who became Methodist included Benton Harris of Worcester County; Henry Airey and Henry Ennalls of Dorchester County; General James Benson, Thomas Harrison, William Hindman, and Henry Banning of Talbot County; Capt. William Frazier, Phillip Harrington, and Henry Downes of Caroline County; Col. William Hopper, William Bruff, Robert Emory, and James Bordley of Queen Anne's County. In Delaware, Methodist converts from the landed gentry included Thomas White, Philip Barratt, and Allen McLane of Kent County and David Nutter, Rhoads Shankland, John Wiltbank, Ezekiel Williams, and Lemuel Davis of Sussex County. Peninsula attorneys and physicians who became Methodists included Richard Bassett of Dover, who also owned considerable land in Cecil County, Maryland; Dr. Abraham Ridgely of Dover; Dr. James Anderson of Chestertown; and probably Dr. Sluyter Bouchell of Cecil County.[27]

Even on Virginia's Eastern Shore, the last sector of the Peninsula reached by circuit riders, Methodist converts of the "middling and lower sorts" were proud to note that their ranks had been joined by the likes of Col. Thomas Paramore of Northampton County, and captains Thomas Burton and William Downing of Accomack County.[28]

"Dull Times"

The drop in membership after 1792—by 1799 membership was down 13 percent from the 1792 figure—was cause for alarm. For the first time in twenty years, Peninsula Methodism was on the defensive. Nationally, Methodism was also having problems, although on a more modest scale. By 1799, nationwide membership was down 7 percent from 1792.

These were, as one itinerant on the Milford circuit put it in 1796, "dull times." There were signs everywhere that enthusiasm for religion was dying. In Dorchester County, a decline in Methodist fervor had been sensed as early as 1786. Eleven years later an Episcopal parish report from Dorchester County admitted that the Methodists were the most numerous religious body, but also added that they didn't seem to be on the increase. The malaise spread north, east, and south, with few societies exhibiting their former vitality. From Wilmington to Easton to Northampton County, Virginia, the story was much the same: religious enthusiasm was on the wane. Itinerant William Colbert found that on more than one occasion no one even showed up to hear him preach.

Opposition from roughnecks, so common during the American Revolution, surfaced again. Wilmington had never been a hotbed of Methodism, causing Asbury in 1791 to cry out in despair: "Alas for poor Wilmington! When will this people open its eyes?" To make matters worse, the handful of Wilmington Methodists were intimidated by mobs that surrounded Asbury Church night after night to denounce the congregation of "scarcely fifty worshippers." Night services in Wilmington had to be abandoned, and even day services were interrupted by the breaking of windows, the stoning of the pastor, and the throwing of snakes and lizards through windows at female worshippers.

Elsewhere the story was much the same, with preachers' sermons interrupted in midstream by disturbances. William Colbert, who had previously reported that a Quarterly Meeting held in 1795 in Milford, Delaware, had been disturbed by thugs, noted six years later how commonplace were interruptions of his sermons at a chapel in Worcester County, Maryland. At Accomac, Virginia, in 1800, itinerant Thomas Smith's courage was tried by the threats of four hostile men intent on spilling his blood.[29]

As intimidating as the threats of violence might be, Methodism had never before been cowed by such activity. Indeed, under the persecution of the revolutionary years, Peninsula Methodism seemed to thrive. Moreover, the violence and threats of violence of the 1790s weren't comparable to the physical beatings that characterized the revolutionary period. Rather, the real problem was a religious lethargy that set in while Peninsula Methodism waited for its second wind.

The decline in religious vitality after 1792 puzzled and discouraged itinerants. On the rare occasion that a fair-sized crowd appeared for preaching, the gathering was labeled "a large congregation for these dull times." One itinerant, while riding the Milford Circuit, visited the homes of lax Methodists to find out why they weren't attending services. All too often their answers "gave little satisfaction."[30]

Yellow Fever

One contributing factor to attendance decline at Methodist meetings was the yellow-fever epidemic, beginning in 1789. The dreaded "yellow jack," as the fever was called, had appeared as early as the seventeenth century in colonial ports, but it wasn't until the late eighteenth century that it caused serious panic.

Yellow fever was spread by the *Aedes aegypti* mosquito during the summer and fall of the year. The onset of the first winter freeze put a halt to the spread of the fever by killing the mosquito. Of course, Americans of the late eighteenth century didn't understand the role of the mosquito as a carrier. Indeed, most Americans were convinced that yellow fever was somehow contagious and that the only safeguard during an outbreak was to avoid close contact with other humans. Large gatherings, such as those for religious worship, were considered dangerous by a population intent on avoiding the horrible contagion.

In 1789, in the Tuckahoe Neck region of Caroline County, yellow fever accounted for 150 deaths in a few months. The resulting panic caused attendance at local Methodist meetings to drop precipitously. In 1793 a yellow fever epidemic that paralyzed Philadelphia for months reached deep into the heart of Delmarva. Wilmington, for some unfathomable reason, escaped unscathed. But in Somerset County, 200 were dead of the fever by the end of the summer.

Francis Asbury spent a week in Philadelphia in early September 1793, observing the horrors of the epidemic firsthand. When he reached Easton in late September, the inhabitants were very uneasy because they feared Asbury might infect them with the disease. After all, during periods of serious epidemics, the traveling preacher carried to the faithful the possibility of a quick death as well as the promise of a new life. In Kent County, Maryland, in 1775, for example, itinerant Philip Gatch infected his host family with smallpox, causing the death of the father and one daughter.

As Asbury rode from Easton to Hillsboro, Caroline County, and then into Kent County, Delaware, he found yellow fever prevailing in every house, although "there are not so many deaths as might be expected from general afflictions." In 1797 and 1798, it was Wilmington's turn. Yellow fever epidemics drove from town all who could leave. All of the churches suffered and Wilmington's Methodists, never very numerous, were reduced to twenty.[31]

The Second Great Awakening

About 1800, the Methodist decline on the Peninsula was dramatically reversed. So successful was this extraordinary turnaround that Peninsula Methodism's membership jumped from approximately nine thousand in 1800 to almost twenty thousand in 1803.

Despite a dramatic increase in Methodists nationally, the proportion of Methodists living on Delmarva jumped from 13 percent in 1800 to almost 19 percent in 1804.

At the turn of the century, beyond the Appalachians in the frontier river valleys of Kentucky and Tennessee, a series of revivals kindled a fire of religious enthusiasm that quickly spread eastward. Because this new manifestation of religious enthusiasm reminded many historians of the Great Awakening of George Whitefield's era, it has been labeled the Second Great Awakening. It is tempting to see the resurgence of religion on the Peninsula as simply an eastward extension of this western-bred religious enthusiasm. But other evidence indicates that regardless of developments beyond the Appalachians, at the end of the eighteenth century the Peninsula was ripe for religious revival.

A Necessary Sense of Sin

To begin with, revivals in America seemed to prosper during economic hard times, which the Peninsula was certainly experiencing at the end of the eighteenth century. But even more significant was a key psychological precondition to religious revival, namely, a widespread perception among the populace that they were alienated from God and steeped in sin. A study of the Baptist surge in Virginia in the decade prior to the American Revolution, for example, points up the relationship of a widespread sense of sin to the success of an evangelical revival.

Out of the decline in religious fervor on the Peninsula during the 1790s grew a consciousness of a moral degeneracy that was not restricted to the unchurched. Even Methodists, it was noted, had fallen victim to the Devil's snares. A case in point was the action forced on itinerant William Colbert during a five-week period on the Milford Circuit in 1796. Colbert had to expel from the society a married man with children and a young single woman for "showing so much love for each other as to bring reproach on the cause of God"; a "backslider" who had been taken in only four weeks earlier; and a local preacher for refusing to comply with Methodist discipline. To make matters worse, one of the class leaders on the circuit had "taken to drinking to the destruction of his soul." It was no wonder that a discouraged Colbert would soon be saying that "retirement is best for me."

Three years later in Lewes, nineteen-year-old William Morgan was dumbfounded at the moral degeneracy he found among the populace in general and the Methodists in particular. Morgan lived with a Methodist who prayed one minute and got drunk the next. Not surprisingly, this profligate introduced Morgan into "wicked company." Even more perplexing were the actions of a Methodist class leader and exhorter who passed around a brandy bottle during religious meetings, causing the praying and singing to become too loud for Morgan's liking. Morgan characterized two other Lewes Methodists that he met the same year "as vile hypocrites as could be named."[32]

An Active God

Among the educated elite of the eighteenth century there was an acceptance of the Newtonian concept that the world was run by immutable natural laws. But the majority of Americans, whether in the Shenandoah Valley of Virginia or on the Delmarva Peninsula, rejected the Newtonian perspective for the more traditional view that events in this world took place under God's direct supervision and control. Although God may have the stern, judgemental qualities of the Old Testament, he was also a benevolent being. Therefore, although the 1790s might be a period of religious apathy and trial, God was bound to cause a revival of religious vitality. Indeed, God allowed the widespread apathy and immorality of the 1790s to teach men the harmful results of being alienated from their Creator. Once men learned this lesson, reconciliation was possible.

The process of reconciliation recognized the central role of God's grace but also emphasized the individual's role. In short, if men would recognize their alienation from God and their resulting sinful state and repent, God would open their hearts to Christ's warming presence and this, in turn, would bring about a resurgence of piety. But how to get men to recognize their fallen state and cry out for God's mercy? The 1790s had provided ample proof of man's fallen state. Now, more than ever before, the time had come for God's ministers to sound the alarm.[33]

The Revival Begins

In 1799, as the wondrous revival meetings on the Tennessee-Kentucky frontier were beginning, a Methodist revival began on the Peninsula in Cecil County, Maryland. A year later it spread to the Methodist General Conference meeting in Baltimore. By the end of 1800 a Methodist revival was surging through the Peninsula.

In Sussex, William Morgan noted "a great revival of religion began to spread through our county." South of Sussex, in Somerset, the once discouraged William Colbert reported "a small shaking among dry bones." Further south on the Eastern Shore of Virginia, an itinerant found Methodist services increasingly ending in a "great shout" as enthusiasm spread.

Freeborn Garrettson had noted that "the excitement of the human passions was a natural part of the conversion process." And certainly the Second Great Awakening brought with it an outpouring of human passions, particularly along the frontier. On the Peninsula, the Second Great Awakening unleashed emotional responses that were a bit more restrained than the excesses reported beyond the Appalachians, but startling nevertheless.

One case in point was a service in Guilford, Accomack County, Virginia, where the people were "falling in all directions . . . the place was gloriously awful." Children were seen holding on to their parents and crying "O papa, come to Jesus! God bless you." The next year at the same place, "the congregation lay in heaps around the altar."[34]

Religious ecstasy was not new to the Peninsula. After all, Whitefield, Nichols, Asbury, Garrettson, and others had aroused emotional reactions in the large crowds that gathered to hear them in the eighteenth century. The uniqueness of the religious outpouring of emotions in the early nineteenth century was in its sustained intensity.

Revival Techniques

Methodism, on the Peninsula as elsewhere, recognized the conversion potential of methodically induced and controlled religious ecstasy. Clearly, the progenitor of the journey from a state of sin to a state of religious bliss was God, but His earthly lieutenants could and should develop and use techniques that would act as catalytic agents to the entire process. Therefore, the revival techniques pioneered by Whitefield were supplemented by new tactics and strategies which originated on the Peninsula as well as in the Wesleyan crusades in England and in the new Protestant offensive beyond the Appalachians.

A large number of conversions occurred at regular circuit meetings. The Philadelphia Annual Conference, which included the Peninsula in its jurisdiction, also produced converts at its yearly meeting. At the Annual Conference in Smyrna in 1800, for example, "one hundred souls were converted to God."

But from almost the very beginning of Peninsula Methodism, the crucial revival event was the Quarterly Conference, which was usually held over a weekend. Large crowds turned out to hear a number of preachers from several adjoining circuits flail away at the Devil. As early as 1779, a Quarterly Meeting near Dover attracted between six and seven hundred people. At subsequent Quarterly Meetings, crowds were even larger and converts numerous. Eventually, the camp meeting superseded the Quarterly Meeting in attendance and in converts. And yet as late as 1806, a Quarterly Meeting held near Dover claimed 1,200 in attendance and 164 converts.[35]

In addition to the Quarterly Meetings, which were held throughout the Peninsula, a very popular week-long revival called the "Union" meeting was annually held in Dover from 1801 to 1804. Two Dover residents, Governor Richard Bassett and Dr. Abraham Ridgely, organized and planned the Union revivals after being inspired by the success of the spontaneous revival that occurred during the Annual Conference at Smyrna in 1800. Evidently, huge crowds attended the Union revivals and often had to be divided into smaller groups for preaching. Sometimes three itinerants would hold forth simultaneously to audiences which ranged from the committed to the curious.

The 1802 Union revival was particularly successful. Commencing on a Friday evening in early June and ending before daybreak the following Friday, the revival attracted daily crowds estimated at three to four thousand. Governor Bassett estimated one day's attendance at seven thousand. The twenty preachers present labored hard and within five weeks the Dover Circuit took in 245 probationary members. These Dover revivals were probably the first planned, protracted Methodist revival meetings on the Delmarva Peninsula.[36]

The Altar Call

During Methodist meetings, emotional outbursts by those awakened to their sinful state often interrupted services. Crying out for mercy, the newly penitent drew some of the already saved to their side to offer prayer and comfort. The congregation buzzed with activity as first one and then other stricken sinners cried aloud for God's saving grace. In the confusion, the continuity of the service was interrupted, and the message and the exhortation that followed were lost in the babble of voices. It was self-evident, particularly with the increasing number of penitants that marked 1799 in Cecil County, that a new technique was needed to keep order while simultaneously dealing with the needs of the newly awakened.

In 1799, at Back Creek (subsequently Bethel) Church near Chesapeake City in Cecil County, itinerant William Chandler invited awakened sinners to come forward to the altar. Once kneeling at the altar, the penitents were counselled in an orderly fashion, and the power of God's word to change lives was dramatically demonstrated in front of the entire congregation. The altar call quickly spread to other areas of the Peninsula, appearing as far away as the Milford Circuit by 1800. From the Peninsula the practice spread across the nation and soon became a fixture with evangelical Protestants.[37]

The Camp Meeting

Much of the credit for the dramatic increase in religious enthusiasm and church membership that characterized the Second Great Awakening is given to the camp meeting. The first regular camp meeting was held in Logan County, Kentucky, in 1800. Initially interdenominational in its appeal, the camp meeting increasingly became a strictly Methodist event as it spread eastward. Immensely popular, the institution reached Delmarva five years later.

On July 25, 1805, near Smyrna, Delaware, the Peninsula's first camp meeting was opened by a sermon preached by Jesse Lee. The intent of the sermon was clear; it showed "the awful end of the wicked." Hundreds, it was claimed, were converted. A month later, a second camp meeting was held in Pungateague, Accomack County, Virginia, where 450 conversions were claimed. After an extraordinarily successful camp meeting in Kent County, Maryland, in 1806, apprentice attorney John Emory wrote that there never has been a "more favorable" institution than the camp meeting for spreading of the gospel of Christ.

Peninsula Methodism grew at a spectacular rate during the Second Great Awakening. From 1800 to 1805, membership increased from 8,705 to 18,985, or by almost 120 percent. During the first few years of the camp meeting era, the spectacular rate of increase continued, reaching almost 25,000 by 1807. But then the number of Peninsula Methodists went into a slight decline, dropping below

22,000 by 1810 and dropping to approximately 21,000 by 1820. Although these figures raise some questions about the long-term impact of the camp meeting on church membership, there is no denying that the advent of the camp meeting was a significant event in the history of the Delmarva Methodism. One observer claimed that the introduction of the camp meeting ushered in "a new era of Methodism" for the entire region.[38]

The Chapel Branch Camp Meeting

Because it was the prototype for the future, the Peninsula's first camp meeting was very significant. Located at Chapel Branch (also called Farson's Hill) in "a beautiful grove of trees" a few miles from Smyrna, the meeting lasted from Thursday, July 25, to Monday morning, July 29, 1805. Jesse Lee, much experienced in camp meetings in other sections of the United States, thought that the Chapel Branch gathering "exceeded anything I ever saw, for the conversion of souls and for the quickening influence of the Holy Ghost upon the hearts of believers."

William Chandler, a sometime physician converted to Methodism in 1790 and the moving force behind the first stirring of

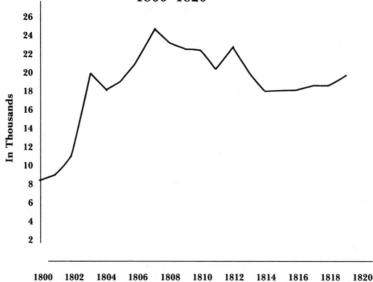

**Number of Methodists on the Delmarva Peninsula
1800–1820**

revival in Cecil County in 1799, was presiding elder at the Chapel Branch camp meeting. He estimated that crowd sizes varied from three thousand on Thursday to nine to ten thousand on Sunday. At night, the people slept in tents, covered wagons, and carts. The bodies of the wagons and carts had been taken off their axles and set on the ground on the north side of the meeting area. Along with a stream to the south, a fence on the east, and gigs on the west, the covered wagons and carts completely enclosed the preaching area. Only one way in and out was left open, making the camp a compound. The Chapel Branch meeting was peaceful, but in future years limited access proved very useful in controlling troublemakers.

In the middle of the enclosed clearing stood a preachers' platform, elevated four feet above ground level. Because Methodist preachers did not read their sermons from a prepared text, there was no need for a podium. There was, however, a "rest board" for preachers with long-winded tendencies. To one side of the preachers' stand was a large, crude wooden shelter in which the itinerants ate and slept. No one else was allowed in except by special invitation.

In front of the preachers' platform, the white audience was seated according to a geometric plan that separated men from women and set up "streets" and "courts." Evidently this seating pattern, with open lanes for crowd passage, was found to be the most efficient arrangement in previous camp meetings in the West. In a precedent followed in subsequent years, blacks were seated behind the preaching platform.

At the north end of the enclosure, under a crude shelter of sticks and tree limbs, was a mourner's bench for men. To the south end, under a similar shelter, was the women's bench. "When any person wished to be prayed for, he or she was invited to these bowers, the men laboring with men; and the women with women only."

At 5:00 A.M. two trumpets signaled morning prayer. At 8:00 A.M. trumpets again sounded to announce preaching, and repeated the call at 3:00 and 8:00 P.M. Between preaching and throughout the night, the faithful prayed, sang, and talked. More than thirty itinerants and approximately the same number of local preachers were present to proclaim the word, exhort, counsel, and pray. Evidently they did their work well in arousing people to their sinful state. "It was said that the noise occasioned by the cries of the distressed and the shouts of the saints was heard the distance of three miles."

Laymen, organized into guard squads, acted as ushers, policemen, and convert counters. William Morgan, one of the guards, maintained that the number of converts was grossly exaggerated because of the actions of Dr. Chandler. There might be, for example, ten guards assigned counting duties during a service that produced three professed converts. Each guard would report the same three converts to Dr. Chandler, who then totaled all of the counts, swelling the number of converts to thirty. The preachers and a foreign observer estimated three to four hundred converts over the four days at Chapel Branch, but William Morgan felt that "one-tenth" of that figure was more accurate.

Whatever the final figures, most of those present proclaimed the Peninsula's first camp meeting a grand success. At the close of the meeting on Monday morning Jesse Lee, who had given the opening message, spoke again. The preachers then gathered at the platform, embraced and wept in each other's arms, and dismissed a weeping congregation. A visiting Englishman later exclaimed: "O, my God! What a scene! The impression it made upon my heart and soul are indelible."[39]

Claims and Problems

The spread of camp meetings to other parts of the Peninsula was accompanied with mind-boggling claims. Methodist itinerant Henry Boehm maintained that those early camp meetings helped break up "the strongholds of the Devil" and "almost revolutionized the Peninsula."

Methodist figures seemed to support Boehm's claims. According to Francis Asbury, there was good reason to believe that camp meetings on the Peninsula produced more than four thousand converts in less than three months in 1806. A camp meeting near Laurel, Sussex County, in June of that year reported 1,165 converts; a camp meeting near Dover a month later claimed 1,320. Crowd estimates reached ten to fifteen thousand at some of the meetings. In November 1806 Asbury rejoiced at hearing "that Delaware and the East of Maryland [Eastern Shore] fire spreads on the Western Shore."

Even taking seriously William Morgan's caveat concerning statistical inflation, one is still left with a feeling of awe at what was going on. Whether assembled crowds were five or fifteen thousand wasn't all that important. What was important was that the preaching of the gospel, Methodist-style, was attracting enormous crowds highly susceptible to extraordinary outbreaks of religious emotionalism. In 1807, for example, at a camp meeting near Wye

Mills, Queen Anne's County, the large crowd so filled the air with cries of distress and shouts of triumph that preaching had to be suspended for one day. One participating preacher was so impressed that he later wrote that the Wye meeting may have been "the greatest meeting ever held in America."

The potential for civil disturbances at camp meetings was considerable. The combination of the emotional intensity of the participants and the desire of some outsiders to ridicule what was going on caused real concern. At that first camp meeting at Chapel Branch, worried civil authorities assigned seven justices of the peace and seven constables to keep order. No real problem developed, but that wasn't the case with some subsequent camp meetings. Often roughnecks invaded the camp site, scuffled with the Methodist guards, and generally made a nuisance of themselves. Despite efforts to keep it out, liquor flowed freely around the fringes of the encampment, exacerbating the situation.[40]

The presence of liquor was a particularly acute problem in Delaware. In 1815 petitions signed by 213 Methodist and other residents of Kent County were sent to the Delaware General Assembly, asking for a law to protect camp meetings from

> people of the worst character, creating stalls and selling spiritous liquors and thereby drawing together a number of people of the vilest character near said meeting, who after getting drunk will come into said meeting and frequently disturb those who wish to be engaged in the worship of God.

The petitioners asked that liquor sales be outlawed within three miles of camp meetings or any other religious services held out-of-doors. In 1818, after receiving more petitions, the Delaware legislature outlawed liquor sales within two miles of outdoor religious meetings, but exempted sales from establishments already in existence. Violaters were to be fined $1 to $20. Eight years later, Delaware enacted a law punishing interference with religious services with fines ranging from $8 to $60.

Maryland's legislature also took steps to halt the sale of liquor near camp meetings, but only in selected counties. In 1816, booths for selling liquor within two miles of camp and Quarterly meetings were outlawed in Dorchester, Cecil and Kent counties, with fines not to exceed $100. There is no indication that similar restrictions on liquor sales were established in Maryland's other Eastern Shore counties or the Eastern Shore of Virginia prior to 1820.[41]

Before the enactment of state laws, keeping order at the camp meetings was primarily the responsibility of the presiding elder and the Methodist guards. Dr. William Chandler, the presiding elder at most of the early Delmarva camp meetings and the one individual responsible for orchestrating the revival sweeping the region, had little patience with troublemakers.

The first large camp meeting to have discipline problems was held two miles from Laurel, in southwestern Sussex County, in June 1806. A number of disturbances broke out, causing Chandler to seek legal advice from Richard Bassett, an attorney and former Delaware governor. Chandler was told that the area within the camp was a place of worship and that he had the right to arrest and imprison any disturbers of the peace within that area. Accordingly, he had a slab jailhouse erected and, on the order of an associate judge of the Court of Common Pleas, had two trouble-makers tied up and held in the jail. Then, on Chandler's orders, Methodist guard squads searched the camp, breaking brandy bottles and even destroying brandy cakes. William Morgan, also a guard at the Laurel meeting, was so disgusted with Chandler's high-handed methods that he decided never to be a guard again.

A month later, Chandler's tactics led to trouble with civil authorities in Virginia. In July 1806 the second camp meeting to be held at Pungoteague, Accomack County, briefly erupted into mass violence. The Reverend John Chambers chastized a man by the name of Oliver for ignoring camp rules against smoking. Oliver, or someone else, promptly knocked the preacher to the ground and a brawl followed. James Kellam, mistaken for Chambers's assailant, was overpowered and tied hand and foot. Kellam's outnumbered friends retreated to the edge of the camp, where their threats of renewed violence kept the camp in turmoil through the night. The next morning Kellam was brought before the injured Chambers only to have the latter insist that the wrong man was being held. Kellam was promptly released but, unfortunately for the Methodists, proved to have political connections. Within a few hours, the local sheriff and a posse arrived and arrested Chandler and—depending on the source—three or four other preachers for breach of peace and false arrest. William Seymour, a wealthy local preacher who lived on Onancock Creek, paid the unusually heavy fines amounting to $2,000 and the Methodists were immediately released. Collections were taken up on circuits from Smyrna south to reimburse Seymour. Needless to say, William Morgan refused to contribute.

Within a few years of its introduction, the camp meeting was an annual event throughout the Peninsula. After 1810, however, some of the extraordinary religious excitement that marked the camp meeting's earlier years began to fade. By 1813, for example, attendance at the annual camp meeting near Snow Hill, Worcester County, was reported to be the lowest ever. Although such meetings would last into the twentieth century, by the mid-nineteenth century it was evident that some Methodists had serious reservations concerning them. One Methodist preacher even felt obliged to insist, in 1850, that on the Peninsula "the days of the camp meeting are not numbered"[42]—probably a case of protesting too much.

As the extraordinary religious enthusiasm of the Second Great Awakening gradually gave way to duller times, Methodists took stock of their position on the Peninsula. No one was more pleased than Francis Asbury when he noted, in 1810, that on Delmarva the Methodists now had approximately one hundred church buildings (still generally referred to as chapels), more than twenty-two thousand members, and 238 local and itinerant preachers. While Asbury sadly noted that most of his old friends had died, he was pleased that, for the most part, their children and grandchildren were baptized Methodists.

Methodists were both numerous—in 1810 they represented 21 percent of the Peninsula's adult population—and "respectable." But this was not an unmitigated blessing. In 1811 Asbury warned that although Methodists "are becoming great on the Peninsula," they should be careful, for "woe unto you when all men shall speak well of you." Indeed, "never in any past period have we had so much hope or fear as a society." Asbury clearly recognized that on the Peninsula, a new era for Methodism as dawning. The years of extraordinary growth were over. In the future, Peninsula Methodism would concentrate on consolidating its recent gains and would reflect in its development the changing socioeconomic nature of its membership.

Despite a membership decline since 1807, in 1820 nearly 20 percent of the Peninsula's adult population remained Methodist, continuing to make the Methodist Episcopal Church the dominant religious force on the Peninsula south of Presbyterian New Castle County. Nationally, however, Peninsula Methodism was losing its significance. Although 31 percent of American Methodists lived on the Peninsula in 1784, the figure dropped to 13 percent in 1800, jumped to 19 percent in 1803, but declined to 8 percent in 1820.[43]

Chapter 4

The Attractions of Methodism

In 1800, apprentice cabinetmaker William Morgan of Lewes, Delaware, was about to make a major decision. Only nineteen and very concerned about his future, Morgan was convinced that a religious affiliation would give needed direction to his life. Shopping around for a suitable faith, he finally narrowed his choice to Episcopalianism or Methodism.

Cornelius Wiltbank, an elderly Episcopalian, advised young Morgan to join with the Episcopalians so that he could have religion and still enjoy himself. Wiltbank assured Morgan that "God did not require so much strictness as the Methodists said he did." Morever, Christ's yoke

> is easy and his burden is light. I am sure there is no harm in civil mirth, in going to balls and taking a civil dance; enjoying one's self among young people, hearing the fiddle; it revives one's spirits.[1]

Wiltbank's entreaties were appealing and his logic convincing. How could anyone choose the dour, strict world of Methodism over the enjoyments of Episcopalianism? Yet Morgan and thousands of other Delmarvans chose "strictness" over "enjoyment" and became participants in the Methodist revolution, for reasons we will examine.

The Ethnic Factor

During the colonial period, Delmarvans with English roots were drawn to Anglicanism because it was their ancestral faith. Although the American Revolution brought an end to the colonial Anglican Church, the rise of the American Protestant Episcopal

Church from Anglican ashes continued to provide Peninsula Anglo-Saxons with an "English" church. After all, Episcopalianism was really colonial Anglicanism minus direct ties with England and the presence of troublesome evangelicals called Methodists. Although fresh from declaring their independence from the Church of England in 1784, Methodists also pointed to Anglican roots and, by doing so, offered Delmarvans a second "English" church.

The contest between Episcopalians and Methodists for the hearts and minds of the Peninsula's predominantly Anglo-Saxon population was decisively won by the Methodists for a number of reasons. Of considerable importance was the fact that the Methodists could claim a faith every bit as "English" as Episcopalianism, a faith that was attractive to the descendants of Englishmen. William Morgan's mother was of English stock and an Anglican. When her son finally narrowed his choice to two churches, it was predictable that they were both "English." It was no accident that on the Peninsula and elsewhere in early America, Methodism had its greatest success in areas previously dominated by the Church of England and the descendants of Englishmen.

The movement of Delmarvans from Anglicanism to Methodism is amply chronicled in a number of biographies and autobiographies. Ezekiel Cooper, Joseph Everett, and Joshua Thomas of Maryland's Eastern Shore and Isaac Davis of Delaware all reflect the same pattern: Anglican-English family roots and subsequent conversion to Methodism. At times the sequential pattern included an Episcopalian interlude prior to Methodist conversion. The latter pattern was particularly true in those areas not yet visited by circuit riders at the time of the Anglican collapse, such as Virginia's Eastern Shore, scattered areas of Maryland's lower Eastern Shore, and the islands in the lower Chesapeake. Joshua Thomas of Tangier Island, Captain Thomas Burton's family of Accomack County, and Josiah and Hester Mitchell of Worcester County, for example, were all Episcopalians before becoming Methodists.

Predictably, Methodism's opponents tried to discredit the "English" nature of Methodism. They called attention to circuit riders of non-English extraction to make their point. When Joshua Thomas announced, in 1807, that he was going to camp meeting, his uncle tried to dissuade him by declaring that Methodist preachers were "nothing but a parcel of Irishmen who ran away from their own country to keep from being hanged." Asbury was sensitive to this issue and hesitated to assign preachers of non-English background to the Peninsula, particularly if they had heavy accents.[2]

The Demographic Factor

Peninsula Methodism received its greatest support in the countryside. Wesley's itinerancy system seemed ideally suited for reaching isolated farmers and watermen as they worked the flat land and the creeks and sounds of the Chesapeake and Delaware bays. Riding his horse over fields, through forests, around marshes, and across rivers, the circuit rider made himself available to most of the rural folk of Delmarva. Where his horse wouldn't carry him, a waterman's log canoe would.

This effective rural ministry was made possible by Francis Asbury's support of the itinerancy system. Before the American Revolution, Methodist preachers Joseph Pilmore and Richard Boardman objected to itinerating and opted instead for a settled urban pastorate. Asbury would have none of that and fought hard to retain the itinerancy system because he knew that a settled pastorate could never bring God's word to the unchurched masses in the American countryside. Because the Peninsula, as well as the rest of America, was overwhelmingly rural, Asbury's victory in the itinerancy dispute assured the predominantly rural nature of Methodism in the New World. In England, by contrast, the Wesleyan faith never really caught hold in most rural areas because Anglican roots were too deep to be dislodged.

The location of chapels reflected Methodism's rural strength. By 1784 Peninsula Methodists had built twenty chapels, and eighteen were in the countryside. Chestertown and Dover had the only in-town chapels, and even in Dover the chapel was "somewhat out-of-town." Many well-established communities didn't construct Methodist meetinghouses until well into the nineteenth century. The future Methodist bishop Levi Scott noted the lack of an in-town Methodist church during his entire childhood in Odessa, Delaware, in the early nineteenth century.

Like most rural movements, Peninsula Methodism was a bit suspicious of towns and town dwellers. Wilmington, New Castle, Dover, and Elkton were all subjected to criticism, but some of the strongest negative comments were reserved for Chestertown, Maryland. In 1776 one Methodist found it "famous for wickedness," and nine years later Asbury called the grain port along the Chester River a "very wicked place."[3]

The cultural antipathy between countryside and town came to a head in Georgetown, Delaware, in a bizarre controversy called the "Great Pig Issue." In 1791 Georgetown was created by legislative fiat to be the new county seat for Sussex. As the newly founded community began to rise on former swamp and farm lands, two distinct visions emerged concerning Georgetown's future. On the one hand, in-town Episcopalians, many of them judges, lawyers, and county officials, wanted their county seat to become aesthetically attractive and sophisticated. By contrast, Georgetown's Methodists, largely residents with rural roots and including some farmers on the edge of town, wanted a community amenable to the rural life-style. The Wesleyans were less concerned with Georgetown's cosmetic appearance than they were with the right to turn their livestock loose to roam through its streets. Consequently, Methodist-owned pigs destroyed Episcopalian flower gardens, and irate Episcopalians demanded redress.

From the beginning, Georgetown was governed by the Delaware General Assembly, and therefore most serious problems that arose in the town had to be dealt with by legislative enactment in Dover. Reflecting political pressure exercised by Methodists as well as Episcopalians, the general assembly banned swine running at large in Georgetown in 1795, and subsequently stiffened, repealed, and finally, in 1821, reenacted restrictions against free-roaming swine.[4] The Great Pig Issue is just one example of the identification of Peninsula Methodism with the rural perspective.

Inactivity of Other Faiths

Methodism's domination of all but the extreme north of the Peninsula was assured by the failure of other denominations to mount effective counteroffensives.

Lacking a clergy that was either numerous or energetic, Episcopalianism seemed capable of only verbal invective to stem the Methodist tide. Rectors focused their attacks on John Wesley, calling him "a fallen Judas" and incorrectly insisting that Methodism's founder had been "disrobed by his [Anglician] Bishop and deprived of all ecclesiastical powers."

But beyond invective, Episcopalianism offered little resistance. Up and down the Peninsula, parishes lacking rectors waited to "be entirely eaten up by the Methodists." Typical was the scene in 1816 at St. Stephen's Parish, Cecil County, where parishioners were joining the Methodists because there was no Episcopal rector. That year, on the entire Peninsula, there were no more than twelve Episcopal clergy to compete with approximately thirty Methodist itinerants and more than two hundred local preachers. By 1820

Episcopalians were lamenting that there wasn't an Episcopal church remaining in all of Caroline County, Maryland.

Lacking the ardor of their Methodist counterparts, the few remaining Episcopal clergy demonstrated a general lassitude, particularly in inclement weather. In Accomack County, right after the American Revolution, English Methodist Thomas Coke was told that the Episcopal clergy "never stir out to church, even on Sunday if it rains."

A weakness for alcohol also seemed to hinder the performance of Episcopal clerics. In Lewes, Delaware, in 1799, the Episcopal parson was reported to frequent taverns, where he got so drunk that his parishioners had to lead him home. In other cases, it was members of the parish who couldn't handle the alcohol. In 1807, at an Episcopal service in Somerset County, the altar was "surrounded by drunkards" and the somnolent vestry failed to take action.[5]

Presbyterians continued to be numerous in New Castle and Cecil counties and, except for Virginia's Eastern Shore, could be found in pockets up and down the Peninsula. As in colonial times, however, their continued insistence on an educated ministry limited the number of available clergy. In 1803 the shortage of clergy on Delmarva led to an urgent request by the New Castle Presbytery that missionaries be sent into all of Delaware south of northern New Castle and into every county of Maryland's Eastern Shore. Evidently, no effective response was made and signs of Presbyterian decline were evident throughout most of the Peninsula. By 1813, for example, four Presbyterian congregations in lower Delaware and one in Dorchester County had disappeared. Even the Presbyterian congregation in Dover was considered "extinct" by 1819.[6]

Baptists were on the offensive throughout the American South, contesting Methodists almost everywhere for the souls of rural folk. In central and northern Delmarva, however, Baptists never mounted a serious challenge. Although the Welsh Tract Baptists, just south of Newark, continued to produce offshoot congregations during and after the American Revolution, Baptist membership figures overall indicate only modest success. By 1812, for example, there were eleven times as many Methodists as Baptists in the First State. On the Eastern Shore of Maryland, Baptists were even less numerous.

The only serious Baptist challenge came from Virginia's Eastern Shore. In 1776 Baptist preacher Elijah Baker left Virginia's Western Shore and crossed the Chesapeake to Northampton County. Two years later, he organized five newly baptized members to form the Lower Northampton Baptist Church, probably the first permanent non-Anglican church on Virginia's Eastern Shore. Despite persecution similar to what Methodists faced further north, Baker and fellow preacher George Layfield eventually organized fifteen Baptist churches on the Peninsula. Six were in Virginia, five in Maryland, and four in Delaware.

By 1785 Baptist churches outnumbered Episcopal churches four to two in Virginia's Eastern Shore, and that region seemed ripe for a Baptist takeover. Ten years later, however, the Baptists were facing a strong Methodist challenge, with Baptists barely outnumbering Methodists in Accomack and Northampton counties by 955 to 848. Baptists were clearly in second place by 1809, as their numbers had declined to 890 while the Methodists had climbed to 1,515. Further north in Maryland and southern Delaware, the Baptist offensive also ran out of steam.

The failure of this lone Baptist offensive to maintain its momentum is partially explained by the death of Elijah Baker in 1798. No one else had the requisite drive and charisma to fill the leadership void. Another significant factor, according to Kirk Mariner, historian of Virginia's Eastern Shore, was the limited appeal of the theology of Elijah Baker and his Baptist congregations. Unlike the free-will theology spawned by the Methodists, Baker brought to the Peninsula a faith incorporating strict predestination, which was far less appealing than Methodist Arminianism. By the time Virginia's Eastern Shore Baptists were willing to abandon predestination in the 1830s, Methodism was too deeply rooted to be supplanted. Mariner also maintains that the Methodist connectional system, with circuits and conferences, guaranteed a constant supply of preachers to Virginia's Eastern Shore. The Baptist congregations, by contrast, were much weaker in their connectional relationships and had no central governing structure that could consistently fill empty pulpits.[7]

Methodism and Other Faiths

At the end of the American Revolution, a bill was introduced into the Maryland Assembly asking for tax support for all of Maryland's Christian churches. The bill was sponsored and supported by members of the Protestant Episcopal Church which, as one of its clergy later noted, "had been accustomed to the countenance of government and hardly knew how to exist without it." Convinced that the bill was a disguised attempt to reestablish Anglicanism in its new Episcopalian form as the state church, Methodists vigorously opposed the measure. Lacking support save from Episcopalians, the bill was never enacted. According to one Methodist source, the furor that accompanied the introduction of the bill aided the Wesleyan cause on Maryland's Eastern Shore.

In Delaware, where no attempt was made by Episcopalians to gain state support, the two "English" churches seemed on better terms and could even cooperate on occasion. A very successful Methodist camp meeting was held in 1806 two miles from Laurel, Sussex County, on the grounds of Christ Episcopal Church at the invitation of the local vestry.

In 1805–6 increased Episcopal criticism of Methodism threatened to end what limited cooperation there was between the two faiths. During those two years, articles by an Episcopalian appeared in the *Easton Star* ridiculing the "emotional manifestations" that accompanied the Methodist rebirth experience and questioning the validity of the Methodist episcopacy. A Methodist writer, published in Easton's *Republican Star*, fired back salvo for salvo. Evidently, the printers of the two papers grew weary of theological invective and declared that if the two sides wished to continue their dispute in print, they would have to use pamphlets or handbills. In 1807 Joseph Jones of Wilmington printed an anonymous Episcopalian's *Inquiry Into the Validity of the Methodist Episcopacy*, which further exacerbated bad feelings between the two faiths.[8]

But even after these vituperative printed exchanges, some cooperation between Methodists and Episcopalians was still possible. As in late colonial times, the Episcopal clergy was split into evangelical and old-party factions. The members of the evangelical faction tended to be less critical of the Methodists, whom they felt close to in spirit. A case in point was William Duke, formerly a Methodist itinerant who had become an Episcopal rector. A member of the evangelical faction, Duke was allowed to conduct Episcopal services in a newly constructed Methodist meeting house in Elkton, Cecil County, in 1814.

Although Asbury and other Methodist preachers had little use for Calvinist theology, they tempered their comments about Peninsula Presbyterians, perhaps because Presbyterians were not overly aggressive proselytizers in the post-Revolutionary era. By contrast, the more aggressive Baptists, led by Baker and Layfield, were a threat and had to be taken seriously.

In 1779, at Sound in southeastern Sussex, Freeborn Garrettson preached to about two hundred people, some of whom were Baptists. When Garrettson finished, a Baptist preacher spoke on the error of infant baptism, calling it "baby sprinkling." At Garrettson's request, the people returned the next day and heard the Methodist preacher vindicate infant baptism and attack the Baptist position. That same year, in the Greenwood region of northwestern Sussex, an alarmed Asbury found Baptists "fishing in troubled water, (they always are preaching water to people) and . . . striving to get into all the houses where we preach." The next day Asbury made it clear that Methodists should oppose the Baptist offensive because "if the people lose their souls, how shall we answer to God?" Indeed, Asbury refused to preach in houses that also received Baptists. But the Baptists were stealthy foes, waiting only for Methodist preachers to leave for Quarterly Conference before going "from house to house, persuading weak people to be dipped and not hear the Methodists." By 1780 Asbury had enough of "John's people" who were "intent to come fishing about when we are gone." That year in southeastern Sussex, Asbury assigned a local preacher to deal with Baptist intrigues while the itinerants were away at conference. The contest between the people of John the Baptist and John Wesley to win souls on the lower end of the Peninsula seemed to invigorate the Methodists. Asbury pledged in 1791 that Methodism would continue its evangelizing even in Accomack County, the heart of Baptist country, "in spite of Satan and the Baptists."

Despite the fact that Deism was never a serious challenge on the Peninsula, Methodist preachers were sometimes paranoid about this rational alternative to "enthusiastic" religion. Thomas Paine's *Age of Reason*, which argued strongly for Deism, was labeled "an abominable book of infidelity." Perhaps some of the Methodist uneasiness stemmed from the Episcopal charge that Methodist preachers were too uneducated "to stand in equal combat with Deism." One circuit rider, however, saw the real Methodist weakness in its struggle against Deism to be the perception that Methodists worshipped "a wrathful God rather than a loving God."[9]

In spite of clashes with and criticism of other faiths on the Peninsula, Methodism could also be tolerant and even friendly to competing denominations. While Methodist and Episcopal clergy argued heatedly over "shouting" and the ordination rights of the Methodist episcopacy, on occasion a Methodist preacher might stop by at an Episcopal sanctuary to hear "an excellent sermon." A circuit rider might even have a friendly talk with Baptist evangelist George Layfield, as William Colbert did in Onancock, Virginia, in 1795.

Quakers, who seemed to resemble early Methodists in so many ways, were sometimes praised by Wesleyans. But on at least one occasion, a circuit rider went to great lengths to emphasize the theological distance between the Society of Friends and the Methodists. Nevertheless, relations between Quakers and Methodists were cordial enough for Methodists to hold Annual Conferences at the Friends' meetinghouse in Smyrna in 1803 and in subsequent years. Despite Asbury's reservations, even the Nicholites were called "Christians" by one itinerant.

Relations with Roman Catholics were a different story. Like Deists, Catholics represented no real threat to Methodist hegemony, and yet the presence of only a few "papists" on the Peninsula was viewed with great alarm. Once in a great while a very liberal circuit rider might dine with a Catholic, as William Colbert did in 1795. More often, they were vehemently denounced, and the pope was pictured as Satan's great lieutenant on earth. Circuit rider Robert Ayres called the Roman Church "Mother of Harlots." John Wesley himself had said that Roman Catholics alone were excluded from those to be tolerated, probably because Catholics themselves seemed so intolerant. Individual contact, however, could mellow the perspectives of Delmarva Methodists. In 1820, William Morgan went to medical school at the University of Maryland in Baltimore and roomed with a Roman Catholic. Morgan returned to the Peninsula with a view that his Catholic roommate was one of the "most pious young men" that he had met.[10]

An Alternative Value System

During the late eighteenth century, a worship service at an Episcopal church in Dorchester County was disturbed by a loud voice crying out, "Choose ye this day whom ye will serve." The challenge came from the lips of a Methodist itinerant as he stood outside the sanctuary. After complaints from the parson, the Methodist remained silent until the congregation was filing out. Then he repeated his stirring challenge with considerable effect, and one old lady responded, "I will serve the living God." Subsequently, the Methodist preacher converted so many of those present that the Episcopal church ceased to have a congregation.[11]

On the surface, this seems a straightforward account of Methodist success in converting Episcopalians. On a deeper level, however, it draws our attention to a compelling aspect of Methodism. The Methodist itinerant was making plain to that Episcopal congregation that one could not serve two masters. Simply put, Methodism maintained that to serve God and His ways required a rejection of the ways of men.

In the Chesapeake world of the eighteenth century, ways and values were forged and shaped by the gentry and then emulated by the "middling and lower sorts." The same dancing, drinking, card playing, gambling, horse racing, cock fighting, and general reveling that marked the gentry's leisure moments also occupied the free time of those lower on the social scale. The "middling and lower sorts" showed their approval of another aspect of the gentry's value system by dreaming of the day that they too would be masters of black slaves.

But there were many who were increasingly uncomfortable with the dominant culture and its underlying values. They found little that was attractive in a life-style that emphasized frivolity, competition, brutality, and deference to higher social rank. Moreover, to those who were ambitious, it was self-evident that many of these ways were self-destructive and that adopting them, on a personal level, spelled nothing but disaster.

Earlier Peninsula evangelists such as George Whitefield and Joseph Nichols tapped some of this discomfort with the Peninsula's dominant mores, but it wasn't until the arrival of the circuit rider that the entire Peninsula was offered a way to deal with it. The Methodist prescription called for a revolution in values. In order to move from the ways of man to the ways of God, the Methodist message demanded the substitution of seriousness for frivolity, cooperation for competition, compassion for brutality, and egalitarianism for deference.

To those seeking deeper human relationships than found in the surface comraderie and the alcoholic haze surrounding the card game, horse race, or gala party, Methodist societies offered a supportive community. To a people facing a lifetime of long, harsh days that drained youth and high spirits prematurely, Wesleyan societies offered far more than just a way to fight the boredom and loneliness of farm life. There was a real sense of psychological security when Methodist brothers and sisters were there to offer physical and financial help or lend a sympathetic ear in time of tribulation. Moreover, while the Methodist class meetings kept members on the road to perfection, they also encouraged each member to bare the innermost depths of his or her soul. What a wonderful catharsis! This type of activity could not go on in the outside world, dominated as it was by the competitive, self-assertive values of a gentry who regarded self-revelation, particularly among males, as a sign of weakness.[12]

The "Better Sort"

That the Methodist challenge to the mores established by the Peninsula's gentry excited and attracted members of the "lower orders" is understandable. More surprising was the willingness of some of the "better sort" to become Methodist, to adopt a serious, pious air, and to abandon revelry, gambling, sports, frivolity, and slavery. Evidently, many of the region's planters and their social peers were also searching for a new set of values to live by.

The unusual number of Methodist conversions among the Peninsula's upper class can also be credited to two other developments: the strength of "old Methodism" and the resulting conversion and subsequent evangelistic activity of some key aristocratic families. Because of the dominance of "old Methodism" in the region during the American Revolution, Peninsula Wesleyans regarded themselves as Anglicans and willingly worked in harmony with the Church of England. For this reason, the Anglican gentry found Peninsula Methodism quite congenial and could comfortably support and even join Methodist societies while simultaneously remaining loyal to the Church of England. With the collapse of Anglicanism, some Peninsula gentry simply continued their Methodist connection, while others joined Methodist societies because, in most areas, these societies were all that remained of Anglicanism.

By 1783 Methodism had spread to members of such leading Peninsula families as Barratt, Bassett, and White in Kent County, Delaware; Anderson in Kent County, Maryland; Bruff and Benson in Talbot County; Downes and Frazier in Caroline County; and Airey, Ennalls, and Hooper in Dorchester County. By the end of the American Revolution, the Methodist seed had been scattered among the gentry and even the Methodist declaration of independence from the Church of England, in 1784, could not halt germination and growth. By contrast, the schismatic nature of early Methodism beyond the Peninsula, particularly south of the Potomac, made Methodism elsewhere less attractive to Anglican gentry.[13]

Blood relationships in general and sibling relationships in particular helped spread Methodism among the Peninsula's elite. The Ennalls family is a case in point. Ann, Catherine, Mary, and Henry Ennalls were born into a planter family near Cambridge, Dorchester County. Ann Ennalls married the future governor of Delaware, Richard Bassett, of Bohemia Manor, Kent County, Maryland, and Dover, Delaware. About 1779 Ann Ennalls was converted to Methodism while living in Dover. Soon after, her sister

Catherine, probably after visiting Ann, also became a Methodist, returned to Dorchester, and converted Mary. Subsequently, through the efforts of Catherine and Mary, brother Henry Ennalls and their wealthy relative Henry Airey, who lived nearby, were also converted. When individual gentry took Methodism seriously, they apparently worked hard at converting other family members.

The desire to convert relatives was particularly strong in Henry Ennall's heart, but his evangelism didn't always meet with success. Some years after his own conversion, Ennalls was at Governor Bassett's home in Dover with James Bayard, who was Bassett's son-in-law, husband to Ennalls's niece, and a future US senator from Delaware. Bassett had long urged Bayard to become a Methodist, but to no avail. At family prayer that morning, Ennalls "prayed with much zeal." Evidently Ennalls, much to Bayard's distress, asked God to save Bayard from the fires of eternal damnation. After walking the floor in an agitated fashion, Bayard turned to Ennalls and demanded, "Henry, what did you mean by shaking your brimstone bag over me?" Ennalls shot back, "To save you from Hell, sir; I thought this a breakfast of plain dealing." Although Methodist Ezekiel Cooper preached at his funeral, there is no indication that Bayard gave in to the urgings of Bassett and Ennalls. Cooper's presence at the funeral probably reflected the continuing Methodist connection of Bayard's wife, Ann Bassett Bayard.[14]

On the Peninsula in 1800, a circuit rider noticed that both "the rich and the poor came freely to the throne of grace." In coming before the throne of grace, the "better sort" shared with the poor the same desire to savor the emotional side of Methodism.

Rachel Bruff, a member of a Talbot County planter family, was a case in point. Once convinced of her own unworthiness for salvation, she entered a period of depression and distress. Then followed the joyful realization of God's saving grace through her own acceptance of Christ. Subsequently she had visions of Christ visiting her. Rachel, who married Richard Bassett after his first wife, Ann Ennalls Bassett, died, was seen at the Peninsula's first camp meeting near Smyrna in 1805, shouting with religious ecstasy and, in her enthusiasm, indiscriminately embracing black and white sisters in the faith.

That some of the wives and daughters of the well-to-do would embrace "enthusiasm" was understandable to their male relatives. Methodist critic James Lackington theorized in England in 1796 that women were easy converts to "enthusiastic" religion because they were more emotional than men. Some of the Peninsula's well-to-do males, however, proved every bit as emotional as their wives

Allen McLane
(Courtesy, Delaware State Archives)

and daughters. At a camp meeting near Dover in 1806, for example, the customs collector of the Port of Wilmington, Allen McLane, was observed "on his knees wrestling with the Angel of the covenant with tears rolling down his cheeks . . . and he was made pure in heart and enabled to see God." Richard Bassett was also present and, "full of faith and the Holy Ghost," gave an emotional testimony before thousands. Six years earlier at the Annual Conference at Smyrna, Bassett became so emotional that some Methodist critics labeled his actions those of "a fool."[15]

If the gentry chose not to personally participate in emotional outbursts, they often liked to see it in other worshipers. In the early nineteenth century at a chapel in southern Accomack County, one of the local gentry felt that shouting was a necessary component of proper worship. If the service was about to end and no outbursts had as yet occurred, he insisted that the service be prolonged until the shouting began.

At times the gentry's religious emotionalism expressed itself outside of the formal worship service. A few years after the American Revolution, following a Quarterly Meeting at Barratt's Chapel, a circuit rider went to a "gentleman's" home to have dinner. After

Richard Bassett
(Courtesy, Historical Society of Delaware)

the meal, with a number of people present—presumably of the "better sort"—the itinerant asked if anyone could sing a hymn. A planter from Dorchester County (possibly Henry Ennalls) led the singing and was joined with such spirit by the others that the impact was extraordinary. The hymn-leader's wife and two others fell to the floor, while several others fell during a subsequent prayer. The net effect was that the man of the house, "a backslider, got restored." As one contemporary noted, "Methodism had not, as yet, put on brocade slippers and gold spectacles."

On the Peninsula, probably a higher percentage of the gentry and their peers became Methodists than anywhere else in the United States. The enthusiasm with which many of the wealthy and influential embraced Peninsula Methodism wasn't lost on the "middling and lower sorts." Accustomed as the latter two groups were to trying to mimic the activities of the gentry, many followed some of their "betters" into the Methodist camp. Riding the Dover Circuit in 1802, a Wesleyan preacher pointed out that the conversion to Methodism of so many wealthy and influential people in Delaware "had a happy influence on the common people." This statement was also true for the rest of the Peninsula.[16]

The "Middling Sort"

The "middling sort" were primarily landed farmers, but also included successful craftsmen, most merchants, and those professionals yet to reach the zenith of their legal or medical careers. While these people sometimes owned a few slaves, they fell short of the gentry in the number of slaves possessed, acres owned, and deference commanded.

But falling short had little place in the future ambitions of many of the "middling sort." They dreamed of upward mobility, worked at it, and a few were even confident that some day they too might be called "squire," with the deference that commanded. It isn't surprising that the "middling sort" found Methodism very congenial, because Methodism reinforced the very life-style and work ethic that ambitious young men recognized as crucial to economic advancement.

Isaac Davis is a case in point. He was born in 1765 near Milford in Kent County, Delaware, to a landed family in "the

Isaac Davis
(Courtesy, Delaware State Archives)

middle circumstances of life." At an early age, Davis adopted the "habit of Labor, and [the] constant pursuit of activity and temperance." By joining the Methodists as a young adult and by taking seriously their emphasis on hard work and temperance, Davis reinforced his previous living and working attitudes, which eventually led him to the presidency of the Bank of Smyrna, appointment to the Delaware Supreme Court, and considerable wealth.

In addition, ambitious young men like Davis found that the Methodist God provided "all things needful" for this world as well as "for eternity." Looking back from old age, Davis felt that his own life justified faith that God would provide for the earthly needs of his people. As a young man he had been "disobedient" to God's "repeated calls." Thereupon, God, "like Job . . . afflicted me." A lightning storm burned his home to the ground and left Davis deeply in debt. A shaken man, he turned to Methodism and later felt that much of his worldly success came from God's subsequent intercessions on his behalf. Like Davis, many who were eager for worldly success were drawn to Methodism because it provided them with the confidence that God was on their side.

In business, it was also important to have Methodists on your side. A natural inclination to favor brothers in the faith while engaging in commercial activity was strengthened by specific directives in the Methodist *Discipline*, telling Methodists to buy from each other and employ each other when practical. Because approximately 21 percent of the Peninsula's adult population was Methodist by 1810, Wesleyans represented a very significant share of the buying and employing public. Moreover, because many of the gentry had become Methodists, and since the gentry, in particular, were heavy purchasers of the products of craftsmen, the wares of merchants and storekeepers, and the services of attorneys and physicians, there was considerable economic pressure on many of the "middling sort" in the business or professional community to find truth in the Wesleyan persuasion. At the end of the eighteenth century, a Talbot County critic of Methodism cynically pointed out that businessmen and professionals "are apt to join in with those amongst whom they are most likely to succeed best."

Being appointed to Methodist boards of trustees could create economic opportunities. Often the construction of a new church or the repair of the old one was contracted to a trustee who was a builder. But a church contract wasn't always a blessing. In the early nineteenth century in Georgetown, Delaware, the local Methodist church was unable to pay all of its construction bills, which created considerable friction among the trustees and particular consternation among those who submitted the unpaid bills.[17]

Poor Whites

The Methodist message in both England and America was particularly aimed at the downtrodden, the impoverished, and the unfortunate. Methodism offered the "lower sort" the same possibilities sought by the Parisian mobs during the French Revolution— liberty, equality, and fraternity—but in a religious rather than a political context. Understandably, poor whites were stirred by the circuit rider's message of hope for this world as well as for the world to come.

To be poor—that is, to be a tenant farmer, laborer, or owner of only a few acres—left one particularly receptive to "true religion." Francis Asbury shared this view with evangelists of many faiths. Wealth, by contrast, sometimes caused men to "forget that they are Methodists." On a nostalgic trip through the Peninsula in 1810, Asbury admitted that now the houses of some of the rich were open to him, but prayed, "O God, give us the poor." At Brown's Chapel on the Sussex-Caroline border, even some of the principal leaders "had not been financially successful." Then again, "had they prospered in their pursuits, perhaps they never would have sought God."

Because membership records for Peninsula Methodism prior to 1820 have almost completely disappeared, it is impossible to give a precise estimate of the number and percentages of Peninsula Methodists who were of the "better," the "middling," and the "lower sort." There is considerable evidence, however, that sizeable numbers of Delmarva Methodists were found in all three socioeconomic classes. There is no doubt that poor whites represented a very significant percentage of the Methodist total. On the Eastern Shore of Virginia in 1789, a concerned Francis Asbury lamented the difficulty Methodism had in raising money. "We have the poor but they have no money, and the worldly wicked rich, we do not choose to ask." Indeed, Methodism on the Peninsula, as elsewhere, attracted large numbers of whites who "have no money."[18]

Poverty, however, wasn't necessarily viewed as a virtue in itself. When Asbury encountered the economically deprived members of Brown's Chapel, he did not tell them to feel blessed by their unfortunate economic circumstances. Rather, he advised that they break the shackles of poverty by migrating "to the western country

[Ohio], where the means of . . . advancing in the world, were within the reach of the inhabitants."

To those unwilling or unable to move westward, Methodism offered escape from economic destitution through the adoption of a religious life-style that rejected the old, poverty-inducing habits. The Methodist regime called for rising before the sun, working hard and long, and showing little interest in and even less patience with idle chatter, amusements, and other forms of self-indulgence. The type of family that needed Methodism most to set its economic house in order was that found by Asbury in Delaware in 1781, "lying in bed until sunrise, and drinking a dram after they are up."

George Morgan lived in poverty in Northwest Fork Hundred, western Sussex County. His son, William Morgan, realized at an early age that his father's weakness for alcohol "made him poor and kept him poor indeed." Determined not to follow his father's path, the son decided to avoid intemperance and gambling and to work hard at learning a trade. But Morgan also realized that he needed membership in a Methodist society to help himself avoid his father's fate.

Far to the southwest on Tangier Island in the Chesapeake, Joshua Thomas also grew up in poverty. He too recognized that personal vices—in this case alcoholism and idleness—were the buttresses of economic destitution. Thomas, as he grew older, understandably loathed intemperance and was considered remarkably industrious. It seemed only natural that Thomas became a Methodist, a faith in which he found support for the temperance and industry necessary to lift himself from the depths of poverty.[19]

Belonging to a Methodist society also offered crucial economic insurance. The basic units making up the local Methodist society were the class meetings, each having anywhere from ten to thirty-five members. The purpose of the class meeting was to encourage and to monitor spiritual growth through soul-revealing testimonies directed by the class leader, who demanded every member's participation. Because members aired their most private thoughts at class meeting, economic concerns of an urgent nature were bound to surface. In the process, material sharing became a natural extension of spiritual sharing. At times, aid might even come from Methodists outside the local society. In 1796, for example, a sick member of the Georgetown, Delaware, society received money donated by Methodists belonging to other societies on the same circuit.

As the years went by and Methodist congregations became more formal in their organizational structure, financial aid to poor

Methodists became a more structured undertaking. In 1822 in Wilmington, for example, Methodists established a benevolent society to offer aid to indigent and distressed Methodists in the city.

Poor whites must have also valued the egalitarian way in which Methodists addressed each other. Certainly, French revolutionaries were no more democratic in their demand that all Frenchmen be addressed with the common prefix "citizen" than were Methodists who cheerfully called each other "brother" and "sister." Although most local lay leadership positions on the Peninsula may have been filled by the "middling and better sort," this still didn't detract from the heady feeling produced when a poor farmer heard himself called "brother" by a wealthy and esteemed member of the gentry.[20]

White Women

Like other movements in early American history, Peninsula Methodism was male dominated. All clerical and lay leadership positions were reserved for men. White women weren't even allowed to vote for local church trustees and were segregated from men at religious services. Paradoxically, the same white women who had so little overt power probably represented, according to fragementary sources, a clear majority of Peninsula Methodism's white membership.

There is evidence that in some regions of the United States, a few women may have been exhorters—lay speakers who encouraged the congregation to heed the sermon just delivered—but there is no evidence of this on the Peninsula. Perhaps the closest was Mary White, wife of Judge Thomas White, who on occasion led class meetings and religious exercises, and probably would have preached had Francis Asbury been more encouraging.

Asbury Methodist Episcopal Church, Wilmington, gives an example of the sexual segregation that characterized Peninsula Methodism. Husbands and wives arrived together for Sunday worship, but outside the brick wall in front of the church they parted company. They entered through separate gates, through separate doors, to a sanctuary divided down the middle by a four-foot-high partition that prevented either sex from viewing the other while seated. Husband and wife might not see each other again until meeting outside in the street after the service. It wasn't until 1832 that Asbury's husbands and wives were allowed to enter the sanctuary by the same door, and not until 1845 that they could sit

together. In village and rural churches, sexual segregation continued beyond mid-century. An example was Camden, just south of
Dover, where women and men were separated until the 1860s.[21]

Although sexually segregated and barred from leadership roles,
white women made very significant contributions to Methodist success on the Peninsula. They particularly excelled at person-to-per-
son evangelism. Indeed, tradition has it that the first Methodist
evangelist in Queen Anne's County was a blind woman by the
name of Mrs. Rogers.

Wives were particularly important in bringing their husbands
into the Methodist fold. Among those of considerable means who
were led, or probably led, to Methodism in this manner were Delawareans Allen McLane, Richard Bassett, and Judge Thomas White,
as well as Capt. Thomas Burton of Accomack County, Virginia,
and Robert Emory of Queen Anne's County, Maryland. Among
males of lesser means, white women were equally active in making
converts. An Episcopal rector, unhappy with the large number of
Methodist conversions in Talbot County in the postrevolutionary
years, observed that the religion of "not a few" men seemed "to be
guided by their wives and sweethearts' " apron strings. Too many
of these female evangelists, according to the rector, had "inherited
the curiosity of Lot's wife and the confidence of their mother Eve."

White women made other significant contributions to the success of Peninsula Methodism. According to testimonies of the influence of maternal piety, female Methodists played a crucial role in
family devotions and in providing a general religious ambiance that
nurtured pious sensibilities in children.[22]

In the face of their second-class status, it is difficult to explain
why white females found Methodism so attractive and why they
worked so hard for its success. In the past, observers have often
accounted for the religious bent of women by noting that females
have a greater predisposition than men for piety. Moreover, the
very real threat of death in childbirth must have increased the
religious sensibilities of some women.

A second explanation rests on the sociobiological argument
that genetic inheritance considerably influences human personality.
The father of sociobiology, Edward O. Wilson, maintains that
females are predisposed, by modest genetic differences, to be more
intimately sociable than men. The one institution on the Peninsula
that could meet these female social needs was the Methodist Church.
Indeed, the propensity of women to gather at their segregated
entrance for a bit of socializing after Sunday service brought such
complaints from impatient husbands that the trustees at Asbury

Church, Wilmington, did away with segregated entrances in 1832. Like a greater disposition of women for piety, however, this explanation is impossible to substantiate.

A third explanation rests on what Peninsula families expected of their daughters. While sons were trained and educated in the practical skills necessary for making a living on the farm, on the bay, in the store, or in the courtroom, daughters were trained to be good mothers and wives. In many Peninsula homes, an education in spiritual values was considered every bit as important as learning to cook and sew. Although Nancy Mitchell of Worcester County was from a family of some means, her father decided against the frivolous education of the boarding school where she would have been taught "belles lettres and merely fashionable learning, such as how to drink tea and make curtseys." By remaining home, Nancy Mitchell "obtained a far better education," which included how to "behave herself in the house of God." Far to the northwest, in Chestertown, Anna Matilda Moore was brought up "with a strict and scrupulous regard for her spiritual and eternal interests." It was very natural for young women, whose spiritual training had been fairly rigorous, to have an inclination for church attachment. A case in point was the first wife of Isaac Davis of Kent County, Delaware, who had a religious education, "wanted religion," and subsequently became a Methodist.[23]

Perhaps the most compelling reason why Methodism attracted more Peninsula women than men was that Methodism met the female need for independence, self-esteem, and power. For men, this need could be fulfilled by simply playing out traditional male roles at home or in the commercial and political arena provided by the outside community. To most Peninsula women, however, only the local Methodist society offered the same opportunity.

As opposed to other decisions concerning their families and themselves, Peninsula women—as the sexual imbalance in Wesleyan societies indicates—often acted independently of their husbands in deciding to become Methodists. This independent step and the resulting deep attachment to a movement beyond the control of non-Methodist husbands must have seemed a bit threatening to some men. Perhaps it was to keep an eye on this threat that some non-Methodist husbands accompanied their wives to chapel services.

Not surprisingly, some men objected to the religious intensity shown by their wives. On at least one occasion, these objections led to a bizarre scene. In 1802 during a service at Green's Chapel, not far from Dover, a woman cried out for God's mercy and her enraged husband ordered her out of the chapel. Defiantly she insisted that first she would make her peace with her Maker. Although the irate husband quickly seized his wife and physically removed her from the chapel, she continued her monologue with God even while being dragged down the aisle and out the door. Despite meeting some resistance from their menfolk, women found that attendance at religious services and, particularly, at all-female class meetings not only conjured up a sense of female solidarity but also offered some a respite from their husbands' direct control.

Although the Methodist sermon was delivered by men, it praised such idealized feminine traits as patience, love, gentleness, sensitivity, humility, and submissiveness, and rejected the competitive values of the male-dominated spheres of commerce, politics, and sport. One had only to look to the behavior of Freeborn Garrettson and other itinerants in the face of brutal persecution during the American Revolution for a compelling demonstration of the personality traits that Methodists considered Christ-like.[24] By lifting up these so-called feminine traits for praise, circuit riders affirmed female self-esteem. In doing so, the itinerants must also have softened resentment over the lack of overt female power in the Methodist polity.

But women did exercise considerable covert power, particularly over the itinerants. Because they were dependent on Methodist women for their room and board, quite naturally circuit riders did what they could to please their hostesses. Since the itinerants were usually young and single, older matrons often became surrogate mothers who provided circuit riders with sympathetic understanding, advice, and encouragement to go along with a bed and meals. While serving in Dorchester County in 1800, a young and discouraged Henry Boehm considered abandoning the itinerancy after less than a year in the saddle. Sarah Ennalls, wife of Henry Ennalls, put an end to these thoughts by reminding Boehm that his eternal salvation might depend on the course he was about to take. Two years earlier, a second circuit rider's doubts about remaining in the itinerancy were also ended by Sarah Ennall's counsel. Even the few older itinerants relied on feminine advice and encouragement. One example was Benjamin Abbott, who was substituting on the Dover circuit for his son when he reported that Mary White, wife of Judge Thomas White, "took me by the hand, exhorting me for some time. I felt very happy under her wholesome admonitions."[25]

Certainly women, who could exercise such influence over the itinerants, were a formidable force to contend with when displeased. Not only could Methodist women show their displeasure by refusing their moral support and by closing their homes to hard-pressed itinerants, they could also cut back on their financial contributions and persuade those husbands who were Methodists to do the same. This wouldn't be the first nor the last time that the power of the purse was used to drive home a message to a basically authoritarian institution.

Blacks

Free and enslaved blacks joined white women in presenting the same interesting paradox. Despite being segregated and being denied leadership roles and voting rights in the Methodist polity, both groups were inordinately drawn to Peninsula Methodism. But while white women were treated as second-class Methodists, blacks of both sexes were relegated to a third-class status. Blacks were restricted to the back of the church or the gallery during regular worship, were limited to an area behind the speaker's platform at camp meetings, and could only join all-black class meetings, which were often led by white men. There is even some indication that while in the gallery, blacks were forced to stand.

Segregation of blacks was standard procedure from almost the very first. During the American Revolution, for example, both Asbury and Garrettson spoke to segregated audiences on the Peninsula. But there is some evidence that segregation of blacks, as well as of white women, was less formal in smaller churches. One case in point was Concord Methodist Episcopal Church, east of Seaford, Sussex County, where the question of where to seat blacks wasn't settled until the early nineteenth century. Although some blacks, such as Harry Hosier, were effective preachers, all regular circuit appointments on the Peninsula were reserved for white men.[26]

Yet enslaved and free blacks became Methodists in impressive numbers. In 1787, the first year of a complete count of Peninsula Methodists by race, blacks numbered 1,839, or 30 percent of all Delmarva Methodists. By 1793 the black number was up to 3,549, though it leveled off in the subsequent "dull times" that followed. Starting with the Second Great Awakening in 1800, black membership shot up to over nine thousand by 1808, representing 38 percent of the Peninsula's Methodists. With the waning of some of the enthusiasm generated by the Second Great Awakening and changes in the Methodist position on slavery, black Methodists dropped below eight thousand in 1814. But because of an even greater slippage in white membership, 43 percent of the Peninsula's

Methodists were black. Over the next six years, black membership decreased slightly while white membership totals increased. By 1820 black membership had declined to 36 percent of the Peninsula's total.

It is clear that a higher percentage of Peninsula blacks than whites became Methodists. In 1810, for example, about 25 percent of Delmarva's adult blacks sixteen years of age and over were Methodists. That same year, slightly less than 20 percent of the Peninsula's adult whites were Methodists.[27] Probably the majority of black Methodists were women, but there isn't enough extant evidence to be sure.

Why did blacks find Methodism so attractive? To start with, there is the familiar explanation that Methodism, by stressing the conversion experience more than religious instruction, made itself easily accessible to illiterate blacks and whites. In addition, no other religious group on the Peninsula treated blacks better. Early Methodist itinerants worked very hard to make black converts and spoke out in a clear voice against slavery. By contrast, at least some clergy of other denominations seemed disinterested in blacks, and a few supported slavery. Even the Quakers and Nicholites, who spoke out vehemently against slavery, showed little interest in recruiting black members.

From an early date, John Wesley had been very sympathetic to the plight of blacks, holding that they were in no way inferior to whites. Moreover, Wesley saw to it that the Methodist General Rules of 1743 took a clear stand against slavery. These same General Rules were brought to America by Methodist missionaries. In subsequent years, Wesley's antislavery position hardened, particularly after he read a persuasive abolitionist pamphlet by the American Quaker Anthony Benezet.

Francis Asbury, who seemed strongly influenced by Wesley's antislavery sentiment, was pleased by black responses to his preaching on the Peninsula. While in semiseclusion in Delaware in 1778, Asbury decided that Methodists must follow the Quaker lead and support abolitionism or suffer God's displeasure. Subsequent stands taken by Methodist Conferences in America clearly labeled slavery an evil to be firmly opposed.

On the Peninsula, circuit riders attacked slavery in vigorous fashion and continued to flail away at that peculiar institution into the first decade of the nineteenth century. At first the crusade was led by English-born Methodists such as Asbury, but soon American-born preachers were leading the charge. An example was Joseph Everett, born and raised in Queen Anne's County, who not only preached against slavery "with all his might" but also refused to eat with slaveholders. In 1797 in Talbot County, an Episcopal rector complained that the Methodist preachers "relish the manumitting subject as highly as the Quaker preachers and spread the evil far and wide." Methodist preachers did not hestitate to warn that the institution of slavery might provoke divine wrath. In 1801 a circuit rider told his congregation in Somerset County to assume that "the clouds of vengeance are collecting over the heads of the inhabitants of this country for their cruelty to the poor distressed Africans."[28]

By the beginning of the nineteenth century, economic and institutional realities began to affect the Methodist crusade against slavery. Irate slaveholders increasingly refused to allow Methodist preachers access to their slaves. While in Delaware in 1778, Asbury was aware of this problem and warned that in promoting the freedom of black bodies from bondage, some might overlook the primary importance of black souls. Without hearing the gospel, blacks would become "vassals of Satan in eternal fire."

To Methodists, saving blacks from becoming the "vassals of Satan" was paramount. Unlike Quakers, who depended on the guidance of the inner light, Wesleyans held that preaching the gospel was central to soul saving. But now, what a terrible conundrum! If irate slave masters continued to bar Methodist preaching, the saving grace of God might be denied black slaves. What then was more important for the black slave: freedom from earthly bondage or freedom from eternal damnation? Peninsula circuit riders responded to that question by stressing soul saving, and consequently toned down their antislavery rhetoric.

Certainly other factors also contributed to the new, softer approach to slavery. The desire to attract slaveholders to Methodism, even if this meant abandoning previous principles, was prompted by traditional institutional needs and concerns. Simply put, slaveholders' contributions helped fill Methodist coffers. Methodists also justified the admission of slaveholders to membership on the grounds that exposure to the gospel would imbue them with the spirit of Christian charity and compassion which, inevitably, would lead to better treatment of their slaves.

Whatever the justification, on the Peninsula and across the nation the Methodist antislavery crusade lost much of its fire after 1800. The black community, which had taken due note of the earlier Methodist position, was aware of the change. The slow erosion of black membership on the Peninsula after 1810 probably reflected the fact that Methodism was no longer seen by blacks as a vigorous and unequivocal enemy of slavery.[29]

Blacks seemed to be drawn to the emotional side of early Methodism, and often their vocal outbursts proved a godsend to Peninsula preachers unable to stir lethargic whites. With a feeling of great satisfaction, itinerants reported that black audiences responded to the message by praising the Lord "in the song, in the shout and in the dance." When black emotionalism went too far, however, blacks were reined in by being reminded of "the impropriety of being governed by our passions."

Although whites might give free rein to their own passions at religious gatherings, many whites were uncomfortable in the presence of black emotionalism. In 1800 northwest of Berlin, Worcester County, a service was being carried on in a newly constructed house of worship. As blacks responded to the message with increasing verbal enthusiasm, whites in the congregation fled the building for fear that they too would be expected to cry aloud and fall to the floor, "very much exposing themselves." One slave master in southwestern Sussex became so uncomfortable with black Methodism that he even gave an old female her freedom because "she had too much religion."[30]

But it would be a mistake to see black Methodism as just a highly emotional variant of white Methodism. Some of the Peninsula's blacks had been born in Africa, while many if not most of the rest remembered or heard stories of parents, grandparents, and great-grandparents who had crossed the Atlantic in the holds of slave ships. Over the years most of the culture and language of Africa was lost, but some remnants of the African heritage did survive. It is easy to see, for example, a strong residue of African behavior patterns in the joyful, unrestrained actions of blacks at religious services. Perhaps foremost was the positive celebration of life that characterized blacks in worship and led them to reject the sense of guilt that seemed to pervade white Methodism.

To be more specific, the black style of demonstrative worship during religious services—which seemed so alien, and therefore so threatening, to many Peninsula whites—had its roots in the religious practices of the African village. As Albert J. Raboteau's study of slave religion has shown, among American slaves the gods of Africa soon gave way to the God of white Christianity, but the African style of worship didn't die. Rather, it found a home in Methodism, as well as in some of the other evangelical faiths. And so it was that Peninsula Methodism, as refracted by black sensibilities, preserved in its services the cultural shards of the

African past. Put another way, Peninsula Methodism provided a theater in which the sons and daughters of Africa could reaffirm, through joyful, emotional participation, just who they were.[31]

At times, black emotionalism caused damage to Methodist chapels. In 1801, at a service in Moore's Chapel in southwestern Sussex, blacks were so enthusiastic that their movements brought the gallery crashing down on the whites below. Fortunately, the large crowd below was able to support and then lower the collapsing gallery to the floor without injury to anyone. In 1803 at Asbury Methodist Church in Wilmington, blacks were blamed for breaking benches during class meetings. At Barratt's Chapel in 1814, the board of trustees had to assign one of its members the responsibility for repairing any damage caused by black worshipers. In addition, one trustee had to be present at every meeting of blacks in the chapel.[32]

White presence at black religious meetings was not just to prevent physical harm to Methodist buildings. Thanks to Methodism, blacks were coming together for the first time in very large groups. The possibility that these occasions might be used to air black grievances which, in turn, could lead to violent rebellion was not lost on the white community. Given white anxieties, it isn't surprising that when blacks assembled for religious services they were harassed by whites.

But what a marvelous release it must have been for so many blacks to meet together, to wax emotional through shouting and singing, and to feel, as did white women, a shared sense of solidarity surging through the group. The presence of whites might stop the flow of words critical of the status quo, but it could do little to dam the flow of emotions that had been stoically stored in black hearts since slavery's introduction to the Peninsula during the seventeenth century.

White paranoia about slave rebellion and white prejudice against blacks could be found everywhere on the Peninsula, but it was probably greatest on the Eastern Shores of Maryland and Virginia, where slavery was most heavily concentrated. Even in Delaware, where by 1810 slavery was considerably weaker and free blacks clearly outnumbered slaves in every one of the state's three counties, there was uneasiness about the actions of both free blacks and slaves. One might suspect that Wilmington would have been the least paranoid community on the Peninsula, but even there white Methodists wished to keep an eye on their black brothers and sisters.[33]

In 1800 or 1801, frustrated at being treated as third-class

Methodists, black members of Asbury Methodist Episcopal Church, on Third and Walnut streets in Wilmington, began holding their own religious services in black homes and in shady groves along the edge of the city. Simultaneously these blacks continued to attend Asbury, where they were relegated to the gallery during regular services but were allowed to use the main floor for class meetings when the church was empty. In June 1805 Asbury's trustees accused black members of breaking benches and leaving the church "so defiled by dirt . . . as to render it unfit to meet in." The trustees then issued an ultimatum to the black members, telling them that the only place they could hold future meetings would be in the gallery. This ultimatum evidently ignited long-smoldering resentment, and the black members of Asbury left in 1805 to build Ezion Church, a stone structure on Ninth and French streets some six blocks from Asbury. Built with the financial help from the white community, including some members of Asbury, Ezion became the first all-black Methodist Episcopal Church on Delmarva.

According to Peter Spencer, a local preacher and one of the founders of Ezion, "We thought we could have the rule of our church." Ezion did have its own board of trustees, class leaders, and lay preachers, but it had to accept the same white pastor who was assigned to Asbury Church. Nevertheless, Ezion's members assumed that they had the right to "refuse any that were not thought proper persons to preach for us." But in 1812 Ezion's white pastor, James Bateman, informed the black congregation's leaders that they had no right to reject a pastor and that he exercised ultimate authority over the church and its activities. Ezion refused to acknowledge Bateman's claims. Bateman responded by accusing Ezion's leadership of breaking the Methodist *Discipline,* and then summarily dismissed the trustees and class leaders without so much as a hearing. Led by Spencer, thirty-one black families left Ezion in 1813 and, with financial support from wealthy Quakers, erected the African Union Church, or Old Union as it was called, nearly opposite Ezion. Spencer became the pastor of a congregation that maintained it was Methodist but not Methodist Episcopal. Old Union was the first truly independent black church in the United States and the parent body of the African Union Methodist Protestant and the Union American Methodist Episcopal churches.[34]

The Old Union story demonstrates that, in Wilmington at least, white Methodism was willing to allow blacks to establish their own congregation and build their own church. The type of independence that Peter Spencer and his followers yearned for,

Peter Spencer
(Courtesy: Dr. James Newton, University of Delaware)

however, was not tolerated by white Methodism. To achieve real independence from white control, black Methodists were forced to cut all ties with the Methodist Episcopal Church. Prior to 1820, no other group of blacks on the Peninsula organized a separate Methodist Episcopal congregation similar to Ezion or took the additional step of following Old Union's example to complete independence. Except for Spencer's movement, there is no further evidence on the Peninsula of black agitation for independence from white Methodism until 1822, when some members of Richard Allen's African Methodist Episcopal movement, based in Philadelphia, were accused of trying to win over black Methodists in the Smyrna, Delaware, area.

In addition to its early stand against slavery, its eagerness to preach to blacks, its ability to provide a conduit for the pouring forth of black emotions, and its willingness to provide blacks with an opportunity to meet in large numbers and reaffirm their collective identity, Peninsula Methodism attracted blacks through the content of its sermons, hymns, and prayers. The Methodist message that men are responsible for their own spiritual destiny and that after death the kingdom of God was open to all men regardless of race and previous condition of servitude was a heady tonic.

In Talbot County in 1782, Freeborn Garrettson found blacks "in vassalage" but happy in the consolations of Christianity. The Methodist message excited blacks because it contrasted so much with the sorrow of their daily lives. A circuit rider found in lower Somerset County in 1801 that "those poor creatures who have to work hard all day under the lash of tyranny" came out at night through frost and snow to attend Methodist meetings and then went home again "rejoicing."[35]

Through the preaching, Bible readings, and hymns, blacks saw the parallel of their own difficult journey to the trials and tribulations of the ancient Israelites. The enslavement of the Hebrews in Egypt and their eventual deliverance from bondage by God was not lost on the sons of Africa, held captive on a peninsula in a distant land. Moreover, if deliverance in this world was not imminent, certainly the chains of slavery and the barriers erected by prejudice would disappear when the souls of the dead faced final judgement. And that final judgement would not be based on skin color, wealth, power, and worldly goods, but on how pure and holy in Christ one's life had been lived.

The Promise of Salvation

To the circuit riders itinerating through the Peninsula and to the large crowds that came to hear them preach, this world was important, but the world beyond death had even greater significance. Overwhelmingly, the subject that the circuit riders addressed and the message their listeners most wanted to hear was how to be saved from the fires of damnation and enter the Kingdom of Heaven.

No matter how unpleasant life might be for the Peninsula's blacks and poor whites, the termination of that life was a traumatic event to contemplate. To the Peninsula's "middling" and "better sort," death was an increasingly difficult specter to deal with. The increased discomfort that marked the gentry's dealings with death grew out of the decline of Anglicanism's spiritual hold on the "better sort" in the second half of the eighteenth century.

Spiritual deadness was also typical of the rest of Peninsula society. Ezekiel Cooper, born in 1763 to an Anglican family of the "middling sort" in Caroline County, found spiritual death among almost all of his acquaintances. He observed that it "was almost a miracle to find a man of real piety."[36] Because of this dearth of piety and faith, physical death among all classes was increasingly dealt with in the context of family relationships and secular values. To many on the Peninsula, this was less than satisfying; it was not enough.

George Whitefield and other evangelists of the First Great Awakening brought to the Peninsula an awful awareness of the twin possibilities that followed death: an eternity in Heaven or Hell. As subsequent years dimmed Delmarvan memories of Whitefield and company, concern with life after death became less central but remained important. While some, consciously or unconsciously, rejected the Church of England's answer to the question of immortality, others turned to the Church for assurance only to find a lack of theological certainty that must have been unnerving.

In 1773 Samuel Keene, rector of St. Luke's Parish in northern Queen Anne's County, summed up the Anglican position on life after death. Locked in debate with a Methodist itinerant, Keene told his audience that "he knew nothing of sin being forgiven, or of being converted." He did, however, have "hope, as all Christian people had, of being saved, and that was all any of us had." But Delmarvans wanted something more solid than just "hope."

When the Methodists arrived on the Peninsula, they preached

not "hope" but "certainty." The people on Delmarva were ready and waiting for this message. The need to confront the specter of death with spiritual confidence cut across all races, classes, and ages. Indeed, the ability to meet the need for "certainty" may have been the single most important factor in explaining Methodist success on the Peninsula.

Methodists not only preached "certainty," they practiced "certainty." Typical of this was the way three Methodists met death. Sarah Coulter of Lewes, Delaware, had been delivered from "the bondage of sin and its consequences, the fear of Death and Hell" soon after joining the Wesleyans. On her death bed in 1789, she "cried out with a strong distinct voice, 'O death, where is thy sting, O grave, where is thy victory.' " In the early nineteenth century, the wife of Isaac Davis of Smyrna, Delaware, just before dying, "audibly and distinctly said 'Here I go to Heaven' and died without a struggle or a groan." In 1813 in Queen Anne's County on Spaniard's Neck, west of Centreville, planter Robert Emory lay near to death. He was asked by his son John, a circuit rider and future bishop, "Do you see your way clear to heaven?" Robert Emory answered, "Yes, I am as sure of it as that two and two make four." A few minutes later he "tranquilly breathed his last." The confidence with which these and other Methodists faced death caused non-Methodists to stand up and take notice.

But probably no death excited the interest of the general populace as did that of John Laws. As a young man living in the St. Johnstown area just east of Greenwood in northwestern Sussex, Laws contracted a terminal illness and was subsequently visited and converted to Methodism by Asbury. Prior to his death in 1779, Laws spoke persuasively to his family and acquaintances of his new-found faith and how it enabled him to face death with confidence. A large number who heard Laws were moved "to reform their own lives and seek the Lord." Approximately a thousand people gathered at Law's funeral and heard a sermon preached by Asbury. That same year a Methodist society, inspired by Laws's words and example, was formed at St. Johnstown.[37]

Chapter Five

The Broadcasters of Methodism

The new confidence with which many Delmarvans lived their lives and then met death reflected the circuit riders' extraordinary success in spreading the Wesleyan message. Prior to 1820, approximately 250 different itinerants were assigned to the Peninsula. Of the 158 whose birthplaces can be identified, 102, or 65 percent, were born on Delmarva. Many other native sons took up the itinerancy on circuits in other regions of America. The disproportionately large number of Delmarvans who became Methodist preachers is said to have caused Asbury to label the Peninsula his "preacher garden."[1]

Educational Background

In 1773 in Queen Anne's County, an Anglican cleric argued that a certain Methodist itinerant should not be allowed to preach because he lacked a college education. In subsequent years this complaint became a familiar litany, and for good reason. Before 1820 only a few Methodist preachers had attended college. Indeed, most had only a few years of formal schooling. Many could be labeled "uncultured," and at least a few were semiliterate or illiterate. Joseph Cromwell, for example, an unusually effective preacher who was one of the pioneers in bringing Methodism to Talbot County in 1777, could not write his name.

But then many itinerants and laymen felt that if God called a man to preach, God would provide the necessary gifts. Moreover, if literacy levels elsewhere in the United States are any indication, a majority of Delmarvans were either illiterate or semiliterate until well into the nineteenth century. Under these circumstances, the circuit rider's limited formal education proved advantageous because, instinctively, he understood how to communicate with the large number of Delmarvans who had little familiarity with the written word. Because their own formal education was limited, many of the "middling" and "better sort" could also relate to sermons couched in the language and imagery that appealed to the "lower sort."

Early Methodists agreed that it was conversion and not education that made one fit for the ministry. While in hiding at John Fogwell's in 1778, Asbury declared that "holiness is preferable to the greatest wisdom." Thirty-eight years later Ezekiel Cooper, a product of Caroline County and a former itinerant on the Peninsula who had gone on to head the Methodist Book Concern, restated the Methodist position on the education of its clergy:

> Though language, arts, and sciences ought to be encouraged, and, no doubt, have their various excellent uses, yet nevertheless, they are not the essential, nor preeminent qualifications of an apostolic, primitive or modern Christian minister or bishop. The scriptures are clear and full on this point—the apostles were not learned men. We are also informed that many of the primitive fathers were not learned men.[2]

As Cooper pointed out, most Methodists didn't feel a good, formal education was necessary for a career in the ministry, but they did think "it ought to be encouraged."

By the standards of the day, a few Peninsula itinerants did have fairly impressive academic credentials. John King, one of the first to preach on the Peninsula, was said to be educated at Oxford and hold an M.D. degree from London Medical College. William Chandler, who sparked the Second Great Awakening on the Peninsula, was supposed to have studied medicine under early America's best-known physician, Dr. Benjamin Rush of Philadelphia. Thomas Haskins was reading law in Dover when he was converted by Freeborn Garrettson in 1780. Two years later Haskins was riding the Somerset Circuit. John Emory received a fine classical education from private schools in Easton, Maryland, and Strasburg, Pennsylvania, and at Washington College in Chestertown, Maryland. Like Haskins, Emory too read law. After starting his own legal practice in Centreville, Queen Anne's County, in 1808, Emory decided to become a Methodist itinerant and was serving the Caroline Circuit by 1810.

Although Wesley and Asbury didn't demand much formal education of their preachers, they did insist that the itinerants read extensively for their own spiritual growth. While on the Peninsula in 1779, Asbury noted that the demands of the job were such that "in many circuits, the preachers have hardly an opportunity of reading their Bibles, much less anything else." Asbury thought that it would be well, "under such circumstances, if the preachers could have one spare day in every week for the purpose of improving themselves."

Self-improvement through reading generally meant religious books and tracts, but not entirely. While some itinerants limited themselves to spiritual works, others read more widely, roaming particularly through works on history and medicine. William Colbert, who spent a number of years on the Peninsula, is a case in point. In addition to the usual, spiritually oriented materials, Colbert also read a biography of Benjamin Franklin, some of Franklin's essays, and histories dealing with the United States and classical antiquity. Colbert's personal observation that life was a painful travail was confirmed by these readings. After finishing a volume on ancient Rome, Colbert sadly noted, "What a field of blood is this world."[3]

On Being Saved and The Call to Serve

Christopher Spry of Talbot County led a life of youthful dissipation until he "was awakened" in 1791. But the process of being born again wasn't easy. Spry tells us, "I fasted twice in the week and prayed . . sometimes 17 times a day; yet I was nine months before I got the blessing." The symbolism suggested by the nine-month waiting period before Spry could be born again as a "new man" is arresting. Spry went on to become a Methodist itinerant and spent a number of years riding the circuits of Delmarva.

Spry's conversion followed a pattern familiar to the lives of other itinerants who served the Peninsula. Convinced that they were stained by personal sin, some had deliberately turned to a regimen that promised a rebirth experience. In the Arminian-Methodist tradition, God's work was aided by the actions of those seeking his peace and pardon.

In many cases the desire for conversion was generated by a heightened sensitivity to death. A sudden awakening to mortality might be caused by the loss of relatives and friends, a close personal brush with death, or by a hellfire and brimstone sermon delivered by a wandering itinerant.

Death was a constant companion, and probably no one was more personally touched by it at an early age than Thomas Smith, a native of Kent County, Maryland. While very young, Smith lost both parents, two sisters, and a brother to a smallpox epidemic. At the age of eight, a classmate at school alerted him to the agonies of Hell, and Smith determined not to end up there. The next year he had a conversion experience.

For most Peninsula itinerants, however, the conversion experience occurred in the middle or late teens, and it usually was credited, as in the case of Christopher Spry, with saving him from a life of dissipation. Whatever the event that triggered the conversion, most itinerants could give the exact date, time, and place of their "awakening."[4]

The degree of intensity of the conversion experience probably explains, in part, why some white males decided to become spiritual shepherds and why others were content to be part of the flock. Joseph Everett of Queen Anne's County actually experienced two conversions, separated by fifteen years of "backsliding." The intense feeling of euphoria and freedom felt after the first conversion led him to write

> I rode on the sky,
> Freely justified I!
> Nor envied Elijah his seat:
> My soul mounted higher
> In a chariot of fire,
> And the moon it was under my feet.

Also rising skyward like a passenger in a helium ballon was Levi Scott of Odessa, Delaware. His conversion in 1822 "was an ecstatic moment," when he seemed to be "flying through the midst of heaven."[5]

A Change in Vocation

As a group, itinerants were not born to privilege and wealth, nor did they generally have a superior education. But, on the whole, they did seem to be considerably more capable and energetic than the average Peninsula resident. Some abandoned promising futures in business, law, and medicine for the uncertainties of the Methodist circuit. Solomon "Devil Driver" Sharp was a merchant in Camden, Kent County, Delaware, and Thomas Smith owned a successful business in Chestertown. William Williams of Worcester County had a medical practice, while John Emory, Thomas Haskins, and

John Emory
(Courtesy, Methodist Collection, Drew University, Madison, NJ)

Lawrence Lawrenson gave up promising futures in the legal profession. Probably most toiled on the family farm, like Joseph Everett of Queen Anne's County, or were artisans like tailor William Gill and shoemaker Joseph Wyatt, both of Kent County, Delaware.[6]

In contrast to the economic security provided by their previous jobs, the itinerancy offered very low pay and working conditions that, at best, were physically debilitating. Adding to the circuit rider's insecurity was the right of Methodist bishops to assign the itinerant to a circuit anywhere in the United States.

Understandably, not all of the circuit riders' relatives approved of this change in vocation. Despite the fact that he was a devout Methodist, John Emory's father was so upset with his son's decision to abandon law for the insecurity of the ministry that he refused to communicate with his son for two years. Joseph Everett had his hands full with an obstinate wife who so strongly objected to his itinerancy that she "made a great noise which gave me much trouble." Most of the other itinerants did not experience Everett's problem—they weren't married.

Steps Up the Ladder

Moving from personal conversion to circuit rider involved a number of intermediate steps. Those who were newly awakened took on increasingly more important leadership roles in their local Methodist societies, and by doing so attracted the attention of the itinerants. John Emory, for example, was "saved" on August 18, 1806, and went on to become class leader, exhorter, and by 1809, local preacher. Somewhere along the line of ascending steps, a decision was made to enter the itinerant ministry.

If the circuit itinerant was impressed with the young candidate's leadership and speaking abilities and if the Quarterly Meeting approved, the young man was invited to the Annual Conference to take an oral examination to test his religious orthodoxy. Usually the exam was administered by Francis Asbury. In the case of Thomas Ware in 1783, one of Asbury's questions was: "Have all men since the fall of Adam been possessed of free will?" Ware responded affirmatively.

If, like Ware, the candidate satisfactorily answered all of the questions and otherwise met with Conference approval, he was assigned to work with older, more experienced circuit riders for two years of on-the-job training. During those two years, he was considered "on trial." At the end of the trial period the candidate's work and personality were evaluated, and he was quizzed again concerning his doctrinal views. If found acceptable by the Annual Conference, he was declared a preacher in "full connection."

After 1784, full connection usually meant ordination as a deacon with the right to baptize, perform marriages, and to assist an elder in the administration of the Lord's Supper. After serving as a deacon for at least two years, a circuit rider could be elected an elder by the Annual Conference, which meant that he would be fully ordained. Experienced and trusted elders were appointed by the bishop as presiding elders to act as superintendents of districts made up of a number of circuits. In 1801, for example, Thomas Ware was presiding elder over the Delaware and Eastern Shore District, which included all of the Peninsula except New Castle and Cecil counties and counted nine circuits and nineteen circuit riders. The final rung on the ascending ladder was reached by election to the episcopacy. John Emory of Spaniard's Neck, Queen Anne's County, and Levi Scott of Odessa, Delaware, were elected bishops in 1832 and 1852 respectively.[7]

A Calling to Poverty

A majority of circuit riders didn't remain in the itinerancy long enough to move very far up the rungs of the ecclesiastical ladder. One reason was the low salary that made the Methodist itinerancy a brotherhood of poverty. As far back as 1774, a uniform salary for all itinerants was established by Annual Conference. In subsequent years, additional salary supplements were established for circuit riders with families. In 1800, the annual salary was increased from $64 to $80, and the supplement for a wife was set at $80 with lesser sums for each child under fifteen years. In 1816, the annual salary and the supplement for a wife were both increased to $100. Unfortunately for the itinerants, these low figures represented a ceiling rather than a guaranteed salary base. In reality, many itinerants were paid far less because Methodist circuits and districts were constantly strapped for funds.

An itinerant could request reimbursement for money spent in maintaining himself and his horse on the circuit. Food for rider and horse, fees for ferry crossings, and the cost of horseshoeing were all reimbursable expenses. But again, the circuit rider would be lucky to collect in full. To help meet this shortfall in reimbursements, after 1792 circuit riders were allowed to accept payment for performing marriages, provided that the fee was divided among the preachers in the district who had not been fully reimbursed for expenses.

Occasionally circuit riders received gifts from individual laymen. In 1802, for example, Thomas Smith was presented with $100 as he was about to leave the Northampton Circuit, on the southern tip of the Peninsula. But monetary gifts were not very common, and a preacher counted himself fortunate to receive one.

A comparison with incomes of Americans in other occupations clearly shows how poorly itinerants were paid. Through the last quarter of the eighteenth century, the annual salary for an unmarried circuit rider was set at the equivalent of £24 Pennsylvania currency, or about $64. Probably few itinerants received the full amount due them, but even if they did, their annual income was significantly less than what an unskilled American laborer could make in a year. Skilled artisans, such as carpenters, might make four times as much as a bachelor itinerant.

Unless the neophyte itinerant had some funds of his own, he was clearly entering a life of economic destitution. A case in point was Philip Cox, who served a circuit in the Kent County, Delaware, area in 1777–78. The circuit rider was expected to provide his own horse. But because he couldn't afford a horse, Cox became a pedestrian itinerant and carried what little he owned in a "linen wallet" slung over a shoulder. Out of pity, Judge White's daughters made Cox some undergarments and some local Methodists finally donated enough money for him to buy a horse.

On paper, married itinerants could do considerably better after a salary supplement for supporting a wife was established, first on a selective basis in 1784 and then broadened to include all married itinerants in 1796. But few itinerants collected the full supplement, and even when they did it was far from enough.

Typical was the case of Caleb Boyer, who was born and raised just south of Dover. Converted by Freeborn Garrettson in 1778, he became an itinerant about twenty months later. A great extemporizer, Boyer was soon considered one of early Methodism's finest preachers. After marrying, however, he found that the $160 produced by his annual salary and supplement was simply inadequate. He located in or near Dover in 1788 and served as a local preacher for twenty-five years. Not surprisingly, few itinerants could afford to have a family until well into the nineteenth century.[8]

Relations With Women

Along with economic hardship, itinerants' wives had to tolerate long periods of separation from their husbands. But for wives who were convinced Methodists, their husbands' work was so significant that it justified the sacrifice. The spirited opposition of Joseph Everett's wife to his new vocation, for example, ended when she was converted.

The preponderance of single itinerants reflected the low salary, but it also reflected the preference of Francis Asbury and some others for a celibate ministry. Asbury's support of celibacy was implicit in his many tributes to celibate circuit riders and in the fact that he made his own life of celebration of celibacy. While the preference wasn't unanimous among other leaders of early American Methodism—Bishop Coke, for example, supported the idea of itinerants having families—it was evidently shared by many. It surfaced at the Philadelphia Annual Conference held at Smyrna in 1803, when great opposition was expressed to allowing married men ride circuits. By the time of Asbury's death in 1816, the celibacy concept for the Methodist ministry was on the way out, but its importance in early American Methodism deserves attention.[9]

The preponderance of young, single itinerants had a considerable impact on the female population. Delmarva's women were unaccustomed to the type of men that the evangalists seemed to be. Articulate, sensitive, compassionate, and impassioned, the circuit riders set themselves apart from other men by providing women with emotional experiences far different from any they had known. The itinerants' passionate pleas for changed hearts were heard in candle-lit barns or in bucolic settings under shade trees beside meandering brooks and creeks, as well as in the simplicity of newly completed Methodist meeting houses. The combination of the young itinerant, his fervent message, and the romantic setting stirred emotions in female hearts that were a mixture of the sacred and the profane.

In this sensually charged atmosphere, the celibate itinerants were hard pressed to avoid temptation. Thomas Rankin, while in Queen Anne's County in 1775, found himself "uncommonly exercised by foolish and impertinent desires." He struggled "with the remains of a carnal mind," and begged God to give him a "clean heart." Married itinerants were also subject to sexual stirrings. William Colbert, while serving Maryland's upper Eastern Shore in 1805, lamented separation from his wife. Colbert soon found a vicarious outlet in reading some seventy pages of "that masterly piece of eloquence—the trial of Lord Heedfort for the seduction of the wife of Charles Massey, an Irish clergyman."

Sigmund Freud might have explained the circuit riders' exceptional enthusiasm and energy in terms of sexual sublimation, but some Methodist leaders weren't so sure that the sex drive would remain sublimated. John Wesley was particularly sensitive to the problem and warned an itinerant in Ireland to "avoid all familiarity with women. This is a deadly poison both to them and to you. You cannot be to wary in this respect." Asbury shared Wesley's concern. In 1774 he advised an itinerant on Maryland's Western Shore to "stand at all possible distance from the female sex, that you be not betrayed by them that will damage the young mind and sink the aspiring soul and blast the prospect of the future man." Among the articles of religion adopted by American Methodists in 1784 was a warning to itinerants to "converse sparingly and cautiously with women."[10]

Not all itinerants heeded the advice. In 1787 Thomas Chew was one of three presiding elders of a district that covered Maryland's upper Eastern Shore and most of Delaware. A few miles below Milford, Delaware, Chew met with "a Delilah," causing him to be expelled from the itinerancy. Twenty years later a youthful itinerant on the Lewes [Delaware] Circuit had to marry a young woman he had gotten pregnant while on a previous circuit and move to the frontier. Probably no preacher was more controversial than Richard Lyon, who served a number of Peninsula circuits prior to 1807. "Some said that he was a wizard, some that he carried love powders, others that he was in league with the devil." Some even call him a "lyon in sheep's clothing." His last Peninsula position was on the Smyrna Circuit, where he was simply called "vituperative" and forced to leave for the Bristol [Pennsylvania] Circuit. Lyon was later expelled from the Methodist Church for "fornication."[11]

Working and Living Conditions

Physical hardships and unhealthy living conditions also insured that the itinerancy would be a calling primarily for the young. Indeed, so exhausting and debilitating was the life that "locating," because of declining health, was very common. At the Christmas Conference in Baltimore in 1784, Thomas Ware said of his fellow circuit riders, "Although there were but a few on whose heads time had begun to snow, yet several of them appeared to be way-worn and weather-beaten into premature age."

And no wonder! On the Peninsula, itinerants traveled circuits that could be two hundred miles long on horses that were cheaply purchased and, therefore, undependable and even dangerous to ride. In 1785 in Caroline County, one itinerant was thrown by "a strange, clumsy horse," resulting in his partial blindness "for some time." Even if the itinerant wasn't thrown, traveling on horseback could be very unpleasant. In 1801 William Colbert left Salisbury on "a young, wild colt" and experienced "a very dangerous ride."

A typical itinerant's day started very early. In 1780 the Annual Conference in Baltimore affirmed that all preachers ought to rise at 4:00 or 5:00 A.M. and that it was shameful for a preacher to be in bed until 6:00 A.M. Itinerants took these directions seriously. James Moore, on the Talbot Circuit in 1801, actually made pastoral calls before sunrise. A typical day for Thomas Smith, as he labored on Virginia's Eastern Shore in 1800, meant an early rise in order to make two preaching stops, be present at two class meetings, and, if possible, lead a prayer meeting. Then it was off to the home of a Methodist layman for a bed and some food. At times the circuit rider might find lodging with one of the gentry such as Richard Bassett or Thomas Airey, but more often the night was spent sharing a one-room cabin with a large Methodist family too poor to afford a candle. Asbury, while on the Peninsula in 1779, summarized the lot of the itinerant: "In this our labour, we have to encourage hunger, heat and many restless nights with mosquitos, unwholesome provisions and bad water."[12]

The mosquitos were more than just a nuisance. Unknown to the itinerants and their contemporaries, mosquitos were the carriers of malaria as well as yellow fever. The prevalance of malaria on the Peninsula caused Delmarva to be considered a high-risk area for itinerants. Sussex County, in particular, had a bad reputation. Itinerants' journals testify to the spread of malarial fevers among the circuit riders, with those native to the Peninsula faring better than those raised in more elevated regions.

Asbury was very sensitive to the danger of lowland fevers and would often tell itinerant Henry Boehm, "Brother A or B has been too long in the rice plantations [South Carolina] or on the Peninsula; he looks pale, health begins to decline; he must go up to the highlands." A native of Lancaster, Pennsylvania, Boehm was greatly relieved to be transferred from the Peninsula back to his native state in 1802. The change from the "low, level, and unhealthy" Peninsula was "wonderful" to his health and spirits. It was only with great reluctance that many natives of upland America accepted assignment to the Peninsula. Pennsylvanian Robert Roberts, who would be elected bishop in 1816, was very hestitant to serve a Peninsula circuit in 1814 because he was convinced that the Peninsula would "injure his health."[13]

The variable nature of the weather on the Peninsula proved a shock to British itinerants. While at Judge White's during the American Revolution, Asbury found that winter and summer were much more extreme than in England. Moreover, he found that the winter's snow and ice restricted his travels in a manner that Europeans would be hard put to understand.

Methodist preachers could understand the reluctance of Delmarvans to travel in winter conditions, but they were quite puzzled by the unwillingness of the populace to turn out in wet weather. Being new to the region in 1785, itinerant Robert Ayres seemed surprised that, after riding "through much rain to Thomas Layton's, none attended." A more seasoned William Colbert summed up the situation nicely in 1796 by pointing out that there was no sense in keeping preaching appointments if it was raining because "people will not go to meeting in this country if it is wet."[14]

Preaching Skills

Itinerants were willing to tolerate the poverty, physical hardships, and disease that attended their calling because they were extraordinarily motivated. At stake were the souls of men and women, and the circuit rider intended to win them for God. But victory over the forces of evil demanded certain skills as well as good intentions. To start with, circuit riders had to be arresting speakers because Methodism was, above all else, a preaching religion. When Asbury talked of building a house of worship in western Sussex in 1780, he didn't call it a chapel; he called it a "preaching house."

In Baltimore in 1807, a Methodist itinerant said, "I do not deem a reader of sermons deserving the name preacher of the gospel." No Methodist itinerant worth his salt would emulate the example of Episcopal clerics, who usually read carefully written sermons to their congregations. To the Methodists, since God provided inspiration for the appropriate words, there was no need to depend on a written presentation. Indeed, in 1807, a curious Joshua Thomas was drawn to a Methodist camp meeting in lower Somerset

County to see how people could pray without a book and preach without a written sermon.

So effective at extemporaneous preaching did Methodist preachers become that Anglican and Episcopalian divines knew that in spontaneous oratory they couldn't compete. In 1773 in northern Queen Anne's County, Methodist itinerant Abraham Whitworth threw down the gauntlet to the local Anglican rector in front of a large audience, proposing that the right of each to preach the gospel be settled by a test. The Church of England parson would choose a text from anywhere in the Bible, and Whitworth would immediately preach a sermon based on the passage. Then Whitworth would choose the text, the Anglican divine would preach on it, and "the audience could judge who was most fit." The crowd was for it, but the Anglican parson, no doubt convinced that he would lose, quickly excused himself, "saying it was late in the day."[15]

The irony, of course, was that the supposedly spontaneous Methodist sermon, despite the fact that it was dramatically delivered without notes, was a carefully crafted presentation, honed to perfection by constant repetition. On the Peninsula, some circuits were so large that it took an itinerant six weeks to go around once. Since Methodists itinerants were constantly moved from circuit to circuit—by 1804 a year's stay was normal—a preacher could give the same sermon at every stop for six weeks and then use it again his first time around his new circuit the next year. Because one sermon might be repeated twenty or thirty times before being put on the shelf, it is clear why Methodist itinerants didn't need notes or a written text. Indeed, six to eight good sermons could suffice for a lifetime in the itinerant ministry.

To give his carefully practiced sermon, the itinerant needed a loud and projecting voice. Sobriquets carried by the itinerants, such as "Son of Thunder" and "Devil Driver," make the point. A local preacher in Sussex was thought to be gifted because "he had a strong voice and made a great noise, which was estimated as a great talent for a Methodist preacher at that day."

To both literate and illiterate Delmarvans, the Methodist circuit riders were extraordinarily persuasive. It was commonly said that if itinerants William Chandler and Solomon Sharp preached simultaneously from opposite ends of a platform during a camp meeting, such was their oratorical power that "they could preach the devil out of Hell." The listening crowds were fearful that they would die in damnation, and most preachers exploited this fear. Perhaps none did it more explicitly than Joseph Everett, who is remembered for starting his sermons, "It was just six weeks since I was here last and some of you are six weeks nearer Hell than you were then."[16]

Because the early itinerants gave "extemporaneous" sermons, we can't be sure of exactly what they said. Neverthless, the linguistic patterns found in itinerants' journals indicate that, in their battle with the Devil for the souls of Delmarvans, the itinerants communicated with their audiences using metaphors and similes drawn particularly from agriculture, war, and construction. The whole Peninsula or just the state of Delaware became "like the garden of God" or "will become as the garden of the Lord filled with plants of His own plantings." The itinerants projected themselves as "courageous soldiers," using "sharper arrows" to achieve "splendid victories." In describing the development of faith to an inquiring woman, one itinerant pointed out that "wise builders began at the foundation . . . then . . . go forward with the superstructure."

At meetings along the circuit, the itinerant would give the sermon, followed by an exhortation by a local preacher or exhorter. At larger gatherings, however, a number of exhortations by other itinerants might follow the sermon. In 1795, in the heart of Accomack County, a Methodist sermon was followed by three different itinerants giving exhortations, leading to "a great shout" among the listeners. Although itinerants filled the role of both preacher and exhorter, some, like Thomas Ware, felt that their "gift was rather to preach than exhort."

Above all else, the message preached was very basic and easy to understand. The itinerants were not interested in theological fine points but rather in a faith that would cause men to act. Again, the pragmatic doctrine preached is mirrored in the itinerants' journals. Basic Arminianism, which placed responsibility on the individual, is reflected in Joseph Everett's words: "If Christ died for all the world, all the world was savable; and they that were lost, were lost by their own fault." Joseph Pilmore was asked by a lady in Newark, Delaware, about the doctrine of perfection—the Methodist belief that men and women, through their acceptance of Christ, could eventually achieve purity of heart. He responded that "all the perfection I hold is contained in the words of our Lord, 'Thou shalt love the Lord thy God with all thy heart—and thy neighbor as thyself.' "

Unhindered by the need to read their sermons and prayers, Methodist preachers were free to move about while delivering the message. Lawrence Lawrenson, "perhaps the finest preacher ever" on the Annamessex Circuit in lower Somerset County, would leave the pulpit toward the end of his sermon and pace to and fro among the congregation. But often the peculiar setting shaped the preaching technique. Prior to the construction of Methodist meeting houses, itinerants would make preaching stops at homes along the circuit. They would often find themselves in relatively small rooms packed with people like sardines in a can. In at least one case, listeners were sitting and lying on as many as four beds in one crowded room. Often when the house, chapel, or church was packed to overflowing, the preacher would stand in the doorway or next to an open window so that the crowds inside and out could hear the message. Courtrooms and schoolhouses were often opened to Methodist preaching, particularly in areas where many of the gentry were Methodist.[17]

The itinerant often had to shout to drown out competition from yelping canines. William Colbert, for example, once had to "exert" himself "on account of a hateful barking of dogs about the house." But more difficult to handle were verbal confrontations with irate and even insane members of the audience. Like other itinerants, Colbert preached sermons on personal morality, much to the discomfort of some of his listeners. In Somerset Co., in 1800, Colbert's sermon against "whoredom" ignited fireworks. While standing before his congregation, Colbert "was severely tongue lashed by a woman of that stamp," who had left her husband and children for a man who was also in the audience and also angered by Colbert's message.

But that interruption was nothing compared to the excitement at a Quarterly Meeting at St. Martin's, Worcester County, two years later. During a love feast a layman was "engaged with God for the salvation of his soul" when his sister and two brothers, carrying weapons, "came rushing in, full of the devil, resolved to pull their brother out." Colbert demanded that they leave, but the three grabbed hold of their brother. Only after a fight were the three intruders disarmed and thrown out.

Success in the pulpit was usually measured by the emotional reaction of the crowd and the number of converts made. To assure success on both fronts, a few itinerants were not above a little chicanery. Presiding elder William Chandler, for example, knew of an impending eclipse of the sun while a camp meeting near Laurel, Delaware, was in progress in 1806. Playing on the credulity of his audience, at the appropriate moment Chandler announced that the world was about to come to an end. Needless to say, the attendant eclipse caused an extraordinary outpouring of emotions. But Chandler was not without his critics. He was later charged with making off with such a large sum of money, collected at the Laurel camp meeting, "that his four-wheeled carriage broke down under the weight." Actually, one of Chandler's enemies had taken the lynch pin out of the axle and the wheel simply fell off. Later Chandler was exonerated of charges that he used camp collections for his own benefit.

Another example of crowd manipulation is an often told story concerning the actions of the eccentric Lorenzo Dow. Capable of extraordinary physical effort—while on the Peninsula in 1805 he rode eighty miles and preached five times in a two-day period without any sleep—"Crazy Dow" was a most singular itinerant. On his way to address an outdoor Methodist meeting, probably near Pocomoke City in southern Worcester County, Dow encountered a small black boy with a tin horn by the name of Gabriel. With the vision of the Angel Gabriel and his golden horn dancing through his head, Dow decided this was too good a possibility to pass up. He paid the young boy to climb, unobserved, into a big elm tree at the spot where Dow was to address the outdoor Methodist meeting, and then to listen carefully from his perch to Dow's sermon. When Dow cried, "Blow, Gabriel, blow," his young conspirator was to let fly with a blast of his horn.

The meeting went according to plan as "Crazy Dow" preached on life beyond death. Working up to his climax, Dow described the Angel Gabriel poised at the last judgement with his trumpet in hand. Then Dow exhorted Gabriel to blow and the tin horn in the elm tree responded. The congregation fell to the ground, crying for mercy and causing the horses tethered nearby to go into a frenzy. When Dow's accomplice was discovered in the elm tree, the crowd turned hostile. Dow, we are told, was equal to the occasion and addressed the angry crowd, saying that if they were so terror stricken because of the action of a little black boy, how would they respond to the day of judgement?[18]

John Wesley felt strongly that long sermons and long services were counterproductive. As a result, sermons in England were generally limited to no more than forty to fifty minutes and services usually lasted no more than an hour. In America, Wesley's constraints proved less and less significant as the nineteenth century approached. In Baltimore, for example, the average itinerant preached fifty or sixty minutes and the typical service lasted two hours. But the people of Baltimore could, if they wished, hear preaching two or three times every week. Over on the Peninsula, circuit riders usually stopped by only once every two or three weeks. The rural population that assembled for the occasion felt cheated if the sermon wasn't a long one. Delmarvans were understandably upset with itinerant Thomas Smith because his sermons only lasted twenty or thirty minutes. To remedy the situation, Smith took to preaching two or three sermons at a time.[19]

Singing Skills

Indications are that congregational singing was uncommon in the colonial Anglican Church and "generally languid and unaffecting" in the Episcopal Church. By contrast, the Methodists emphasized hymn singing more than perhaps any other Christian faith of the eighteenth and early nineteenth century. Vocal music, according to the *Methodist Magazine* in 1820, raised the worshipper's mind from earthly things and prepared it to receive the gospel. To itinerants, however, the hymns represented much more: they enticed music lovers to Methodist meetings, and they became a very significant aid in teaching Methodist theology. So pivotal was singing that, in addition to a loud and projecting speaking voice, a circuit rider needed the ability to sing out on key.

From the very beginning, hymn singing was an integral part of Methodist services on the Peninsula. The first Methodist to preach on the Peninsula, Robert Strawbridge, had a fine musical voice which he used, no doubt, to lead singing at his pioneer service. Asbury loved to sing and was a great admirer of the hymns of Charles Wesley, John Wesley's brother. At first, hymn books were rare on the Peninsula and the itinerants "lined out" the hymn— that is, they would sing a line and the audience would repeat it. Hymnals soon became more common on the Peninsula; by 1786 Jesse Lee was using them on Maryland's upper Eastern Shore. Still, they were relatively scarce almost until the end of the eighteenth century.

One itinerant noted that "if people did not sing scientifically, they sang in the spirit." But sometimes the singing was too "unscientific" to suit Methodist leaders, and itinerants were directed to have practice sessions with the people to improve their efforts. As Methodism grew older on the Peninsula, some of the town chapels particularly felt the need to upgrade hymn singing. In 1798, for example, Asbury Church in Wilmington established practice sessions after weekly prayer meetings on Tuesday night. Ten years later, at Wesley Chapel, Dover, the trustees agreed to sit inside the altar rail in order to keep order and encourage and regulate the singing.

Singing was fun as well as an expression of worship and a means to learning. Included in those who were brought to Methodism in part because they enjoyed hymn singing was Joshua Thomas, the famed Parson of the Islands. Subsequently, Thomas came to regard the Methodist hymnal, more than even the Bible, as "the clearest and most comprehensive expositor" of God's revelation.[20]

Repeatedly, hymns were used to drive home theological points. Generally, three or four were sung at regular worship services and two at class meetings. Whether the congregation was singing from memory or from a Methodist hymnal, the itinerant would often interrupt to ask, "Now, do you know what you said last?" or "Did you speak no more than you felt?" Within a short time the hymns were being sung daily by Methodists as they worked, traveled, and relaxed.

Delmarvans did not have to depend on the bimonthly preaching visits of the circuit rider to hear the Methodist message. Their own constant singing of Charles Wesley's hymns repeated, over and over, John Wesley's version of God's truth. In medieval times, the stained glass windows of the great cathedrals brought home the Christian message to a population that was overwhelmingly illiterate. During the late eighteenth and early nineteenth centuries, memorized Methodist hymns served the same basic function for literate, semiliterate, and illiterate Delmarvans.

Particularly appealing were hymns of praise, which also held out the promise of a new birth through Christ, no matter what the present condition of the individual. These and other Methodist hymns reflected, in their words, the strongly democratic nature of Wesleyan theology in its promise of salvation to the poor as well as the rich, to blacks as well as whites. Of Charles Wesley's compositions, "O for a Thousand Tongues to Sing" was a favorite. Itinerant William Smith liked to start worship with it, and William Morgan jotted down the first verse in his autobiography. Some of the "lower sort" couldn't help but be attracted by Joseph Hart's "Come Ye Sinners Poor and Needy." For those of better economic means, hymns that emphasized the possibility of spiritual peace were favored.

The personal impact of a Methodist hymn could be extraordinary. A case in point was William Morgan as he walked from Lewes to Georgetown for a Quarterly Meeting in 1801. Morgan was a Methodist convert, but not yet of the "shouting" variety. Along the road he practiced singing Charles Wesley's "O How Happy Are They the Savior Obey." Soon he began to tremble, his bodily powers "gave way," and he "sank down helpless." When he came to, he was "exceedingly happy," could "praise God aloud," and became a "shouting" Methodist. (Evidently, "shouting" included bodily movements along with vocal exertion.) Morgan viewed the entire incident as God causing "a deeper work of grace in my soul."[21]

The Image

Along with preaching and leading hymn singing, the circuit rider exercised other responsibilities that brought him into contact with Delmarvans on a more intimate basis. To be effective on this level, it was important that people see the itinerant as a very special being, set apart from other men. The itinerant's appearance did just that.

To begin with, the circuit rider's dress was unusually ascetic, making him identifiable with great distances. Most itinerants followed Francis Asbury's sartorial example. A contemporary described Asbury as looking somewhat like a Quaker except for the substitution of black for gray in later life.

> He wore a low-crowned, broad brimmed hat, a frock coat, which was generally buttoned up to the neck, with straight collar. He wore breeches or small clothes with leggings. Sometimes he wore shoe buckles.

Breeches and leggings continued to be worn by itinerants until 1810 when, much to the consternation of Bishop Asbury, "several left them off." Methodist circuit riders, with a few exceptions, wore their hair combed smoothly down over the forehead. Their faces were clean shaven, "exhibiting neither mustache, goatee or other fanciful arrangement."

When itinerants first rode the circuits of the Peninsula they carried very little excess baggage.

> The equipment of a Methodist preacher was a horse, saddle, and bridle; one suit of clothes, a watch, a pocket Bible, and a hymn-book. Anything more . . . would be an incumbrance.

It wasn't long, however, before itinerants' saddle bags included religious books to be sold along the circuit. The first Methodist *Discipline* directed circuit riders to make sure that every society "be duly supplied with books," particularly with Richard Baxter's *Saints Everlasting Rest*, as edited by John Wesley, and Wesley's *Instructions for Children* and *Primitive Physick*.

As early as 1775, American printers had issued more than three hundred distinctly Methodist items. On the Peninsula, the first Methodist works to be printed were a Charles Wesley sermon and hymn, issued by James Adams of Wilmington in 1770. While itinerants were regularly selling books prior to the American Revolution, the first record of that sort of activity on the Peninsula occurred in 1780 when Asbury, while confined to Judge White's during bad weather, "was principally employed in assorting books for sale." Indications are that Methodist hymnals joined religious tracts in the itinerant's saddle-bag inventory by the end of the American Revolution. Apparently, hymnals sold better throughout the United States than any of the other early Methodist publications.[22]

Usually itinerants found Peninsula residents eager to open their homes and provide free meals and lodging, and for good reason! According to itinerant Henry Boehm, those who opened their doors to "the messengers of God" prospered far more than those who failed to offer hospitality.

In addition to God's blessings, the itinerant brought the latest news of friends and relatives from up and down the circuit to isolated farm families. Some itinerants also brought with them some of the skills of a country physician, picked up from practical experience and the reading of John Wesley's best-selling *Primitive Physick*. Itinerant William Colbert, for example, seemed to routinely bleed "unwell" Methodists along the Somerset Circuit at the turn of the century.

Generally, the itinerants projected a very serious, even dour exterior. After circuit riding on Maryland's upper Eastern Shore prior to the American Revolution, William Watters was representative when he wrote, "Let others plead the innocence and usefulness of levity, I cannot." But to naturally exuberant young men, the total rejection of levity was very difficult. We can only sympathize with a distressed William Colbert, on the Northampton Circuit in 1795, as he cried out against "my airy turn of mind. O that I were more solemn."[23]

Disciplinarian

The circuit rider's serious, even dour, image was crucial to the success of one of his most important responsibilities: keeping order in the local Methodist societies. Keeping order was a key to

Wesleyan success on both sides of the Atlantic. In America, this meant getting individual societies to accept and support decisions made at Annual and General conferences, and to see that Methodists patterned their lives according to the *Discipline* of the Methodist Episcopal Church. In this scheme of things the itinerant was the enforcer, and his somber visage befitted the role.

One disciplinary weapon wielded was the denial of the Lord's Supper. While serving the Northampton Circuit in 1795, William Colbert turned away from communion an older woman of whom he had heard bad things. Later, however, Colbert had some misgivings about his actions.

More commonly, the itinerants simply expelled from society those Methodists who broke the rules and the spirit of the faith. Prior to 1800, offending members were brought to trial before the itinerant who, after hearing the evidence, decided whether or not to expel the defendant. By 1800, however, the decision to expel had become a prerogative of the local membership through a majority vote, with the itinerant then reading the offending member out of the society.

In the early years, when they possessed the sole power to expel members, itinerants didn't let family influence and connections interfere. While he was serving the Milford Circuit in 1795, for example, William Colbert reported that he had "the disagreeable piece of business" of trying the wife of one of the "most respectable" local Methodists. Despite her husband's standing in the local society, Colbert expelled her. If this particular case had come up ten years later, when the decision was in the hands of the local society's members, one suspects that the outcome would not have been the same.[24]

The Local Preacher and the Itinerant

A Methodist society saw an itinerant only once every two or three weeks. In his absence, a local preacher conducted the services and delivered the message. Eventually, some local preachers applied for and were accepted into the itinerancy. Most, however, remained farmers, craftsmen, or storekeepers and preached in their free time. They were licensed by the Quarterly Conference, and some were consecrated as deacons with the right to perform baptism and marriage ceremonies. Local preacher Joshua Thomas was even ordained an elder. Regardless of consecration, however, local preachers took directions from the itinerants. Moreover, membership in the Philadelphia Annual Conference was restricted to the itinerants. Since the Annual Conference made decisions critical to the future of Delmarva Methodism, local preachers resented being excluded.

The local preacher–itinerant relationship worked out well in some cases. In Somerset County, for example, Joshua Thomas got along with a number of itinerants and had a particularly warm relationship with Lawrence Lawrenson. But sometimes the extraordinary power exercised by the circuit rider over the local Methodist society gave rise to a certain arrogance that infuriated strong-minded local preachers. Anticipating such a problem, the Methodist *Discipline* reminded itinerants to be humble, because the preacher of the gospel was a servant to all. But, according to some local preachers, many of the Peninsula's itinerants didn't take that injunction very seriously.

In 1807 in Sussex, for example, local preacher and class leader William Morgan described his relationship with a circuit rider as a case of "ecclesiastical dictation." Morgan and fellow local preacher and class leader Daniel Baker had been holding unauthorized Methodist meetings in the woods near Asbury Church, about six miles east of Seaford. Itinerant John Collins put an end to the meetings by threatening to remove Morgan and Baker as class leaders. That same year at nearby Concord, circuit rider Thomas Emory finished his sermon only to have Morgan rise and give an exhortation that caused some of the congregation to break into "a shout." Despite the fact that local preachers exhorted after itinerants' sermons on other circuits, Emory thought it "down right impudent for local preachers to get up and exhort after an itinerant minister." Emory went on to tell Baker that if Morgan didn't stop the practice, he "would have him before the Conference." As previously noted, Peter Spencer of Wilmington was still another local preacher unhappy with the dictatorial ways of some circuit riders.

Despite their problems with circuit riders, local preachers— white and black—performed effectively and enthusiastically. A good example was local preacher and exhorter Argil Bloxam of Virginia's Eastern Shore, who could give "a thundering exhortation" that left some of his audience "in extacies." An impressed circuit rider noted, "I believe this man enjoys religion." Of course, no man had more fun in religion than local preacher Joshua Thomas. Whether hailing people from his twenty-foot log canoe, *The Methodist*, or dancing and shouting in the pulpit, it was obvious that the Deal Islander was really enjoying himself.

More than even the circuit rider, the local preacher spoke the patois of his listeners as he applied the gospel to their specific needs. His sermons were sometimes criticized by his congregation, but even here the local preacher would respond in a colorful, pungent language familiar to his audience. One white local preacher, for example, compared critics of his sermons to Zachaeus, "a climbing up sycamore trees to git above the common people. . . . Fact is some of these folks know no more about preaching nor a hog knows about making mince pies."[25]

Black Preachers

On Delmarva, white paranoia denied blacks the opportunity to speak before large groups. There was, however, one exception. From an early date, white itinerants encouraged blacks to speak out at Methodist meetings of the religious stirrings in their hearts. Denied other outlets, black eloquence poured forth to proclaim the gospel. As early as 1779 in Kent County, Delaware, Asbury was pleased to report that a newly freed slave

> gave such an extraordinary account of the work of God in his soul, and withal displayed such gifts in public exercises, that it appears as if the Lord was preparing him for a peculiar usefulness to the people of his own colour.

Some black preachers played a significant role in spreading the Methodist message among whites as well as blacks. Although blacks were never assigned responsibility for a specific circuit, a few traveled extensively in the company of white itinerants, usually following white sermons with black exhortations.

The best known of these traveling blacks was Harry Hosier, known as Black Harry, who accompanied the likes of Asbury, Coke, and other white preachers in their travels through the Peninsula in 1781, 1784, 1804, and 1805. An illiterate, small, and very black North Carolinian, Hosier was gifted with extraordinary oratorical skills. In 1784, after itinerating for a number of days through the Peninsula with Black Harry, the urbane, Oxford-educated Thomas Coke wrote from Accomack County

> I have now had the pleasure of hearing Harry preach several times. I sometimes give notice immediately after preaching, that in a little time, Harry will preach to the blacks; but the whites always stay to hear him. Sometimes I publish him to preach at candle light as the negroes can better attend at that time. I really believe he is one of the best preachers in the

Harry Hosier
(Courtesy, Methodist Collection, Drew University, Madison, NJ)

world, there is such an amazing power attends his preaching,
though he cannot read; and he is one of the humblest creatures
I ever saw.

One day Bishop Asbury was scheduled to speak in Wilmington. A number of curious non-Methodists, wishing to hear the
bishop, found the church overflowing with people. Forced to stand
outside where they could hear the sermon but not see the pulpit,
they didn't realize that Black Harry rather than Asbury was speaking. Hosier's voice and message were so compelling that the listeners
outside remarked that if all Methodist preachers preached like the
bishop, they would be in constant attendance at Methodist meetings. The bishop's image was further enhanced when those outside
were told that they had been listening to Hosier, not Asbury. The
bystanders reasoned that if Asbury's black assistant could preach
like this, what an extraordinary preacher the bishop must be. The
truth was, as one nineteenth-century Methodist historian put it,
"that Harry was a more popular preacher than Mr. Asbury, or
almost anyone else in his day."[26]

Unlike Hosier, most blacks who preached on the Peninsula were local preachers or exhorters. Because most were illiterate, they have left us few records of their number and daily activities. Although the General Conference of the Methodist Episcopal Church decided to permit blacks to be ordained as deacons in 1800 and as elders in 1812, there is no indication that any Peninsula blacks received ordination while preaching on Delmarva prior to 1820.

While such blacks as Abraham Thompson and a preacher known only as Jeffry were very effective in moving crowds at Methodist meetings, by all odds the most famous black local preachers on Delmarva were Richard Allen of Kent County, Delaware, and Peter Spencer of Wilmington. Indeed, these two products of Delmarva, along with James Varick of New York City (father of the African Methodist Episcopal Zion movement), were the three major contributors to the early development of African Methodism in the United States.

Richard Allen was born to slavery in Philadelphia in 1760. He was sold, evidently while in his early teens, to a farmer by the name of Stokely Sturgis who lived near Dover, Delaware. Although Allen had no love for slavery, he later characterized his master as a "tender, humane man" who was "more like a father to his slaves than anything else." At the age of seventeen, Allen was converted to Methodism. Subsequently, he held prayer meetings in his master's home and then persuaded Sturgis to open his home to Methodist preachers. Francis Asbury preached there on August 13, 1779.

Freeborn Garrettson also stopped at Sturgis's home and spoke out strongly against slavery with considerable effect. Persuaded by Garrettson's preaching that slavery was wrong, Sturgis offered Allen the opportunity to buy his freedom in five yearly installments. Allen agreed and began, in January 1780, to earn the requisite money. Starting first as a woodcutter and then an employee in a brickyard, Allen eventually found himself hauling salt from Rehoboth Beach to Dover. Along the way to and from Rehoboth, Allen made many preaching stops and by 1782 was officially licensed to preach. In 1783 he left Kent County and lived for a while in Wilmington, where he became the first black to preach to a white congregation in that city. Allen interspersed work with itinerant preaching from South Carolina to New York over the next few years before settling down in Philadelphia as a free man in 1786. Allen and Harry Hosier were the black presence at the Christmas Conference in Baltimore in 1784.

The rest of Allen's life was primarily spent in and around Philadelphia, where the racial prejudice of white Methodists at St.

Richard Allen
(Courtesy, Methodist Collection, Drew University, Madison, NJ)

George's Church drove him to break away from white Methodism and found the African Methodist Episcopal Church in 1816. Although Allen's most notable activities took place after he left the Peninsula, the religious faith and sense of black dignity that undergirded his role in the development of black Methodism were shaped during his years on Delmarva.[27]

No doubt other Peninsula blacks were just as successful in preaching the gospel as Peter Spencer and Richard Allen. The reputations of these other black preachers were enshrined in the hearts and minds of their Methodist audiences. When the last members of those audiences died, however, buried too were the reputations of their preachers. By contrast, successful organizations and movements consciously preserve for posterity the identities of their founders. Because they were both founders, the names of Peter Spencer and Richard Allen live on, while Abraham Thompson, Jeffry, and the other compelling black preachers are largely forgotten.

Chapter Six

The Impact of Methodism

In 1782 Samuel Tingley, the Anglican rector at Lewes, Delaware, complained of putting up with "the enthusiastic notions of ignorant Methodists" for the past three years. Tingley accused the Wesleyans of trying to "overturn all order and decency in the Church." In declaring that the Methodists had disruptive "notions," Tingley was correct. He was wrong, however, in thinking that only the Anglican Church was threatened. The Methodist revolution was far more inclusive than that.

Methodism took exception to so many of the basic assumptions that undergirded eighteenth-century Delmarva society that it put almost every aspect of the old order on the defensive. Within a few years, the radical Methodist message penetrated so deeply into the Peninsula's collective consciousness that the way many Delmarvans lived, worked, and thought was dramatically altered. Indeed, in its zeal for spiritual rebirth, Methodism produced a new breed of men and women on the Peninsula, whose pattern of behavior was quite at odds with the "ways of men."

The New Man

"Born again" was an apt phrase to describe the striking change brought about by conversion. Methodists used it to make the dramatic point that Wesleyan converts were now free of the shackles of sin and, therefore, free to become what God meant them to be. The Methodist goal was quite simple: to produce a "new man," free of past human frailties and error. This new man not only stood out as a recipient of God's loving grace but was also driven to work hard for the coming of God's kingdom on earth.

The passive nature of Anglicanism/Episcopalianism rendered

that religious body incapable of producing such a new man. The hellfire and brimstone of Calvinism could produce him, but Calvinism had more difficulty than Methodism in sustaining him against the temptations of backsliding. After all, as William Morgan pointed out, Calvinism preached "once elect always elect." By contrast, Wesleyan theology accepted the possibility of falling from grace. This meant that Methodists were constantly on guard against backsliding. Moreover, once saved, Methodists were under compulsion to push on toward a personal reconciliation with God, a process that they labeled "going on to perfection."[1]

In the most dramatic rebirth experience in history, Saul of Tarsus was converted while on the road to Damascus. On the Peninsula, Methodists were pleased to point to many mimetic examples of Saul the Persecutor turned Paul the Apostle. That some avowed enemies of Peninsula Methodism ended up in the Wesleyan camp is not surprising. Often opposites, even while locked in antagonist combat, are drawn to each other by some inner fascination. It seems that many persecutors of Peninsula Methodism showed up at Wesleyan meetings or physically confronted Methodists out of a compelling attraction as well as a desire to be abusive and disruptive.

Joseph Everett of Queen Anne's County was a case in point. Although a determined enemy of Methodism, he was inexorably drawn to their meetings until that night in the spring of 1778 when he heard Asbury at Judge White's. Everett was converted and became a circuit rider and, ultimately, presiding elder for the entire Peninsula in 1802.

Other enemies of Methodism who became converts included the assailant who gave itinerant Caleb Petticord such a severe beating in Dorchester County in 1780. Bartholomew Ennalls, another opponent of the Wesleyans in Dorchester, became a staunch Methodist and played host to Asbury in 1786. In Worcester County, Elijah Laws followed the same path to Methodism. Captain Thomas Burton, a member of the gentry of lower Accomack County, "was to Methodism a Saul of Tarsus." He often said that he would horsewhip the first itinerant who entered his gate. In 1800 an anti-Methodist harangue by the local Episcopal rector backfired, driving the listening Burton into the Methodist camp. Subsequently, he became an important lay leader, and Burton's Chapel was named for him.

Methodists wore the conversions of their enemies like trophies, but they were just as euphoric about the far more numerous converts who hadn't been previously antagonistic. The transformation that took place in the lives of both types of converts was there for all to see. Even Anglican James Kemp, an' inveterate enemy of Methodism during his nineteen-year rectorship in the Cambridge area, admitted that Methodism changed people. A second Anglican rector commented that in Maryland—presumably Eastern and Western Shore—the Methodists caused "a reformation in morals" that should not be undone. An outward sign of this reformation occurred in western Somerset County, where Devil's Island and nearby Damned Quarter were notorious dens of pirates and other undesirables. On conversion to Methodism, the inhabitants demonstrated their changed nature by renaming their communities Deal Island and Dame's Quarter.

Typical were the observations of Quaker physician Nathaniel Luff. Many residents along the Mispillion River, which marked part of the border between Kent and Sussex, had engaged in "libertine" practices during the American Revolution. After converting to Methodism, these former libertines appeared to Luff to be "earnestly devoted to the cause of truth" and were very intent on reforming mankind. It seemed that this "new man" was ushering in the dawn of a new era. Asbury increasingly sensed all of this as he rode through the First State in 1806. Laconically he noted, "In Delaware, the Millenium has begun."[2]

Sin

Asbury was a bit premature. After all, before the advent of the millenium, sin had to be conquered. Although a new breed of men and women, spawned by Methodism, was putting the Devil on the defensive throughout the Peninsula, few talked seriously of the impending death of sin. Because sin wasn't about to disappear, the fight against it continued to be of central importance. Before sin could be fought, however, it had to be defined. Since Methodists were a Bible-oriented people, they naturally turned to Scripture for an inclusive definition. Out of their Biblical studies, Methodists concluded that all human action should be judged sinful if it didn't glorify God.[3]

Based on this understanding of Scripture, Peninsula Methodists found much that was offensive in the conduct of the region's rural gentry and wealthy townsmen. It was self-evident that the life-style of the "better sort" was really based on a value system that approved of personal vanity and self-indulgence. In short,

Delmarva's gentry and wealthy townsmen seemed intent on glorifying themselves rather than God. As mentioned previously, the sinful life-style of the upper class was particularly upsetting to Methodists because of the mimetic tendencies of the rest of society. Because it was practiced by the gentry, the same wrong behavior became highly acceptable to many of "the middling and lower sort."

Dress

To start with, Methodists objected to the ostentatious mode of dress that characterized the wealthy. Clothing and jewelry were, after all, an indication of vanity and an earthly heart. With that caveat in mind, Wesley cautioned his followers to dress in the most simple attire. In America, the Methodist *Discipline* reinforced Wesley by insisting that a Methodist should not wear any apparel "which tends to feed his own pride."

On the Peninsula, Wesleyans took these admonitions seriously. In addition to circuit riders, lay leaders were particularly careful to set a good sartorial example. Among the latter was Dr. James Anderson of Chestertown, who wore the lawned stockings and broad-brimmed hat that became the Methodist uniform. After conversion, even the "princely rich" such as Richard Bassett, who had been a very fashionable man, lived and dressed plainly without display or extravagance. Hair style was very important because it was an extension of the mode of dress. Emulating the itinerants, laymen combed their hair straight down over their foreheads in what was considered "the Methodist fashion in those days."

Young couples, like the one converted by Thomas Smith in Northampton County, Virginia, in 1801, "came out in plain Methodist dress to become members of the Methodist Episcopal Church." Young females were particularly prone to dress "fashionably," only to turn to simple apparel after conversion. Typical were two "very gay young women" from Talbot County who began wearing plain attire after being converted by Freeborn Garrettson in 1778. The first Methodist *Discipline* barred the wearing of such superfluous ornaments as enormous bonnets and ruffles. For that reason a Methodist woman in western Sussex was counted "on the safe side" for wearing a plain white muslin bonnet to every church service.

As with dressing in "fashionable" clothes, the wearing of jewelry spoke of vanity and self-indulgence. Itinerants attacked the wearing of necklaces, earrings, and finger rings as superfluous ornaments. On Maryland's lower Eastern Shore in 1802, for example,

William Colbert shamed a young woman into giving up wearing all three, leaving her "crying to God for mercy." Not surprisingly, the plain dress and the rejection of personal ornaments by early Methodists initially attracted some Quakers to Methodist meetings.[4]

Eating

Ascetism shaped the Wesleyan perception of eating. Although food was essential to fuel men and women so that they could do God's work, too much of it or the wrong kind reflected self-indulgence. Moreover, as local preacher Joshua Thomas pointed out, a full stomach was debilitating and stood in the way of hard work and the exercise of faith. The Methodist *Discipline* (1789) directed circuit riders to practice self-denial by being temperate in eating habits and by not eating meat for supper. By inference, the itinerants' eating habits would be emulated by the laity.

Fasting was common among early Methodists. The *Discipline* of 1789 asked itinerants for a greater commitment to fasting, and Asbury, in particular, set a personal example. On the Peninsula, a day of fasting at each Quarterly Conference may have been standard operating procedure. But Methodist fasting wasn't always quite as severe as it sounded. Often it only meant abstaining from such luxury items as tea, coffee, chocolate, and meat. But for that independent-minded Sussex Countain William Morgan, fasting in any form was so unappealing that he demanded Biblical justification. It must have pleased Morgan that by 1812, Methodist fasting across the nation had become almost obsolete. On the Peninsula, the only exception to this national trend seemed to be Joshua Thomas, Parson of the Islands.[5]

Drinking

Liquor could prevent men and women from praising and faithfully serving the Lord. Moreover, it brought about economic as well as spiritual ruin. These facts were clear to Methodists at an early date. John Wesley began the official Methodist offensive against alcohol in 1743 by proclaiming that buying, selling, and drinking of liquor, unless absolutely necessary, were evils to be avoided. American Methodism shared Wesley's concern and took stands at Annual Conferences, General Conferences, and in its *Discipline* against the manufacture, sale, purchase, and use of alcohol by its membership. As in fasting, the circuit riders were to set the example. In the *Discipline* of 1785, for example, itinerants were directed "to teach the people by precept and example to put away this evil." But at times, early Methodists seemed to equivocate on some of the particulars. Should all alcoholic consumption be banned, or only drunkenness and the distilling and selling of alcohol?

Asbury was particularly sensitive to the interrelationship of abstinence and the serving and praising of God. While visiting Lewes, Delaware, in 1790, Asbury rode out to Cape Henlopen to visit Methodist lighthouse keeper J. R. Hargus. The Methodist bishop was pleased to write in his journal, "I could but praise God that the house was kept by people who praise and love Him; no drinking or swearing here." Asbury seemed to infer that abstinence and the glorification of God were so interdependent that they represented a tandem essential to the Christian character. Ten years later near Chesapeake City, Cecil County, Asbury drove home the point that abstinence opened the heart to the Holy Spirit. The people, he said, "sang and leaped for joy of [the] heart; they have beaten down strong drink and the power of God has come."[6]

Some lay Methodists took seriously their church's warnings and regulated their lives accordingly. One extreme example was Henry Baley of Wilmington, who threatened on several occasions to burn the "dram shops" of relapsed Methodist Allen McLane, customs collector for the Port of Wilmington. For his threats, Baley was expelled from his society. More typical was Isaac Davis of Smyrna who wrote, at the end of his days, that he had "followed after soberness and temperance and had never been intoxicated by strong drink in my life." William Morgan of Sussex and Joshua Thomas of Somerset County, both sons of alcoholics, could have made similar statements concerning their lives after conversion.

Perhaps the most colorful example of a Methodist renouncing the "ardent spirits" was the case of Thomas Barbon, a Portuguese veteran of the Battle of Trafalgar who settled in White Haven, southwest of Salisbury along the Wicomico River. In 1818 Barbon was converted to Methodism while attending a camp meeting on Tangier Island; but it took a temperance address, some nine years later, to cause Barbon to act. He hurried home, rolled out his own barrels of wine and hard cider and, with his ax, bashed in the head of every cask. The liquor poured out on the ground, forming puddles from which Barbon's chickens, turkeys, and pigs drank. The affair ended with his domestic animals enjoying a general drunk.

Barbon's case is amusing but also instructive. When Delmarvans became Wesleyans, they generally abandoned their fashionable clothes for the plain attire demanded by early Methodism. The use of alcohol was also strongly discouraged by early Methodism and yet, for nine years after his conversion, Barbon didn't feel obligated to give up this aspect of his former life-style. Indeed, the reluctance of some early Methodists to refrain, after conversion, from the use of liquor seemed to be a nation-wide problem. The General Conference of the Methodist Episcopal Church, meeting in 1812, lamented that the "use of ardent spirits" was "so common among the Methodists." Supporting the General Conference's concern were plenty of horror stories from the Peninsula, some of which even featured itinerants and local preachers. Specific examples were black orator Harry Hosier; Abraham Whitworth, who served the Kent Circuit in 1773–74; the unlettered Joseph Cromwell, who introduced Methodism to Talbot County; and Major Taylor, a local preacher on the Smyrna Circuit. All four became alcoholics in later life.[7]

Alcohol was, however, such an integral part of eighteenth-century life and culture that heavy drinking was standard behavior. Not only was alcohol seen as an opiate, a social catalyst, and a centerpiece to any celebration, it was also reputed to possess considerable medicinal value. Even John Wesley, in his *Primitive Physick*, prescribed the use of wine and brandy. Alcohol also served a significant ceremonial function, with the gentry particularly prone to sealing business and political agreements with drinks all around. In short, the heavy consumption of alcohol was so deeply ingrained in the life-style of the Peninsula that even the Methodist presence only partially curtailed its use. Moreover, the production and sale of alcoholic beverages was an important business which, quite naturally, resisted Methodist reforms.

Increasingly there were indications that some laymen and even a few preachers distilled, sold, and consumed alcohol and yet remained in good standing in their local societies and Annual Conferences. Indeed, even some tavern keepers were Methodists. After all, it could always be pointed out that at Methodist communion, wine was served. Faced with these factors, by the turn of the century American Methodism was taking a more ambivalent stand. Although the *Discipline* and official minutes of Annual and General conferences continued to put official Methodism unmistakably on the side of temperance, the willingness to discipline errant preachers and church members was less evident than in former times. At the

General Conference of 1812, for example, a resolution condemning all preachers who sold any form of liquor was defeated. Four years later, the General Conference did agree that all preachers who distilled or retailed spiritous liquors should lose their licenses. However, the production and sale of malt liquors (beer) were exempted from the ban.

Indicative of Peninsula Methodism's ambivalent attitude toward alcohol is the case of Sussex County local preacher William Morgan. Determined to avoid his father's poverty-inducing alcoholism, young Morgan became so disgusted at the sight of his father and a Baptist minister "over their grog" that he "entirely abandoned religion." Moving from Northwest Fork Hundred in Western Sussex to Lewes in 1799, Morgan apprenticed himself to a carpenter-joiner and boarded with a Methodist who would pray one minute and get drunk the next. Despite his declaration about abandoning religion, somehow Morgan found himself at a class meeting where a brandy bottle was being passed around. Morgan resolved to have nothing further to do with the Methodists, only to find that the Presbyterian and Episcopal divines in Lewes also had a real weakness for strong drink. At this point, Morgan rejected the Presbyterians and Episcopalians, reciting to himself an old Jewish proverb: "Like priests, like people."[8]

The next year, while cutting down walnut trees, Morgan drank some of his employer's brandy. "I took so much that in a few minutes I could not strike twice in the same place; and for fear of chopping my feet I lay down on the ground." This experience left Morgan resolved to never again get intoxicated.

It was soon after that the Second Great Awakening brought a great revival of Methodism to the Lewes area, and Morgan was converted. Despite his own bad experiences with alcohol and the Methodist emphasis on temperance, however, Morgan continued to drink "small beer." In 1817 while living in Milton, some nine miles directly east of Lewes, Morgan built a sloop, filled it with brandy, and set off for New York. Morgan's business venture turned into a fiasco after his sloop was accidently rammed and "rascally strangers" cheated him out of his entire cargo of brandy.

William Morgan's case history makes the point that a committed Methodist, while seemingly reluctant to consume hard liquor, didn't hesitate to drink beer or to try to make a few dollars on the weakness of others for "spiritous drink." Obviously, Methodism's strong drive for total abstinence was decades away. A symbolic watershed in that drive was the year 1864, when the Methodist

Episcopal Church recommended, in an appendix to the *Discipline*, that grape juice be substituted for wine in the serving of communion.[9]

Amusement and Recreation

All levels of American society enjoyed horse racing, the sport of kings. Methodism, however, labeled this a sinful practice. When Francis Asbury rode through lower Kent County, Delaware, during the American Revolution, he found the region "given to horse racing as well as to other kinds of sport and wickedness." Some local enthusiasts took exception to Asbury's attacks on their favorite pastime and decided to embarrass the Methodist itinerant. Unknown to Asbury, they temporarily made off with his horse Spark and practiced the Methodist's mount on a nearby race track. Soon after, with a startled Asbury in the saddle, Spark took off on the course—it may have been a crudely marked straight course rather than an oval track—and didn't stop until crossing the finish line. The episode pleased "the wicked" because they could now say that Asbury's horse had run a race with the head Methodist preacher in the saddle.

But sometimes Methodist criticism of Delmarva's leisure time activities led to a less imaginative response. In 1789, for example, Broad Creek Chapel in southwest Sussex had its windows broken because, according to the Methodists, a recent Quarterly Meeting had spoken out against "revellings." And no wonder! To the minds of many, Methodists were killjoys, bent on doing away with all of life's fun and frivolity.[10]

In addition to horse racing and "revelling," Methodists condemned gambling, fox hunting, dancing, card playing, reading and singing for entertainment, the theatre, unnecessary conversation, swearing, and the use of snuff and tobacco. Opposition was based on the same theological and practical concerns that caused Methodists to oppose fashionable clothes and intemperance in eating and drinking. Because these were aimed at pleasing certain base human instincts rather than at glorifying God, they were judged sinful. Moreover, many of these activities were held in settings that reflected the immorality and laxness of the world, and so could tempt the unwary into backsliding. In addition, Methodists pragmatically pointed out that each of these activities wasted valuable time and energy that could be better spent in honest labor.

Certainly, Delmarvans were enthusiastic about their leisure-time vices. In 1809 the complaint came from Centreville, Queen

Anne's County, that inclement weather prevented church attendance, but it didn't "deter the servants of the devil from going to horse races and other demonical institutions." But just as certainly, the advent of Methodism dealt a blow to many of those "demonical institutions."

A few brief examples are instructive. A passionate fox hunter who lived near Centreville gave up riding to the hounds after conversion. Further south, on Virginia's Eastern Shore, "Fox-hunting Tom Burton" abandoned chasing the hounds upon joining the Wesleyan persuasion. John Emory, also of the Centreville area, reflected the Methodist contempt for small talk by refusing to indulge in trifling conversation and not liking "course" jesting. Rhoda Laws, of a Worcester County planter family, "had been raised in the view that [Anglican] church people then generally had, of the innocency of dancing and other wordly amusements." On being told by an itinerant that dancing was a sin, she gave it up to become a Methodist. In Accomack County, Christina Newton's conscience was stirred by an itinerant's message. Subsequently, in spite of her newly adopted Methodist inclinations, she was persuaded to attend a ball. Afterward, a contrite Christina symbolically renounced her dancing proclivities by throwing her ball-going attire into a fire and watching it burn to ashes.[11]

Methodists were of two minds concerning music. Vocal music, as long as it praised God, was good. Vocal music for self-enjoyment was condemned, along with almost all instrumental music. Even the use of such accompanying musical instruments as the organ was generally banned during church services because Methodists closely connected musical instruments with frivolity, mirth, and decadence. When the Methodist Church in Camden, just south of Dover, finally purchased an organ in 1860s, it caused such a great controversy that some of the "old Fogies" temporarily left the church.

Fiddles were rejected by Methodists because they conjured up images of dancing and other forms of boisterous revelry. A case in point was William Morgan of Lewes who, upon conversion, gave up his beloved fiddle for a Methodist hymnal. An even more compelling example took place on Tangier Island in Somerset County. John and Charles Parks, cousins of Joshua Thomas, were accomplished fiddlers native to the island. After being converted in 1807, the Parks brothers restricted their fiddling to accompanying Methodist hymns. But soon doubts were raised that fiddles should be used at all, "since they revived memories that were associated with sin." The fiddles were then thrown into a fire, destroying forever those "unwitting 'agents' in levity and frolicking." It seemed that the new life offered by the Methodist message demanded the abandonment of all the old symbols that conjured up images of the convert's former life.

But just as with alcohol, there was a certain ambivalence exhibited by some Methodists toward music and musical instruments. An example was itinerant William Colbert, native of northern Somerset County (part of Wicomico County today), who liked secular as well as spiritual music. Colbert tells of stopping at a Methodist home in Dagsboro, Sussex County, in 1806, where he was "agreeably entertained" by his host who sang and played the clarinet. A few months later, probably in Queen Anne's County, Colbert enjoyed playing his host family's organ.[12]

The Work Ethic

Out of an asceticism that rejected or at least seriously modified many self-indulgent practices, a Methodist personality developed that was committed to a regimen of hard work and frugal living. The commitment to industriousness had long been encouraged by Wesley. As early as 1739, the founder of Methodism warned his followers to avoid indolence and sloth and to give Methodism's enemies no opportunity to accuse Wesleyans of being idle. Always be employed and don't waste time were Wesley's admonitions. Because they were unwilling to waste time, British Methodists were accused of confining their lives to chapel and business.

Joseph Everett of Queen Anne's County summed up the Methodist perspective from the Peninsula by pointing out that "a life of idleness is a life of wickedness." Before "getting religion," Everett "lived without labor for the most part of the time." But as soon as he "got religion," he "set out to labour." Subsequently, as Everett related in his autobiography, "I now earned my bread by the labor of my hands: and believe that no man can live long in the favour of God, without using proper care to provide for himself and his household." Even more to the point was John Emory's description, in 1809, of the Methodist perspective on work. The Queen Anne's County native explained that religion "requires us first to never be idle or unemployed; secondly, never to be trifling or uselessly employed; but thirdly, always be well and profitably employed."

While he worked as a carpenter in Sussex County in 1810, William Morgan's typical day reflected the Methodist emphasis on hard work and optimum use of every moment. He rose early, had private devotions, washed—Wesley preached that cleanliness was next to godliness—and, because he was preparing to become a physician, read medical books for a half-hour. He then worked until breakfast. At the end of breakfast, "while others were chatting or picking their teeth," Morgan read some more. He "did the same . . . at dinner." While laboring during the day, he would lay his open book in such a position that he "could learn two or three lessons in the day while at work." At night, because he rarely had a candle, Morgan's two to six hours of reading were "by the light of pine or lightened knots."

The Methodist workday, with a small adjustment to make time for religious devotions, seemed to come right out of the pages of Benjamin Franklin's *Autobiography*. But then Methodists and Franklin shared a common attachment to the work ethic. If only Franklin could drop his scepticism concerning "revealed religion," Methodists would find him a very congenial figure. Some ten years after Franklin's death, William Colbert, while itinerating through his native Somerset County, discovered such a Franklin. After reading "the life of the celebrated Dr. Benjamin Franklin, with some of his essays," Colbert thought that Philadelphia's most famous citizen, "by his late writing," seemed to see the error in denying revelation.[13]

Revelation was important, make no mistake about that. Divine truth, as revealed through Methodism, saved souls for eternity and yet girded men and women with the necessary self-discipline and industry to deal with the economic demands of the temporal world. A good example of revelation leading to a dramatic financial turn-around was the case of a Methodist convert met by Quaker Nathaniel Luff in Kent County, Delaware, in 1797. Prior to becoming a Methodist, Luff's acquaintance was a horse racer, dancer, and general "libertine" who owed considerable amounts of money. On becoming a Methodist, he gave up all his former pastimes and concentrated "a more close attention to his domestic affairs." The revolution in personal habits led the reformed "libertine" down the road to economic prosperity.

Methodist preachers were pleased by the change in work habits brought about by the Wesleyan message. Freeborn Garrettson, when he first itinerated through southeastern Sussex County, noticed that the people were poor and preferred hunting and fishing to cultivating the land. But after Methodist itinerants spread the message among them, the people of the region became industrious, tilled their fields, and built houses. Garrettson observed that "there is nothing like the gospel in its purity to meliorate both the temporal and spiritual condition of man."

Near Newark, Delaware, was an iron-rolling mill owned by Quaker Abraham Sharpless. A Methodist society was formed among the mill workers in 1807 by itinerant Henry Boehm, and a Methodist church was built in the neighborhood ten years later. Subsequently, Sharpless admitted to Boehm that a great change had taken place in his workers since Methodism had been introduced among them. Sharpless particularly praised his workers' new-found industry and sobriety. What a contrast with their condition before Methodism, when liquor dominated their Sundays and rendered them ineffective workers until Wednesday. Now, according to Sharpless, "all he had to do was tell his people what he wanted done and how, and it was accomplished."[14]

The Methodist work ethic may have made many Delmarvans more industrious, but it didn't necessarily make them wealthy. To start with, the Peninsula was hardly the land of economic opportunity. According to the 1820 census, approximately 83 percent of Delmarva's white work force was engaged in agriculture, 13 percent in manufacturing (primarily in New Castle and Cecil counties where Methodists were least numerous), and 4 percent in commerce. Obviously, the overwhelming majority of Peninsula Methodists had to depend on the soil for their livelihood. And yet, because of the region's worn-out soil, farming on the Peninsula offered very little opportunity for economic advancement. Even the self-discipline and industriousness introduced by Methodism was unable to make Delmarva's farm land as productive as the newly opened, more fertile lands beyond the Appalachians.

Many Peninsula Methodists were prevented from reaping considerable economic benefits from their disciplined working and living habits because of their commitment to the church community. Indeed, the desire to fulfill community obligations competed with the impulse to pursue private economic gain, causing considerable psychic tension among those early Methodists and often leading to agonizing reappraisals of priorities. The extraordinary demands of Methodism, which called for attendance on Sundays and weekdays at regular services as well as prayer, class, camp, and quarterly meetings, consumed time and energy. Lay leaders were expected to make even greater commitments of time. In addition, Methodists were taught to regard each other as brothers and sisters, with commensurate responsibilities for each other in time of economic need. William Morgan, for example, gave away large amounts of his income, because "I had to help everyone that asked me that call themselves Methodists." He thought it "a breach of godliness not to help those of [the] faith." Morgan later grew disillusioned,

William Morgan at sixty-seven
(Courtesy, Historical Society of Delaware)

finding "there were many that would take the bread out of my mouth and turn me out of doors."

No Methodist had a right to be more disillusioned than Levin Conoway, who lived between Laurel and Georgetown in Sussex County. Following the Methodist way, he freed his wife's slaves, gave to the needy, spent considerable time and energy at Methodist meetings, and boarded circuit riders and their mounts on a regular basis for fifteen or twenty years. (The latter was no small obligation. One circuit rider on Virginia's Eastern Shore demanded at each stop no less than eighteen ears of corn and a proportionate amount of fodder just for his horse.) As a result of his generosity, Conoway's temporal fortunes turned sour, and he was forced to depend on a son for financial support.

Other Methodists who joined Conoway in experiencing a decline in their earthly fortunes included Eastern Shore gentry Henry Ennalls of Dorchester County and William Hopper and William Bruff of Queen Anne's County. Even local preacher William Morgan, after working hard his entire life as a cabinetmaker, drygoods merchant, farmer, and physician, was forced at age sixty-five to write his memoir for his grandson as "perhaps the only legacy that I will be able to bestow upon you." To the southwest, the equally hard-working Joshua Thomas fared a bit better. At the age of seventy-five, the local preacher, waterman, and farmer possessed real estate on Deal Island valued at $1,000.[15]

Slavery

We preached against slavery and persuaded our brethren and those who were converted to liberate their slaves, and we were often successful.

Thus spoke itinerant Henry Boehm of his experience on the Peninsula in the first decade of the nineteenth century.

From the very beginning, many American Methodists heeded the urgings of Wesley, the admonitions of their circuit riders, the directives of the Methodist *Discipline*, and even natural law and freed their slaves. Probably no other group of American Methodists matched the manumitting enthusiasm shown by Peninsula Wesleyans. This received strong support from the Philadelphia Annual Conference, which included the entire Peninsula in its jurisdiction.

During the first decade of the nineteenth century, with the General Conference of the Methodist Episcopal Church increasingly willing to compromise Methodism's traditional opposition to slavery, the Philadelphia Conference continued to take a firm stand. Indeed, it was the Phildelphia Annual Conference—39 percent of whose members were Peninsula itinerants—that unsuccessfully challenged the General Conference in 1808 to return to a less equivocal stand against slavery.[16]

Manumission

While nationally Methodism's support of manumission began to weaken, the Philadelphia Annual Conference continued to call on Methodists to liberate their slaves. In 1807 the latest regulations of the Philadelphia Annual Conference were read to a Quarterly Conference meeting in Laurel, Delaware. The listening Methodists were directed to free all of their slaves according to a delayed manumission schedule based on age. Generally, all slaves were to

Henry Boehm
(Courtesy, Methodist Collection, Drew University, Madison, NJ)

be manumitted after serving between seven to ten years. Methodists who didn't abide by the regulations were to be treated as "contumacious persons." Although the General Conference of 1808 put an end to this particular attempt to force manumission on Methodist slaveholders, the Philadelphia Annual Conference didn't give up. In 1810, at its meeting in Easton, Talbot County, it asked every preacher and Quarterly Conference "to use their lawful and prudent influence to promote the freedom of slaves."

Although most Peninsula Methodists weren't wealthy enough to own slaves, those who did manumitted thousands of blacks. They did so because, as William Parramore of Accomack County pointed out, slavery was "repugnant to and a violation of our blessed Christian religion." In 1787 Francis Asbury noted, while in lower Somerset County, that "most of our members in these parts have freed their slaves." In Caroline, Dorchester, and Talbot counties alone, 1,833 blacks were freed between 1783 and 1799. The manumitting masters "in all probability were almost all Methodists." From 1800 to 1833, more than three thousand additional slaves were freed in the same tri-county area, most by Methodists. Wesleyan gentry who led the way included Thomas Airey of Dorchester County, who manumitted thirty blacks, and Henry Banning of Talbot, who liberated forty-five.

Although Delmarva Methodists were strongly urged to liberate their slaves, generally they weren't coerced. The only exceptions were a six-month period in 1785 when the *Discipline* denied communion and membership to those unwilling to free their slaves, and the previously mentioned 1807–8 period when the Philadelphia Annual Conference directed that slaveholders be treated as "contumacious persons." But for those who purchased or sold slaves, it was a different story.[17]

The Slave Trade

Like the Quakers, early American Methodists were convinced that the institution of slavery would shrivel up and die if only the buying and selling of slaves could be halted. Not surprisingly, many Peninsula Methodists held slave traders to be the most despicable of human beings. Native Delmarvan William Colbert called them "the grandest sets of villains on this side of Hell." Evidently, Georgia slave traders made regular purchases at a slave mart in Snow Hill, Worcester County, to sell for profit in the deep South. With understandable pride, Henry Boehm boasted that Peninsula Methodism "made a mighty change here [at Snow Hill] and destroyed the inhuman traffic."

The Methodist *Discipline* of 1796 took a strong stand against the buying and selling of slaves. Methodists who sold slaves were to be expelled from society, and those who purchased slaves were to manumit them according to schedules worked out by respective Quarterly Conferences. The responsibility for carrying out these two directives was left in the hands of Annual and Quarterly conferences and individual societies. As might be expected, in most of the slaveholding South this responsibility was largely ignored.

On the Peninsula the rules of 1796 were enforced, with the Quarterly Conferences quite willing to take decisive measures against Methodists who bought or sold slaves. In 1801, Methodist layman Nathaniel Dixon who lived near Salisbury was expelled from society for selling a slave. Five years later, Roger Robertson of Dorchester County was "disowned as a member" for selling a slave despite the fact that Robertson maintained "ignorance of the rules of society."

Generally, the Quarterly Conferences drew up schedules for delayed manumissions of recently purchased slaves, which the

Methodist slave owners were then required to carry out. In 1805, for example, the Dorchester Quarterly Conference stipulated that a slave named Roger, twenty-five years old, was to be freed nine years from the date of his purchase; fourteen-year-old Rose could be held until she reached twenty-one; and fifty-year-old James Hicks had to be freed two years from the date of his purchase. If, like Joseph Meekins, the slave owner refused to abide by the conference's manumitting schedule, he was "expelled for noncompliance." By 1814 even local societies were called on by the Philadelphia Annual Conference to form committees to draw up delayed manumission agreements with owners of newly purchased slaves.[18]

Other Antislavery Activity

In addition to manumitting slaves, some Peninsula Methodists found other ways to demonstrate their deep-felt objection to slavery. William Morgan, briefly leaving Sussex County for Yorktown, Virginia, wrote that although he found Virginia attractive, "that desperate thing called slavery spoiled all." (Evidently, human bondage on Delmarva seemed less "desperate.") Morgan returned to Sussex County after his opposition to slavery caused Virginia to regard him "as an enemy of the country."

A few Peninsula Methodists became leaders in antislavery societies. Wilmington port collector Allen McLane was elected president of the Delaware abolitionist society in 1803. Andrew Barratt of Kent County, who served as sheriff, judge, and member of the Delaware General Assembly, was the son of Philip Barratt of Barratt's Chapel and a leading Methodist in his own right until his death in 1821. In 1796, following a practice set by his Methodist father and later emulated by two brothers and a cousin, Andrew Barratt manumitted his thirteen slaves. He then went on to become one of the earliest leaders in Delaware's abolitionist movement.

In 1788 an abolitionist society was founded in Dover, with Methodist Richard Bassett one of its leading members. By the mid-1790s, however, it ceased to exist. The abolitionist society of Sussex County was formed in 1809 with the immediate goals of ending the county's domestic slave traffic and the kidnapping of blacks to be sold into slavery. Caleb Rodney, a leading Methodist from Lewes, was its first president, and Daniel Hudson and William Russell, trustees of Wesley Chapel, Georgetown, served as the society's first secretary and treasurer.

For the most part, however, Peninsula Methodists didn't rally to abolitionist societies. In the early nineteenth century the Quaker-dominated Delaware abolitionist society tried to encourage the formation of local societies that would attract downstate Methodists, but only the Sussex group responded.

More vigorous were the efforts of some leading Methodists, particularly in Delaware, to enact legislation against slavery. According to a law passed in 1767, Delawareans had to provide £60 security for each slave they liberated in case the slave became a ward of the county. This requirement prevented many from manumitting their blacks. In 1787 Representative Richard Bassett successfully introduced a bill into the General Assembly that ended the payment of this security and also made illegal the sale of Delaware slaves beyond the state boundaries. Bassett, who manumitted his own slaves, was joined in subsequent legislative efforts to abolish slavery and to establish limited rights for free blacks by such other leading Methodists as Caleb Rodney of Sussex County, Isaac Davis of Kent County, and Allen McLane of Kent and New Castle counties. Indeed, thanks to the efforts of some of these Methodists and others, in 1797 Delaware came within one senator's vote of legislating a gradual abolition of slavery.[19]

Model Slaves

Unlike Brother Bassett, not all Methodist gentry were comfortable with the idea of manumission, particularly when it became the subject of a sermon. A case in point was Capt. Thomas Burton of Accomack County—formerly "Fox-hunting Tom Burton"—who habitually patted his foot when pleased with the preaching. However, if manumission was broached and the circuit rider thundered to let the oppressed go free, Captain Burton stopped patting.

Some gentry were more expressive in their disapproval. Itinerant Richard Lyon was preaching an antislavery sermon to a Methodist gathering in Accomack around 1804 when an irate slave owner arose from the congregation and started for the pulpit with a cocked horse whip in his hand. A leading layman rushed to the itinerant's aid only to be lashed across the hand for his trouble. Lyon came down out of his pulpit, grappled with the slaveholder, and threw him to the floor. The affair ended without serious injury to anyone, but Lyon's future sermons were carefully monitored by a committee of laymen to avoid further provocations.

Slaveholders resented the Methodist call for manumission because they felt that it enormously increased the possibility of slave disorder and rebellion. Yet there was another side of the Methodist message that admonished slaves to avoid disorderly behavior. Thomas Smith, while riding Peninsula circuits at the turn of the century, noted with approval the many cases of Methodists manumitting their slaves. But what were enslaved blacks to do while waiting and hoping for freedom? In 1801, before perhaps four thousand slaves gathered at a Quarterly Meeting in lower Accomack County, Smith answered that question by using Ephesians 4:5 as his text: "Servants, be obedient to them that are your masters." Obviously, Peninsula Methodism was mixing a peculiar brew for its black followers, combining hope for eventual freedom with the obligation, in the meantime, to obediently persevere. Indeed, the fact that no slave insurrection occurred on the Peninsula may have been partly due to the strong Methodist presence which demanded patience for now, offered the possibility of freedom soon, and promised paradise forever.

Understandably, Methodism was credited with molding—from the slaveholder's perspective—ideal slaves. Thomas Rankin, while itinerating through Kent County, Maryland, in 1774, stopped at the home of Methodist Carvil Hynson. While there, Hynson's wife pointed out to Rankin how impossible it had been to keep slaves from stealing everything in sight. But now, thanks to the advent of Methodism in the area, slaveholders "could leave every kind of food exposed and none [was] touched by any of them." A pleased Rankin responded "that the gospel, in its purity and power, could perform that which the laws faintly attempt to do." Forty-one years later, Episcopalian slaveholder Tench Tilghman of Talbot County noted that "the best disposed" slaves were "attached to the Methodist Church."[20]

Blacks Aren't Brothers

Despite Methodism's ability to turn blacks into "responsible" Christians, the concept of racial brotherhood remained alien to most white Wesleyans. Because of the limited educational level of blacks, itinerant William Colbert felt "that care ought to be taken to keep them humble." But Colbert also insisted that because all races were of similar "passions," blacks ought not to "be spoken to as brutes and slaves." He cited the Apostle Paul, who had exhorted a slavemaster to treat his servant as a brother. After all, Colbert maintained, God "made of one blood all nations of men." While serving the Milford Circuit in southern Delaware in 1795, however, Colbert was rudely awakened to the depth of racial feelings on the Peninsula. At two preaching stops he was rebuked by whites for referring to blacks as "brethren and sisters."

There were a few white Methodists who did treat blacks as brothers and sisters under Christ. One example was John Thelwell, a leading Wilmington Methodist, who began conducting a school for blacks in 1802, sponsored by the Delaware abolitionist society. For the most part, however, Peninsula Methodism was more successful at loosening the fetters of institutional slavery than it was in altering white racial attitudes.[21]

Decline of Anti-Slavery Sentiment

By the second decade of the nineteenth century it was evident that Peninsula Methodists were losing some of their antislavery fervor. Indeed, William Morgan dated the decline in abolitionist sentiment among some Peninsula Methodists from 1808. Despite a plea to the General Conference from the Cambridge Circuit, in 1826, to prevent slaveholders from joining the Methodist Episcopal Church, it was increasingly evident that most Delmarva Methodists were willing to push the evils of slavery to the periphery of their concerns. Reflecting this trend, the number of delayed manumissions of newly purchased slaves recorded by some of the Quarterly Conferences declined appreciably. In the Dorchester Quarterly Conference, the last such agreement was recorded in 1816; in Accomack, in 1824. Subsequently, Dorchester Methodists removed pages from their Quarterly Conference Journal because, evidently, these pages testified to the strong antislavery position of their Methodist ancestors, and that was embarrassing.[22]

The willingness to turn away from the issue of slavery may have resulted, in part, from Methodist success. By the 1820s, Methodism had been the dominant faith of the Peninsula for a number of decades. Largely forgotten were those former days of persecution when violent threats and physical assaults against Methodists, often symbolized by the planter's whip, were an accepted fact of life. In one case, the whip had been in the hand of a former governor of Maryland, Robert Wright of Queen Anne's County, who lashed his son Thomas for becoming a Methodist.

As they received beatings and whippings, those early Methodists must have sensed what it was like to be powerless and to be subject as slaves were to the sometimes whimsical violence administered by planters and their hirelings. Out of this shared experience came an empathy for the situation of the black slave.

By 1820, Methodism reigned supreme south of New Castle and Cecil counties, with the only competition coming from scattered pockets of Presbyterians, Episcopalians, Baptists, and Quakers. Long gone were the days of persecution and the resulting shared experience with at least one aspect of the black slave's life. But much more than empathy for the slave was lost as Methodism moved from persecuted, radical sect to dominant church. As previously noted, Asbury sensed the danger while touring the upper Eastern Shore in 1811. He realized that Methodist success, paradoxically, could lead to failure. Methodists had become "respectable," but that was exactly the problem.[23]

To eighteenth-century Peninsula Methodists, this world was a battleground between the ways of God and the ways of men. Methodists advertised their commitment to God and their unwillingness to bow to the self-centered, "respectable" ways of the dominant gentry by behaving in a manner that set them apart. By 1820, however, Methodists were beginning to cross the line that separated those two worlds. Some of the distinction between the two life-styles began to blur, as the earlier Methodist concerns with eating, drinking, and clothing were gradually pushed aside. Abolitionism, too, lost its symbolic importance as a statement against the corrupt ways of the gentry. Indeed, as the nineteenth century progressed, strong support for abolitionism seemed about to join fasting and plain dress as just another quaint relic from Methodism of another era.

A People Apart

Christ said that his followers were "not of the world, even as I am not of the world." Other Biblical passages reinforced the belief among early Methodists that in order to maintain their Christian purity, they must remain separate from the world. Through their distinctive dress, deportment, value system, and living habits, early Wesleyans emphasized the gulf between God's people and the rest of humanity. Through aggressive proselytizing, Methodists did urge others to cross the gulf and join them, but in a rhetoric that clearly emphasized the differences between the saved and the damned.

In 1802 James Hemphill of Wilmington was on his way to Snow Hill, Maryland, when he was invited to pay a brief visit to the home of George Kennard, a leading merchant and Methodist in Smyrna, Delaware. Before Hemphill was long seated, Mrs. Kennard "attacked in the most severe Methodist strain I ever heard,

[and] told me I was in the broad road to hell." Mrs. Kennard's two sisters were equally adamant, causing the shaken but unrepentant Hemphill to take leave of the Kennards as quickly as possible.[24] The aggressive evangelizing of the likes of Mrs. Kennard and her two sisters awakened some Delmarvans to the perils of godlessness, but it also served to anger others and thus widen the gap between Methodists and many non-Methodists.

To be a people apart, it was important to keep all levels of government at arm's length. To do this, Peninsula Methodism tried to assume many responsibilities traditionally the prerogative of civil authority. It did so with considerable self-confidence, and why not? As itinerant Thomas Rankin intimated, the Methodist message could do a far better job in shaping the actions of men than the laws of government could. In the area of crime prevention, Sussex County was a splendid example. In 1802 Ceasar Augustus Rodney, nephew of Caesar Rodney, noted that "at the last court in Sussex there were very few prosecutions owing" to the progress of Methodist "principles."

On occasion Methodist principles could work in tandem with state laws to put an end to criminal activity. Along the Cornwall coast in southwest England, inhabitants routinely plundered shipwrecked vessels and even set out misleading signals to draw ships to their destruction on the rocks that dotted the rugged coastline. English Methodists struggled hard to stop the plundering and were largely responsible for ending the practice by the early nineteenth century. It seems that many inhabitants of the Lewes area were addicted to the Cornwall practice and routinely looted ships stranded on sand bars off Cape Henlopen. By 1790, the rise of Methodist principles in the area—J. M. Hargus, the lighthouse keeper at Cape Henlopen, was a Methodist local preacher—evidently combined with stricter criminal laws to put an end to the looting.[25]

If individual Methodists were suspected of criminal behavior, they were tried by their local society. In Kent County, Delaware, for example, shoemaker Ebenezer Blackiston had to defend himself against charges of being a thief and a liar, while James Payne denied the accusations that he fathered an illegitimate child. In the latter case, the state wasn't satisfied with society's verdict of innocence and tried Payne in criminal court.

In keeping with their desire to remain a people apart, Methodist societies tried to settle legal disputes between members before they reached the civil courts. During the eighteenth century, the itinerant usually passed judgement on legal controversies between members, but by the early nineteenth century, he routinely appointed a committee of laymen to render judgement. In 1785, for example, circuit rider Robert Ayres settled a legal dispute between two class members near Milford, Delaware. In the early nineteenth century, by contrast, a business dispute involving three society members in Lewes was dealt with by a committee of appointed laymen.[26]

To avoid the temptation of a sinful world, early Methodists generally retreated behind the formidable walls of their local society, class meeting, and family. Recognizing the particular importance of stable families, Methodists worked hard to strengthen familial bonds. Asbury set an example for other itinerants by instructing families on domestic relations. He placed particular emphasis on the duties and responsibilities of husband, wife, and children within the family structure. He often talked about the importance of "family prayer and order." Asbury taught children to recite that they must "learn to read and learn to pray; learn to work and learn to obey." Extramarital sex and living together out of wedlock threatened the sanctity of the family and were vigorously opposed by Methodists. This stand caused James Hudson and Polly Crapper of Somerset County, who had lived together a long time "like man and wife," to quickly marry after becoming Methodists in 1801. That year, three black women from Somerset were expelled from society for having children out of wedlock.

But Methodism could also be a divisive factor in family relationships. Doubtless, upon becoming Methodists, converts were often subjected to ridicule and abuse by unconverted relatives. The willingess of the former governor of Maryland to take the whip to his newly converted son was just one extreme example of the fallout from religious division within Peninsula families.[27]

As the years passed, it became increasingly difficult for Peninsula Methodists to continue their separation from the world. With more and more Delmarvans of all classes becoming Methodists, it was evident that the profane world in general and the political world in particular could not be held at arm's length forever. Indeed, decisions made in the nation's capital or in the state capitals in Dover, Annapolis, and Richmond impinged on the lives of Peninsula Methodists in such a manner that it was difficult to remain totally aloof from the political process.

Political Involvement

Asbury advised American Methodists to steer clear of politics because political involvement distracted them from more significant concerns. At Smyrna, Delaware, in 1791, Asbury noted that "the minds of the people were so occupied by the approaching election, that I fear there was little room for things more important."

Political involvement was also considered risky because it could cause men to abandon their Methodist principles. In 1805 in Sussex County, Federalist and Democratic-Republican rhetoric reached such vituperative extremes that many politicians maintained that their lives were in danger. That July leading county Federalists, including Dr. Jacob Wolf of Lewes and a number of other Methodists, held a meeting in the jury room on the second floor of the county courthouse in Georgetown. Just as the meeting began and Dr. Wolf was being nominated to take the chair, "the most awful flash of lightning" struck "the cupola, ran down the rafters and slivered the front of the courthouse." The thunder clap, which was so loud that it "made the whole town tremble," brought William Morgan running from his nearby home. He found Wolf dead and eleven others seriously injured. To the devout William Morgan, the lightning bolt was a "judgement from heaven" on those who allowed themselves, for political considerations, to be enticed into "traducing and impugning the character and motives of others."[28]

But there were strong counterforces pulling Peninsula Methodists toward political involvement. The attempt by the Episcopal Church in Maryland, right after the American Revolution, to gain tax support for all Christian faiths and the question of war and peace raised by tensions between France and the United States forced Wesleyans to take stands on political issues. Moreover, because Methodists represented the largest organized group on the Peninsula, politicians made every attempt to address Methodist gatherings. In 1804 in Talbot County, Federalist leader Robert Goldsboro was even accused of trying to buy votes by distributing liquor at a Methodist Quarterly Meeting.

Politicians must have sensed that the many hours spent listening to sermons and exhortations made Methodists particularly susceptible to the verbal message. Although Methodists had problems with the accusatory nature of most political rhetoric, political addresses seemed to follow a very familiar pattern. The fervid attacks by politicians on their opponents certainly sounded un-Christian to Methodist ears, but the ability of candidates to portray the coming political contest as a titanic struggle between the forces of light and darkness surely conjured up the image of the itinerant calling on his listeners to side with the angels in the struggle against the sinister forces of Satan. To put it simply, the political stump speech was a form of communication that Peninsula Methodists were especially attuned to and understood.[29]

Methodist Gentry and Politics

Traditionally, most positions of political responsibility on the Peninsula were filled by the gentry.[30] On becoming Methodists, however, the new-found piety of some of the gentry diminished their interest in things political. This Wesleyan trait probably explains the dramatic withdrawal from political activity of such Methodist gentry as Henry Ennalls of Dorchester County, Henry Banning and James Benson of Talbot County, and William Bruff and James Bordley of Queen Anne's County.

But it was difficult for all Wesleyan planters to abandon the leadership roles that they and some of their ancestors had exercised for generations. For this reason, some were willing to risk the spiritual contamination commonly associated with political activity. Examples of the pull of tradition overcoming Methodist reticence included William Hopper and Charles Emory of Queen Anne's County, who continued to serve in local and state politics after conversion. Another Eastern Shore example was William Hindman of Talbot County, who served in a number of local and state positions and then as U.S. congresssman (1793–99) and senator (1800–1). In Kent County, Delaware, Andrew Barratt and Isaac Davis filled local and state elective offices, while family friend and fellow Methodist Richard Bassett was elected U.S. senator (1789–93) and governor of Delaware (1799–1801) and in 1801 became one of President John Adams's "midnight appointments" to a federal judgeship.[31]

An Authoritarian Church

Despite the political involvement of some gentry, many Peninsula Methodists seemed, at times, almost apolitical. Perhaps some of this political apathy could be traced to the authoritarian, undemocratic nature of American Methodism as it was shaped by Francis Asbury and "old Methodism."

At the Annual and General conferences, which were the governing bodies of the Methodist Episcopal Church, only itinerants were represented. Exercising control over these conferences in a manner reminiscent of John Wesley's paternalism was Bishop Asbury. The bishop had little sympathy with the idea of lay representation in the ruling councils of Methodism. He maintained that if laymen really wanted a voice, they should become itinerants.[32]

Of course it might be argued that in spite of the undemocratic nature of its polity, the Methodist Episcopal Church was surprisingly sensitive to the needs and concerns of its members. Because circuit riders wore out in a hurry, their ranks were constantly replenished by young men recruited directly from the farms, stores, or craftshops where they had been in touch with the most urgent concerns of lay Methodists. Moreover, because Methodist itinerants boarded with laymen, they were more aware of the needs of Delmarvans than the stationed clerics of other faiths.

But make no mistake about it, early Methodism's polity was not democratic, and occasionally protests against the authoritarian nature of Methodism surfaced. In 1789, to better govern the rapidly expanding Methodist movement, a council made up of bishops Asbury and Coke and a number of presiding elders was created, which had considerable authority. Of particular interest was the extraordinary power exercised by Asbury through his right to veto any council resolution. Since such a concentration of power ignored the prerogatives of the itinerants, it led to predictable opposition wherever itinerants gathered. At a conference for Maryland's Eastern Shore and Delaware, held at Smyrna in 1790, Asbury heard objections to the council form of government from one or two of the assembled circuit riders. Faced with intense and widespread opposition nationwide, by 1792 Asbury abandoned the council for the far more popular concept of a General Conference made up of all of the traveling preachers meeting quadrennially.[33]

At the first General Conference in 1792, presiding elder James O'Kelly of Virginia's Western Shore and several others challenged the bishop's power to arbitrarily assign itinerants to circuits. O'Kelly proposed that unhappy traveling preachers should have the right to appeal appointments to the General Conference, which, in turn, could force the bishop to assign them to other circuits. O'Kelly's attempt to make the appointment process more democratic was defeated, and he and a number of young preachers then left the Methodist Episcopal Church to form the Christian Church. The O'Kelly schism and subsequent attempts at General Conferences to democratize Methodist polity failed to make an appreciable change in the authoritarian nature of early Methodism.

Except for the actions of Peter Spencer and other Wilmington blacks, on the Peninsula there seemed little support for attempts to reduce the power of the bishops and even less enthusiasm for sending lay representatives to Annual and General Conferences. The reluctance of Peninsula Methodists to challenge the authoritarian nature of the Methodist Church may have been a reflection of the region's continued veneration of Francis Asbury and his "old Methodism."

Asbury died in 1816, and within a decade local preacher William Morgan, now living in southwestern Sussex, was comparing bishops to dictators and presiding elders to vice-regents, and was retrospectively expressing sympathy for James O'Kelly. He also noted that the laity wanted representation at Annual and General Conferences. Obviously the Methodist Protestant schism, which took place in 1828–30 and had a far greater impact on the Peninsula than the O'Kelly schism, had a champion in William Morgan. Writing retrospectively in 1845 as a Methodist Protestant, Morgan maintained

> that a majority ought to govern both in church and state, and that the free male members of any community ought to have the right to elect delegates to make laws by which they should be governed.[34]

Federalists or Democratic-Republicans?

Although unaccustomed to participation in their own church government and reluctant to sally forth into the contaminating world of politics, some Peninsula Methodists did cast ballots in civil elections, but often for the political party which, like their church, had little use for democracy. In Delaware, Methodists generally voted the Federalist ticket. After all, just as Methodism was viewed as an "English" faith, Federalists were seen as the "English" party. Moreover, the opposing Democratic-Republicans were perceived as the Scotch-Irish Presbyterian, radical, upstate party.

Leading Delaware Methodists who ran for political office were usually on the Federalist ticket and, once elected, took good care of their Methodist brothers. Richard Bassett, for example, upon being elected governor of Delaware, appointed Dr. Abraham Ridgley secretary of state and Andrew Barratt judge of the Court of Common Pleas.

Naturally, the Democratic-Republicans attacked the Methodists for their support of the Federalists. In the spring of 1800, Governor Bassett was accused of manipulating Methodists for his own political ends. He was portrayed as a hypocrite who made himself the leader of Delaware's Methodists by loaning money for the construction of Wesley Chapel in Dover. As a result, "a mutual attachment and a reciprocal interest unites the governor of the state with the most numerous religious society." Bassett was further accused of using his influence to have itinerant preachers warn Delaware's Methodists "that no salvation is to be expected" for those who supported Thomas Jefferson in the upcoming presidential election.[35]

Despite attacks of this nature, Delaware Methodists continued to support the Federalist party. Certainly the specter of Jacobin atheism, cleverly associated by Federalist propagandists with the Democratic-Republican party, was much on Methodist minds. Moreover, Methodists were primarily downstate rural folk, wary, as rural folk tend to be, of radical political change. It is understandable that they felt very comfortable with the conservative nature of the Federalist party. With continued Methodist support, Federalist dominance in Delaware continued until 1827, which was later than in any other state.[36]

On the rest of the Peninsula, Methodist political preference was less clear. The same forces that pulled Methodists into the Federalist camp in Delaware were also at work in Maryland and Virginia's Eastern Shore. But in Maryland there was an additional factor not present in Delaware: particularly bad feelings between Methodists and Episcopalians. Right after the American Revolution, relations between the two faiths in Maryland were exacerbated by the Methodist declaration of independence, the Methodist charge that the Episcopalian Church was attempting to reestablish itself as the state-supported church, and later by the Episcopalian attacks on the episcopal prerogatives of Methodist bishops. Moreover, Eastern Shore Episcopalians identified with the Federalist party, and at least one Episcopalian accused Methodists of having "Jacobinite principles."

The hostility of the Episcopalian-Federalists and their efforts on behalf of tax-support legislation for all churches drove many Eastern Shore Methodists into the Democratic-Republican camp. Among other things, the aborted tax-support scheme would have supplied salary support for Maryland's Christian clergy. Episcopalians thought it a necessary measure because of the high cost of supporting their settled or stationed ministers. Methodists, by contrast, found that because their itinerancy system required very little money, they could carry on nicely without state support. Moreover, without state support, the Methodists had a considerable advantage over their rival "English" church in the competition for the souls of Eastern Shore Anglo-Saxons. A government subsidy to both faiths would only diminish the Methodist advantage. No wonder itinerant Ezekiel Cooper signed a petition against tax-supported ministers' salaries, while riding a circuit on the upper Eastern Shore in 1785.

But not all Eastern Shore Methodists voted Democratic-Republican. Early success by Federalists on both Maryland and Virginia's Eastern Shore and the continued leadership in the Federalist party of Talbot County planter William Hindman after his conversion to Methodism indicate that many other Eastern Shore Methodists from Maryland to Virginia probably voted Federalist or didn't bother to vote.[37]

Reaction to war and the threat of war was another indicator of increasing interest by Peninsula Methodists in the political issues of the day. During the American Revolution, Peninsula Methodists held themselves aloof because of strong pacifist convictions. By 1798, however, some Peninsula Methodists seemed primed for war. French ships had interefered with American vessels on the high seas, and American diplomats in Paris were insulted in the famous XYZ Affair. War fever swept the United States, and President John Adams called for a day of fasting to demonstrate national unity in the face of the French threat. In Dover, Delaware, a Methodist meeting was held in response to the crisis. Before a large crowd, a local preacher delivered a sermon that was "very well suited to the occasion and as much in the political way as you can imagine." With a company of uniformed militia in attendance, a patriotic and martial spirit was ascendant. Subsequently the black cockade, a symbol of anti-French feeling, was worn by just about everyone in the Dover area, "even the Methodists." Two years later, Quaker Nathaniel Luff constrasted Methodist pacifism during the American Revolution with the present militarism among some Wesleyans in the Dover area. Indeed, Luff found local Methodists "now, perhaps, most forward in military measures."[38]

Who, Then, Was This New Man?

James Kemp, Episcopal rector of Great Choptank Parish, Dorchester County, disliked Methodists. About 1811, he compared them to Episcopalians and found Methodists unattractive. Episcopalians were "gay, lively and sometimes distracted" but also "charitable, honest, candid, and free of hypocracy." Methodists, by contrast, were "gloomy, morose, and sober." Kemp admitted that Methodist rules prohibited "some open and apparent sins," but he found Wesleyans to be "uncharitable, backbiting, and censorious."

Because Methodists lived their lives with such intensity and seriousness, Kemp's view that they tended to be very sober, even a bit gloomy and morose, is understandable. But at chapel or camp meeting, Peninsula Methodists displayed quite another side. Typical was a scene on Maryland's lower Eastern Shore just after the turn of the century. Itinerant Henry Boehm reported

> the people got so happy and shouted so loud they drowned my voice, leaped for joy, and sometimes they would fall, lose their strength, and lie for hours in this condition, and then come to praising the Lord.

Even at funerals, "in several instances, loud shouts were heard at the grave."[39] Evidently, Peninsula Methodists kept their emotions pretty much bottled up during much of the week, only to release them through loud singing, cries of joy and sorrow, and even leaping during Wesleyan services.

Because they took life so seriously, Peninsula Methodists naturally displayed little tolerance of those who seemed less earnest. To those sunk deeply in sin, Wesleyans held high the banner of hope through Christian redemption. But when redeemed sinners backslid, Methodists could be very "uncharitable" and "censorious."

In 1802 William Morgan and Stephen Redden became partners in a joining and carpentry business in Georgetown, Sussex County. Being zealous Methodists, the two partners would often end the workday praying for particular Georgetown families in need of conversion and then follow up with a visit. Mitchell Scott, the old county jailer, was among those targeted for conversion. At first Scott responded with oaths to the entreaties of the two young evangelists. But when Morgan, accompanied by others, began to sing, "Oh how happy are they the Savior obey," Scott began to weep, tremble, and at length cry out, "What shall I do to be saved?" The commotion brought almost everyone living in Georgetown to the jail. A number of onlookers were deeply moved and an Episcopalian, who had been a persecutor of Wesleyans, was converted. Even the old jailer claimed to have had a change of heart, but within a few weeks he returned to drunkeness and swearing. We can hear the harsh, censorious edge to Morgan's voice as he compares Scott's fall from grace to the return of a dog "to his vomit" or a sow "to the mire."

Sober, censorious, and a good many other things besides, Peninsula Methodists spread a message and created a way of life that can only be called revolutionary. By 1820, however, Peninsula Methodism was well on its way to shedding its radical, sectarian garb for the more circumspect mantle of the dominant church. In the process, some of the earlier Methodist character traits, found so objectionable by the Reverend James Kemp and others, were doubtless modified. But before that original Methodist personality was modified, it sparked a remarkable change in the spiritual and secular life of the Delmarva Peninsula. Indeed, so dramatic a change took place that widely traveled itinerant Henry Boehm observed that "the Peninsula seemed like the Garden of God." As Quaker Nathaniel Luff retrospectively pointed out, Methodists "were then very much in earnest."[40]

Some Afterthoughts

From the beginning, the geographically isolated population of the Delmarva Peninsula developed a strong conservative bent. But then, in the late eighteenth century, Methodism blew across the Peninsula like a fresh wind, challenging this conservative perspective with a radical message that stirred men to think and act in new ways. Even more than the American Revolution, the Methodist movement rejected previously held assumptions and changed individual lives.

But as the nineteenth century progressed, Peninsula Methodism drew back from some of the more radical implications of the Wesleyan message, and the traditionally conservative nature of the region gradually reasserted itself. Indeed, the Methodist offensive that caused such great alarm among champions of the status quo in the late eighteenth and early nineteenth century was the only force to challenge the conservative nature of the Peninsula until the mid-twentieth century.

While urging change in individual lives and raising questions concerning the nature of Delmarva's religious, social, political, and economic institutions, Peninsula Methodism worked hard at preserving the Wesleyan heritage. When this heritage was challenged by outspoken Methodists from other sections of the United States, the Peninsula's strong support of "old Methodism" proved crucial in turning back many of these challenges and in preserving for posterity the Wesleyan tradition of an itinerating ministry serving a connectional church run in an authoritarian manner.

Why did Peninsula Methodism lose some of its early vigor and its willingness to challenge the status quo? Perhaps part of the answer lies in the generally accepted view that revolutionary movements have a life cycle of their own, with the early, radical phase eventually giving way to a more conservative and accommodating phase. Or perhaps it was just a case of powerful social, economic, and demographic forces eventually overriding the dynamic spirit of religious reform. Whatever the reason, by the mid-nineteenth century, Peninsula Methodism had generally abandoned confrontation for accommodation in its search for a "proper" relationship with the secular world.

Notes

Introduction

1. William H. Williams, *A History of Wesley United Methodist Church* (Georgetown, Del., 1978), p. 9; Francis Asbury, *Journals and Letters of Francis Asbury*, ed. Elmer Clark, 3 vols. (Nashville, 1958), 1:274; John Lednum, *A History of the Rise of Methodism in America* (Philadelphia, 1859), p. 211; Henry Boehm, *Reminiscences, Historical and Biographical, of Sixty-Four Years in the Ministry* (New York, 1865), p. 57.

2. Thomas Scharf, *History of Maryland*, 3 vols. (Hatboro, Pa., 1967), 2:5; statistics on blacks were compiled from *First Census of the United States, 1790* (Philadelphia, 1791), passim, and *Fourth Census of the United States, 1820* (Washington, 1820), passim.

Chapter 1: The Coming of Enthusiasm

1. Albert D. Belden, *George Whitefield: The Awakener* (New York, 1953), p. 28; George Whitefield, *George Whitefield's Journals*, ed. Iain Murray (London, 1960), p. 338.

2. Whitefield, *George Whitefield's Journals*, pp. 338, 339.

3. Benjamin Franklin, *The Autobiography and Other Writings*, ed. L. Jesse Lemisch (New York, 1961), pp. 116, 119.

4. Nelson Waite Rightmyer, *The Anglican Church in Delaware* (Philadelphia, 1947), pp. 114, 115; Belden, *George Whitefield*, p. 113; Charles Hartshorn Maxson, *The Great Awakening in the Middle Colonies* (Chicago, 1920), p. 69.

5. Whitefield, *George Whitefield's Journals*, pp. 362–64; *Pennsylvania Gazette*, December 6, 1739.

6. Luke Tyerman, *The Life of the Rev. George Whitefield*, 2 vols. (London, 1890) 2:164, 165, 170, 178, 337, 485; Whitefield, *George Whitefield's Journals*, pp. 424–30, 496–99; John W. Christie, ed., "Newly Discovered Letters of George Whitefield, 1745–46," *Journal of the Presbyterian Historical*

Society (September 1954): 160–64, (December 1954): 259–66; Henry Pringle Ford, *History of Manokin Presbyterian Church, Princess Anne, Maryland* (Philadelphia, 1910), p. 16.

7. Rightmyer, *Anglican Church in Delaware*, p. 11; Leonard Trinterud, *The Forming of an American Tradition* (Philadelphia, 1949), p. 88; William Morgan, Memoir of His Own Life and Time, p. 1, Hall of Records, Dover, Del.; Belden, *George Whitefield*, p. 34.

8. Rightmyer, *Anglican Church in Delaware*, p. 115.

9. William Stevens Perry, ed., *Historical Collections Relating to the American Colonial Church*, vol. 5, *Delaware* (Hartford, 1878), p. 83.

10. Ibid., vol. 2, *Pennsylvania* (New York, 1969), p. 214.

11. Whitefield, *George Whitefield's Journals*, pp. 362–64, 496, 497. In his journals Whitefield, on at least one occasion, writes "William Tennent, Jr.," when he means "Charles Tennent": see p. 362. Evidently Charles Tennent was the least influential of William Tennent's four sons. Trinterud, *Forming of an American Tradition*, pp. 53, 59. For the most recent look at the New Side-Old Side conflict, see Elizabeth I. Nybakken, "New Light on the Old Side: Irish Influences on Colonial Presbyterianism," *Journal of American History* (March 1982): 813–32.

12. John A. Munroe, *Colonial Delaware: A History* (Millwood, NY, 1978), p. 171; *Pennsylvania Gazette*, December 6, 1739; Perry, *Historical Collections*, 5:83.

13. John Link, "Was Lewes Before Philadelphia?" *Christian Advocate* (June 22, 1961): 9. It can be argued that there was an earlier Methodist society organized by John Wesley in Savannah in 1736. Like the Lewes society of 1740, it was short-lived. The Savannah society was founded two years before Wesley had his Aldersgate experience, which emphasized the importance of rebirth in Christ. One can argue, therefore, that Methodism before Aldersgate wasn't really Methodism. One can also argue that the Lewes society, founded by Whitefield, had to be more Calvinist than Wesleyan Methodist. For a different view, see Frank Baker, *From Wesley to Asbury* (Durham, NC, 1976), pp. 14–27.

14. Perry, *Historical Collections*, 5:83, 86; ibid., 2:230.

15. Ibid., pp. 214, 215.

16. Ibid., 5:85, 2:214, 230, 313.

17. See, for example, Lednum, *The Rise of Methodism*, pp. 218, 286; Nathan Bangs, *The Life of the Rev. Freeborn Garrettson* (New York, 1832), pp. 74, 80.

18. Asbury, *Journal*, 1:778.

19. Ibid., p. 336.

20. Kenneth Carroll, *Joseph Nichols and the Nicholites* (Easton, Md., 1962), pp. 13–17; Benjamin Mifflin, "Journal of a Journey from Philadelphia to the Cedar Swamps and Back, 1764," *Pennsylvania Magazine of History and Biography* 40 (1928): 131, 132.

21. Carroll, *Joseph Nichols*, pp. 18–26; Carroll, "Religious Influences

on the Manumission of Slaves in Caroline, Dorchester, and Talbot Counties," *Maryland Historical Magazine* (June 1961): 184, 185; John Woolman, *The Journal of John Woolman* (Gloucester, Mass., 1971), pp. 165, 166; Asbury, *Journal*, 1:336.

22. Perry, *Historical Collections*, 5:114; Nathaniel Luff, *Journal of the Life of Nathaniel Luff, M.D.* (New York, 1848), p. 55; Mary Catherine Downing, *Sydenham Thorne; Clergyman and Founder* (Milford, Del., 1974), pp. 3, 4.

23. George A. Phoebus, *Beams of Light on Early Methodism in America* (New York, 1887), p. 13; Woolman, *Journal of John Woolman*, p. 166; Luff, *Journal of Nathaniel Luff*, pp. 56, 57; Carroll, *Joseph Nichols*, pp. 19, 20; Carroll, "The Influence of John Woolman on Joseph Nichols and the Nicholites," *Then and Now: Quaker Essays Historical and Contemporary*, ed. Anna Brinton (Philadelphia: 1960), p. 172.

24. Carroll, *Joseph Nichols*, pp. 33–44; Woolman, *Journal of John Woolman*, p. 165; Asbury, *Journal*, 1:336.

25. Carroll, *Joseph Nichols*, pp. 46–47; Carroll, *Quakerism on the Eastern Shore* (Baltimore, 1970), p. 118; William and Thomas Evans, eds., *The Friends Library*, vol. 12, *Memoir of Martha Routh* (Philadelphia, 1848), p. 449; Lorenzo Dow, *Travels and Labors of Lorenzo Dow* (New York, 1855), pp. 133, 134; William Duke, *Observations on the Present State of Religion in Maryland* (Baltimore, 1795), p. 40.

26. Leon Thornbury, "The Society of Friends in Maryland," *Maryland Historical Magazine* (June 1934): 105, 106; F. B. Tolles, "Quietism vs. Enthusiasm: The Philadelphia Quakers and the Great Awakening," *Pa. Mag. of Hist. and Biog.* (January 1945): 26–38.

27. See note 22, Perry; note 20, Mifflin; and note 21, Woolman.

28. Edwin Scott Gaustad, *Historical Atlas of Religion in America* (New York, 1962), p. 20; Munroe, *Colonial Delaware*, p. 162; *Peninsula Methodist* (Wilmington, Del.), March 21, 1896, pp. 6, 7.

29. Nybakken, "New Light on the Old Side," p. 825. Of forty-four Presbyterian ministers who could be identified as serving Delmarva congregations from 1735 to 1775, thirteen were definitely New Side and twelve definitely Old Side. In a sectional breakdown, New Side clergy outnumbered Old Side ten to six in New Castle and Cecil counties, but farther south were outnumbered by Old Side clergy six to three, according to Guy S. Klett, ed., *Minutes of the Presbyterian Church of America* (Philadelphia, 1976), passim; Frederick Lewis Theis, *The Colonial Clergy of Maryland, Delaware, and Georgia* (Lancaster, Mass., 1950), passim; William B. Sprague, ed., *Annals of the American Pulpit*, vol. 3, *Presbyterians* (New York, 1858), passim; James Lappen, *Presbyterians on Delmarva* (n.p., 1972), passim; Records of Lewes Presbytery, 1758–1810, Presbyterian Historical Society, Philadelphia, Pa., passim.

30. Kirk Mariner, *Revival's Children: A Religious History of Virginia's Eastern Shore* (Salisbury, Md., 1979), p. 8; Wesley M. Gewehr, *The Great Awakening in Virginia* (Durham, NC, 1930), p. 68; Maxson, *Great Awakening*

in the Middle Colonies, p. 78. Elizabeth I. Nybakken in "New Light on the Old Side" maintains that Irish-born Presbyterian ministers were usually Old Side. My sampling of nine Irish-born Presbyterian ministers who served on the Delmarva Peninsula during the colonial period shows six as Old Side and three as New Side. The New Side edge among Presbyterian ministers in Cecil and New Castle counties is accounted for by the fact that most of the ministers who were born in Scotland and in the colonies were New Side. See note 29 for sources.

31. Theis, *Colonial Clergy*, s.v. "Thomas Yarrell," "Richard Utley," and "John Reinhold Ronner."

32. Morgan Edwards, "Materials Towards a History of the Baptists in Delaware State," *Pa. Mag. of Hist. and Biog.* 9 (1885): 47–51.; J. Thomas Scharf, *History of Delaware, 1609–1888* (Philladelphia, 1888), 2:954; Gaustad, *Historical Atlas of Religion*, p. 11.

33. Edwards, "Materials Towards a History of the Baptists," p. 51. This is based on the assumption that the nation of one's youth creates speech patterns that are very difficult to shake. Evidence is based on nation of birth and childhood, as found in sources cited in note 29, and the fact that Welsh is written on some of the tombstones in the graveyard of Welsh Tract Baptist Church.

34. Mariner, *Revival's Children*, pp. 2, 3; Gaustad, *Historical Atlas of Religion*, p. 7.

35. Perry, *Historical Collections*, 5:75; Carol Lee van Voorst, "The Anglican Clergy in Maryland, 1692–1776" (Ph.D. diss., Princeton University, 1978), p. 123; Theis, *Colonial Clergy*, passim.

36. Frederick V. Mills, *Bishops by Ballot, An Eighteenth Century Ecclesiastical Revolution* (New York, 1978), pp. 19, 85–88, 92, 98; Rightmyer, *Anglican Church in Delaware*, pp. 122–31.

37. See, for example, Rhys Isaac, "Evangelical Revolt: The Nature of the Baptist Challenge to the Traditional Order in Virginia, 1765–1775," *William and Mary Quarterly* (July 1974): 350.

38. Mills, *Bishops by Ballot*, pp. 6, 87, 136–38; Perry, *Historical Collections*, vol. 4, *Maryland*, p. 335; Joseph Everett, "An Account of the Most Remarkable Occurrences of the Life of Joseph Everett," *Arminian Magazine* (1790): 505.

39. Perry, *Historical Collections*, 4:328, 335, 339; David C. Skaggs and Gerald E. Hartdagen, "Sinners and Saints, Anglican Clerical Conduct in Colonial Maryland," *Historical Magazine of the Protestant Episcopal Church* (June 1978): 177–95, passim; Rightmyer, *Maryland's Established Church* (Baltimore, 1856), pp. 97, 98.

40. Perry, *Historical Collections*, 4:93–95, 2:245; Mariner, *Revival's Children*, p. 11; Voorst, "The Anglican Clergy in Maryland," appendix C. Maryland's Eastern Shore clergy charged with moral transgressions included Thomas Thomson, John Urmstone, Hamilton Bell, Matthias Harris, Nathaniel Whitaker, and Neill MacCallum.

41. Rightmyer, *Maryland's Established Church*, p. 106–9; Perry, *Historical Collections*, 4:343–47, 2:430.

42. Perry, *Historical Collections*, 4:363, 5:97, 108; Society for Propagation of the Gospel in Foreign Parts, Correspondence, series B, 15:141, 21:139, Library of Congress, Washington, D.C.; Rightmyer, *Anglican Church in Delaware*, p. 38; Mariner, *Revival's Children*, pp. 7, 8, 12. For a similar pattern of baptisms exceeding number of communicants on the Peninsula see C. H. B. Turner, ed., *Some Records of Sussex County* (Philadelphia, 1909), pp. 214, 221, 238, 239, 241. For a definition of Churchmen, note the premise of Patricia U. Bonomi and Peter Eisenstadt, "Church Adherence in Eighteenth-Century British American Colonies," *William and Mary Quarterly* (April 1982): 252, 253.

43. Rightmyer, *Anglican Church in Delaware*, pp. 138–41; Perry, *Historical Collections*, 2:57, 5:101; Sprague, ed., *Annals of the American Pulpit*, vol. 5, *Episcopalians* (New York, 1859), p. 186. The estimate of the unchurched population (that is, those who did not regard themselves as part of any church community and did not attend church services) of Kent County is based on the estimate that Anglicans made up one-sixth of the county's population, with dissenters such as Nicholites, Presbyterians, and Quakers together representing slightly more than one-sixth of the population. This left almost two-thirds of Kent County's population unchurched. Perry, *Historical Collections*, 5:97, 108. For a discussion of why so few Anglicans took communion, see Bonomi and Eisenstadt, "Church Adherence," p. 252.

44. Isaac and John Comly, eds., *Friends Miscellany: Being a Collection of Essays and Fragments, Biographical, Religious, Epistolary, Narrative and Historical* (Philadelphia, 1883), 4:256–57; Perry, *Historical Collections*, 5:102, 103; Gerald E. Hartdagen, "The Vestries and Morals in Colonial Maryland," *Maryland Historical Magazine* 60 (1968): 360–78; Rightmyer, *Maryland's Established Church*, pp. 25, 52, 93.

45. Gewehr, *Great Awakening in Virginia*, p. 33.

46. Rightmyer, *Anglican Church in Delaware*, pp. 55–67; Weis, *Colonial Clergy*, pp. 79, 80, 85; Downing, *Sydenham Thorne*, passim; Turner, ed., *Some Records of Sussex County*, pp. 238–41.

47. Perry, *Historical Collections*, 4:96, 2:417–20; Trinterud, *Forming of an American Tradition*, p. 55; John T. Scharf and Thompson Westcott, *History of Philadelphia* (Philadelphia, 1884), 2:1348; Norris Stanley Barratt, *Outline of the History of St. Paul's Church* (Philadelphia, 1917), passim.

Chapter 2: The Coming of Methodism

1. Bernard Semmel, *The Methodist Revolution* (New York, 1973), p. 181.

2. Joseph Priestly, "An Address to the Methodists," in Joseph Priestly, ed., *Original Letters by the Rev. John Wesley, etc.* (Birmingham, England, 1791), pp. xvii, xviii; Elie Halevy, *The Birth of Methodism*, ed. Bernard

Semmel (Chicago, 1971), pp. 1–29; Semmel, *Methodist Revolution*, pp. 170–98.

3. Frederick A. Norwood, *The Story of American Methodism* (New York, 1974), pp. 66–69; Wade Crawford Barclay, *Early American Methodism, 1769–1844* (New York, 1949), 1: 17–23; Lednum, *The Rise of Methodism*, pp. 33, 60; E. C. Hallman, "Methodism in Delaware," *Delaware, History of the First State*, ed. H. Clay Reed (New York, 1947), 1: 671. For a discussion of when Strawbridge arrived in America and for other information about him, see Gordon Pratt Baker, ed., *Those Incredible Methodists* (Baltimore, 1972), pp. 1–11. The best treatment of Capt. Thomas Webb is in Frank Baker, *From Wesley to Asbury*, pp. 50–69. For a view that Webb lost his eye at Louisburg and was wounded in the arm at Quebec, see Robert Pattison, "The Life and Character of Richard Bassett," *Papers of the Historical Society of Delaware* (Wilmington, Del., 1900), 29:6.

4. Lednum, *The Rise of Methodism*, pp. 18–20, 22, 126; Jesse Lee, *A Short History of the Methodists* (Baltimore, 1810), p. 39; Boehm, *Reminiscences*, p. 19; Asbury, *Journal*, 1:89n. According to Federal Writer's Project, Church Records, folder no. 10, p. 57, Hall of Records, Dover, Del., Chester-Bethel, in Brandywine Hundred north of Wilmington, was organized by Captain Webb. However, the facts that Webb was in England at this time and that the date 1775 was given by other sources discount this possibility.

5. Asbury, *Journal*, 1:610; Lednum, *The Rise of Methodism*, pp. 55, 56, 65, 73; Joseph Pilmore, *Journal of Joseph Pilmore*, ed. Frederick E. Maser and Howard T. Maag (Philadelphia, 1969), p. 84. Some sources maintain that Captain Webb was preaching in Wilmington as early as 1766. Webb, however, was probably in Albany, New York City, or Long Island at that time. For example of sources maintaining Webb's presence in Wilmington in 1766, see Asbury M. E. Church (Wilmington) Records, vol. 5, first page (unpaginated), Hall of Records, Dover, Del.

6. Thomas Ware, *Sketches of the Life and Travels of Rev. Thomas Ware* (New York, 1842), pp. 84, 85; R. W. Todd, *Methodism of the Peninsula* (Philadelphia, 1886), p. 47; Boehm, *Reminiscences*, pp. 438, 439; Asbury, *Journal*, 1:xiii; *Minutes of the Methodist Conferences Annually Held in America from 1773–1813* (New York, 1813), passim. Henry Boehm disagreed with the view that Asbury was an inferior preacher. See Boehm, *Reminiscences*, p. 440.

7. Asbury, *Journal*, 1:26, 27, 48, 58, 59.

8. Lednum, *The Rise of Methodism*, pp. 133, 126, 121; Pilmore, *Journal of Joseph Pilmore*, p. 201; Asbury, *Journal*, 1:72, 73, 75, 86; E. C. Hallman, *The Garden of Methodism* (n.p., 1948), p. 14.

9. William Watters, *A Short Account of the Christian Experience and Ministerial Labours of William Watters* (Alexandria, Va., 1806) p. 36; Lednum, *The Rise of Methodism*, pp. 59, 117, 120, 121; *Minutes of the Methodist Conferences, 1773–1813*, p. 10.

10. Philip Gatch, Autobiography, pp. 17, 18, on microfilm at Drew University, Madison, NJ; Lednum, *The Rise of Methodism*, pp. 136, 137,

146, 162, 201–3, 255; Henry C. Conrad, in *History of the State of Delaware* (Wilmington, Del., 1908), 2:785, maintains that Methodist itinerants spoke in Lewes, Sussex County, as early as 1774. However, he does not cite his source. Other evidence, such as Garrettson's account, place the arrival of Wesleyan Methodism in Lewes in 1779.

11. Bangs, *Freeborn Garrettson*, pp. 29–35, 43; Patricia Hayes Bradley, "Mark the Perfect . . . Freeborn Garrettson Speaks for Methodism," *Methodist History* (April 1978): 117; Robert Drew Simpson, "Freeborn Garrettson, American Methodist Pioneer," (Ph.D. diss., Drew University, 1954), p. 4.

12. Phoebus, *Beams of Light on Early Methodism*, pp. 13, 19; Lednum, *The Rise of Methodism*, pp. 162–64.

13. Bangs, *Freeborn Garrettson*, pp. 91, 98; Thomas Coke, *Extracts from the Journals of the Rev. Dr. Thomas Coke's Five Visits to America* (London, 1793), p. 15.

14. Asbury, *Journal*, 1:308, 309; Bangs, *Freeborn Garrettson*, pp. 34, 37, 102,170, 222; Bradley, "Mark the Perfect," p. 119.

15. Bangs, *Freeborn Garrettson*, pp. 66–68, 74; Lednum, *The Rise of Methodism*, pp. 216, 217.

16. Bangs, *Freeborn Garrettson*, pp. 74, 84, 85, 87; Freeborn Garrettson, *The Experience and Travels of Mr. Freeborn Garrettson* (Philadelphia, 1791), p. 113; Lednum, *The Rise of Methodism*, pp. 145, 206, 218, 226, 227, 232.

17. Bangs, *Freeborn Garrettson*, pp. 92, 93; William Colbert, Journal of the Travels of William Colbert, typed copy at St. George's U. M. Church Library, Philadelphia, 2:89 (original copy at United Library, Garrett Theological Seminary, Evanston, Il.).

18. Bangs, *Freeborn Garrettson*, pp. 95, 99, 100; Lednum, *The Rise of Methodism*, pp. 74, 76, 162, 213, 214; Asbury, *Journal*, 1:266, 308; Lee, *Short History of the Methodists*, pp. 64, 65.

19. Lednum, *The Rise of Methodism*, pp. 213, 232; Asbury, *Journal*, 1:315; Bangs, *Freeborn Garrettson*, p. 102 n.; Ethan Allen untitled manuscript, St. Peter's Parish in Talbot County, 3:34, Hall of Records, Annapolis, Md.; Ezekiel Cooper, *The Substance of a Funeral Discourse Delivered . . . on the Death of Francis Asbury* (Philadelphia, 1819), p. 87; Coke, *Extracts of the Journal*, p. 20, 49, 54; Hallman, *Garden of Methodism*, p. 286.

20. Lednum, *The Rise of Methodism*, pp. 249, 250; Bangs, *Freeborn Garrettson*, pp. 98–100, 102; Abel Stevens, *A Compendious History of American Methodism* (New York, 1867), p. 130; Asbury, *Journal*, 1:324, 325; Edward C. Papenfuse, ed., *A Biographical Dictionary of the Maryland Legislature, 1635–1789*, 2 vols. (Baltimore, 1979), vol. 1, s.v. "Harry Ennalls" for the first names of girls in the family.

21. Bangs, *Freeborn Garrettson*, pp. 94, 95, 100–6; Asbury, *Journal*, 1:340.

22. Bangs, *Freeborn Garrettson*, p. 107; Garrettson, *Experience and Travels*, pp. 169, 170; Asbury, *Journal*, 1:339, 340. For correspondence relating to Garrettson's arrest in Dorchester County in 1780, see B. C. Steiner,

ed., *Archives of Maryland, Journal of the Correspondence of the State Council of Maryland, 1779–1780* (Baltimore, 1924), 43:103, 104, 130, 438, 439, 444, 445. Samuel Magaw, rector of Christ Church, Dover, and staunch friend of the Methodists, may have played a role in convincing Caesar Rodney to intercede on Garrettson's behalf. For Magaw's relations with Rodney, see *The Peninsula Methodist* (Wilmington, Del.), March 21, 1896, p. 7.

23. Asbury, *Journal*, 1:333n., 339; *Minutes of the Methodist Conferences, 1773–1813*, pp. 24, 35, 256; Cooper, *Substance of a Funeral Discourse*, p. 87; Lednum, *The Rise of Methodism*, p. 264.

24. R. W. Todd, "History of Methodist Episcopal Church, Easton, Md.," unpaginated folder in Hall of Records, Annapolis, Md.; Mariner, *Revival's Children*, pp. 20, 21, 23, 55–58; John Wesley Andros Elliott, "Unwritten History of Eastern Shore Methodism," (ca. 1885, 1886), nos. 2, 3, in possession of the Reverend Dr. Kirk Mariner, Vienna, Va. Because this account contains obvious inaccuracies, it should be used with caution. Asbury, *Journal*, 1:292, 393, 469–71; Lednum, *The Rise of Methodism*, pp. 341, 342. Robert Williams and Joseph Pilmore, the two itinerants most likely to have traveled down the Peninsula in 1772, were not on the Eastern Shore of Virginia in 1772–73, according to their respective journals. For a listing of Methodist chapels on the Peninsula as well as elsewhere in the United States in 1784, see Lednum, *The Rise of Methodism*, p. 417.

25. *Minutes of the Methodist Conferences, 1773–1813*, pp. 9, 10; Allen manuscript, 3:34; Philip Mazzei, *Memoirs of the Life and Peregrinations of the Florentine, Philip Mazzei, 1730–1816* (New York, 1942), pp. 216, 217; Ambrose Serle, *The American Journal of Ambrose Serle*, ed. Edward H. Tatum, Jr. (San Marino, 1940), p. 252; Steiner, ed., *Archives of Maryland*, 16:364, 378; Cooper, *The Substance of a Funeral Discourse*, pp. 81–82; John Littlejohn, Journal, typed copy, p. 107, at Lovely Lane U. M. Church Archives, Baltimore, Md.; Caesar Rodney to George Washington, Middletown, Del., September 6, 1777, quoted in James W. May, "Francis Asbury and Thomas White: A Refugee and His Tory Patron," *Methodist History* (April 1976): 152, n. 44.

26. Bangs, *Freeborn Garrettson*, p. 64; Harold B. Hancock, *The Delaware Loyalists* (Wilmington, Del., 1940), pp. 34, 35; Hancock, *The Loyalists of Revolutionary Delaware* (Newark, Del., 1977), pp. 80–82; May, "Francis Asbury and Thomas White," p. 158; Lednum, *The Rise of Methodism*, p. 214.

27. Lee, *Short History of the Methodists*, p. 64; May, "Francis Asbury and Thomas White," p. 142; Lednum, *The Rise of Methodism*, pp. 208, 214, 253; Ronald Hoffman, *A Spirit of Dissension: Economics, Politics, and the Revolution in Maryland* (Baltimore, 1973), pp. 229, 230; Allen manuscript, 3:34; Bangs, *Freeborn Garrettson*, p. 64; Baker, ed., *Those Incredible Methodists*, pp. 46, 47; Norwood, *The Story of American Methodism*, p. 86; Charles J. Truitt, *Breadbasket of the Revolution, Delmarva in the War for Independence* (Salisbury, Md., 1975), p. 113; Asbury, *Journal*, 1:338, 339; Cooper, *The Substance of a Funeral Discourse*, pp. 80, 81; Richard K. McMaster, "Methodists and War Resistance in the Revolutionary War," *Christian Advocate* (April 12,

1973): 9–10; Thomas Rankin, Diary of the Rev. Thomas Rankin, typed copy at Drew University, p. 161 (original copy at United Library, Garrett Theological Seminary, Evanston, Il.); Everett, "An Account of the Most Remarkable Occurrences," p. 604; Freeborn Garrettson, Journal, pp. 31, 32, Methodist Collection, Drew University, (hereafter cited as MCDU). Ronald Hoffman, in *A Spirit of Dissension*, p. 230, is incorrect when he states that Methodists would not take oaths. In England, John Wesley never took a stand against taking oaths. Semmel, *The Methodist Revolution*, p. 185.

    28. Ware, *Sketches of the Life and Travvels*, p. 70; Asbury, *Journal*, 1:181; Lednum, *The Rise of Methodism*, p. 214; Bangs, *Freeborn Garrettson*, p. 64; Steiner, ed., *Archives of Maryland*, 45:23; Truitt, *Breadbasket of the Revolution*, p. 113; Hoffman, *Spirit of Dissension*, p. 227; Thomas Rankin to ?, September 17, 1777, Methodist Archives, Manchester, England. See chapter 3, note 5 for sources of population estimates and explanations of the 3–4 percent figure representing Methodist percentage of the total population of the Peninsula. John A. Munroe, "Reflections on Delaware and the American Revolution," *Delaware History* (Spring-Summer 1976): 8–10.

    29. Rankin, Diary, p. 145; Asbury, *Journal*, 1:343; Hancock, *The Delaware Loyalists*, p. 55–57; Hancock, *The Loyalists of Revolutionary Delaware*, passim; May, "Francis Asbury and Thomas White," p. 159.

    30. Rankin, Diary, p. 145; Donald G. Mathews, *Slavery and Methodism* (Princeton, 1965), pp. 5–8; Hoffman, *Spirit of Dissension*, pp. 228–30; Asbury, *Journal*, 1:273, 274; Allen manuscript, 3:35.

    31. Asbury, *Journal*, 1:260–62; Norwood, *The Story of American Methodism*, pp. 70–73; Barclay, *Early American Methodism*, 1:43, 44.

    32. Asbury, *Journal*, 1:253–69; Lednum, *The Rise of Methodism*, pp. 115, 204, 267–72; May, "Francis Asbury and Thomas White," pp. 143–62; Everett, "An Account of the Most Remarkable Occurrences," pp. 559, 560; Watters, *A Short Account of the Christian Experience*, p. 36. Judge White's home was recently torn down. It was located a mile southeast of Whiteleysburg, a short distance off Route 59 on Route 291.

    33. Ware, *Sketches of the Life and Travels*, pp. 251–52; Asbury, *Journal* 1:299.

    34. Asbury, *Journal*, 1:285, 287, 313; 2:641, 642, 3:298; Bangs, *Freeborn Garrettson*, p. 76. For implied criticism of Asbury's courage, see Lee, *A Short History of the Methodists*, pp. 64, 73. For a more direct criticism, see Lednum, *The Rise of Methodism*, p. 210. Henry Boehm reports on Asbury's response to Lee's implied criticism in Boehm, *Reminiscnces*, pp. 291–93. See also Asbury, *Journal*, 2:641, 642, 3:298.

    35. May, "Francis Asbury and Thomas White," pp. 160–62; Asbury, *Journal*, 1:262–347, passim; Lee, *A Short History of the Methodists*, p. 67; *Minutes of the Methodist Conferences, 1773–1813*, pp. 10, 19, 20.

    36. Asbury, *Journal*, 1:85; Barclay, *Early American Methodism*, 1:55; *Minutes of the Methodist Conferences, 1773–1813*, pp. 5, 8; For the significance of "old Methodism," I have gained much from reading James W. May,

"From Revival Movement to Denomination: A Re-Examination of the Beginnings of American Methodism" (Ph.D. diss., Columbia University, 1962), passim; and George Phoebus, "The Methodist Episcopal Church," *Historical and Biographical Encyclopedia of Delaware*, ed. J. M. McCarter and B. F. Jackson (Wilmington, Del., 1882), pp. 118, 119. Although the *Minutes* of 1773 bar every Methodist preacher from administering the sacraments, Asbury notes that Strawbridge, "under the particular direction of the assistant" Thomas Rankin, could do so. Asbury, *Journal*, 1:85.

37. Nonjuring Anglican clergy were identified from the chart in Rightmyer, *Maryland's Established Church*, pp. 119, 120, and Weiss, *Colonial Clergy*, passim. Norman Harrington, *Shaping of Religion in America* (Easton, Md., 1980), p. 91; Mills, *Bishops by Ballot*, pp. 171, 172. Approximation of the number of Anglican clergy on the Peninsula in 1780 is based on evidence from Perry, *Historical Collections*, 4:343–47; Rightmyer, *Anglican Church in Delaware*, p. 119; Rightmyer, *Maryland's Established Church*, pp. 119, 120; Truitt, *Breadbasket of the Revolution*, pp. 112, 113; Mariner, *Revival's Children*, p. 15; Ware, *Sketches of the Life and Travels*, p. 93. One Anglican minister whose sympathies were obviously with the American Revolution was Samuel McCroskey of Northampton County, Virginia. See Truitt, *Breadbasket of the Revolution*, p. 112. On Maryland's Eastern Shore, for example, the eleven active Anglican clergy of 1780 had been reduced to six by 1783. See Ethan Allen, *Protestant Episcopal Church Conventions in Maryland of 1780–83* (Baltimore, 1878), pp. 4, 12.

38. Watters, *A Short Account of the Christian Experience*, pp. 36–38; Bangs, *Freeborn Garrettson*, p. 82; Lednum, *The Rise of Methodism*, pp. 85, 115, 128, 137; Rightmyer, *Anglican Church in Delaware*, pp. 116, 117.

39. Rankin, Diary, p. 135; Asbury, *Journal*, 1:300, 310, 319, 342; Rightmyer, *Maryland's Established Church*, p. 205.

40. Hallman, *Garden of Methodism*, p. 14; Scharf, *History of Delaware*, 2:1348; Lednum, *The Rise of Methodism*, pp. 223, 234; Phoebus, "The Methodist Episcopal Church," p. 118; Asbury, *Journal*, 1:299 n., 324, 341, 345, 390, 468; 2:468; 3:28. For the view that Thomas Chapel was not given by Magaw but built from the beginning by Methodists, see Ronald Finch, "Thomas Chapel," typed manuscript, pp. 5, 6, Montchanin, Del.

41. Barclay, *Early American Methodism*, 1:31; Asbury, *Journal*, 1:322.

42. John M'Lean, *Sketch of Rev. Philip Gatch* (Cincinnati, 1856), p. 67; Watters, *A Short Account of the Christian Experience*, pp. 68–72; May, "From Revival Movement to Denomination," pp. 102, 103.

43. Asbury, *Journal*, 1:300; *Minutes of the Methodist Conferences, 1773–1813*, pp. 19, 20; Lee, *Short History of the Methodists*, p. 67; Watters, *A Short Account of the Christian Experience*, pp. 72, 73. Freeborn Garrettson insisted that there were only ten preachers at White's. See Freeborn Garrettson to ?, November 28, 1817, MCDU.

44. Asbury, *Journal*, 1:300, 304, 307; Watters, *A Short Account of the Christian Experience*, pp. 79–81; M'Lean, *Sketch of Rev. Philip Gatch*, pp. 67–70; Lee, *Short History of the Methodists*, p. 69; May, "From Revival Movement to Denomination," pp. 105–12.

45. Asbury, *Journal*, 1:343, 346, 348–92, 393; *Minutes of the Methodist*

Conferences, 1773–1813, pp. 25, 26; May, "From Revival Movement to Denomination," passim; Bangs, *Freeborn Garrettson*, pp. 111, 112; Freeborn Garrettson, Semi-Centennial Sermon, p. 16, MCDU.

46. Lednum, *The Rise of Methodism*, p. 279, 280; Lee, *A Short History of the Methodists*, p. 77; Asbury, *Journal*, 1:345. The membership percentages were computed from *Minutes of the Methodist Conferences, 1773–1813*, pp. 14, 31, 32. The times Asbury preached in Dover are a rough estimate found in Asbury, *Journal*, vols. 1–3, passim.

Chapter 3: Methodism Victorious, 1781–1820

1. Bangs, *Freeborn Garrettson*, pp. 220–23.
2. Asbury, *Journal*, 2:388, 3:343, 350.
3. In *Minutes of the Methodist Conferences, 1773–1813*, p. 28, the site of the Preparatory Conference is given as "Choptank, State of Delaware." Asbury probably cited "Choptank" because the Choptank Bridge (in present-day Greensboro, Maryland) was a few miles from Judge White's and the only town in the area.
4. Ibid., p. 28.
5. Barclay, *Early American Methodism*, 1:103, 104; Leo Pfeffer, *Church, State, and Freedom* (Boston, 1967), p. 95; Edwin S. Gaustad, *The Rise of Adventism* (New York, 1974), p. xiii. Population for the Peninsula in 1775 is estimated at 145,000, based in part on a 140,000 estimate in Truitt, *Breadbasket of the Revolution*, p. 7. Population for the Peninsula in 1784 is estimated at 156,000, based on figures in Stella Sutherland, *Population Distribution in Colonial America* (New York, 1936), pp. 124, 174; and 1790 census figures. Statistics on Methodists are found in *Minutes of the Methodist Conferences, 1773–1813*, passim. Based on 1790 census statistics, a little less than one-half of Delmarva's total population during the late eighteenth century was sixteen and older.
6. Bangs, *Freeborn Garrettson*, p. 82; Barratt's Chapel Record Book, pp. 2–5, Barratt's Chapel, Frederica, Del.
7. Robert Ayres, Journal, October 12, 1785, Historical Society of Western Pennsylvania, Pittsburgh, Pa.
8. Hallman, *Garden of Methodism*, p. 14; Lednum, *The Rise of Methodism*, p. 417; Thomas Coke, *Extracts of the Journals of the Rev. Thomas Coke's Visits to America* (London, 1793), pp. 17, 18; Bridgetown U. M. Church Chronology, Ridgely United Methodist Charge, Ridgely, Md. The strength of Peninsula Methodism was nationally recognized. In 1784, for example, 32 percent of a collection for wives of American itinerants was assigned to Delmarva, according to *Minutes of Methodist Conferences, 1773–1813*, p. 47.
9. Lednum, *The Rise of Methodism*, pp. 338, 342; Ayres, Journal, March, 26, 1786.
10. Ware, *Sketches of the Life and Travels*, pp. 82, 90; Thomas Coke, "The Journal of Bishop Coke," *Arminian Magazine* (1789): 242, 288.
11. Frederick E. Maser, ed., "A Revealing Letter from Joseph Pilmore," *Methodist History* (April 1972): 56–58.
12. John Wesley, *The Letters of John Wesley*, ed. John Telford (London,

1931), 7:238–39; Barclay, *Early American Methodism*, 1:98 n.; Coke, "Journal of Bishop Coke," p. 242.

13. Ibid., pp. 242, 243.

14. Asbury, *Journal*, 1:468; Scharf, *History of Delaware*, 2:1156, 1157, 1177; Lednum, *The Rise of Methodism*, p. 265; Minutes of the Board of Trustees, Dudley's Chapel, 1794–1900, p. 8, Hall of Records, Annapolis, Md.; Hallman, *Garden of Methodism*, p. 236. For vestry room connected to White's Chapel, see photograph in text and Phoebus, "The Methodist Episcopal Church," pp. 118, 119.

15. Asbury, *Journal*, 1:471–73; Ezekiel Cooper, Notebook, Ezekiel Cooper Collection, MCDU; Cooper, *Substance of a Funeral Discourse*, pp. 104–6; Coke, "Journal of Bishop Coke," p. 243; Garrettson, *Experience and Travels*, p. 215; Norris S. Barratt, *Barratt's Chapel and Methodism* (Wilmington, 1911), pp. 36, 48; Cooper, in *Substance of a Funeral Discourse*, p. 104, maintains that there were "about fifteen" American preachers, in addition to Asbury, at Barratt's Chapel.

16. Ezekiel Cooper said that, because of Asbury's demand for election, henceforth the office would be elective and not subject to Mr. Wesley; Cooper, Notebook, Ezekiel Cooper Collection, MCDU. While it is true that the preachers at the Christmas Conference pledged to obey Wesley's commands, Asbury later insisted that he remained silent on the issue. Two years later, the Annual Conference voted to rescind the pledge of obedience to Wesley. See L. C. Rudolph, *Francis Asbury* (Nashville, 1966), pp. 59, 60.

17. Asbury, *Journal*, 3:38. See John Alfred Faulkner, *The Methodists* (New York, 1913), pp. 81–103, and Faulkner, *Burning Questions in Historic Christianity* (New York, 1930), pp. 207–32. Of particular interest are pp. 96, 97 in *The Methodists* and pp. 219, 220 in *Burning Questions*. In 1787, William White of Philadelphia, a leader in the organization of the American Protestant Episcopal Church, was consecrated bishop in England. Before he returned to America, he wanted to meet with John Wesley, but the connection was never made. It is tempting to think that an Episcopal-Methodist union could have come out of the meeting of the two. By 1787, however, Asbury would have had difficulty taking a back seat to any Episcopal bishop, and Wesley no longer exercised control over American Methodism.

18. Garrettson, *Experiences and Travels*, p. 217. Garrettson's personal copy is in the Rare Book Room, Morris Library, University of Delaware.

19. Coke, "Journal of Bishop Coke," pp. 243, 244; Asbury, *Journal*, 1:471, 472; Stevens, *Compendious History of American Methodism*, p. 183. Ezekiel Cooper shared Stevens's view in Cooper, *Substance of a Funeral Discourse*, p. 212; and in the Ezekiel Cooper Collection, n.d., item no. 227, United Library, Garrett Theological Seminary, Evanston, Il. (hereafter cited as GTS.)

20. Coke, "Journal of Bishop Coke," p. 244; Maldwyn Edwards, *After Wesley: A Study of the Social and Political Influence of Methodism in the Middle Period* (London, 1935), pp. 142, 143.

21. Boehm, *Reminiscences*, p. 42; Coke, "Journal of Bishop Coke," p. 243; Garrettson, *Experience and Travels*, p. 215.

22. Coke, "Journal of Bishop Coke," pp. 244, 286–88. Asbury indicates that prior to Coke's visit, Methodists were meeting at Garrison's Chapel in lower Accomack County. However, this chapel was probably a structure originally built for other purposes. Asbury, *Journal*, 1:470; Mariner, *Revival's Children*, p. 22.

23. Coke, "Journal of Bishop Coke," pp. 288–90.

24. Gregory A. Stiverson, *Poverty in a Land of Plenty; Tenancy in 18th-Century Maryland* (Baltimore, 1977), pp. 89, 90, 100, 102, 103, and passim. For dramatic agricultural changes in the Chesapeake region during the antebellum era, see Avery O. Craven, *Soil Exhaustion as a Factor in the Agricultural History of Virginia and Maryland, 1606–1860* (Urbana, Il., 1925). For the change from tobacco to wheat in Maryland's upper Eastern Shore, see Paul G. E. Clemens, *The Atlantic Economy and Colonial Maryland's Eastern Shore* (Ithaca, N.Y., 1980).

25. Luff, *Journal of the Life of Nathaniel Luff*, p. 103; Whitman Ridgway, *Community Leadership in Maryland, 1790–1840* (Chapel Hill, N.C., 1979), p. 17; John A. Munroe, *Federalist Delaware* (New Brunswick, N.J., 1954), pp. 242, 243; Asbury, *Journal*, 1:497, 2:445, 479; *Delaware Gazette*, June 2, 1826; *First Census of the United States*, 1790, passim; *Fourth Census of the United States*, 1820, passim; Lednum, *The Rise of Methodism*, pp. 255–57; Margaret Withgott, "Migration from the Eastern Shore to Ohio," typed manuscript, file folder no. 276, Maryland Room, Dorchester County Library, Cambridge, Md. For figures to support the assumption that the Eastern Shore was materially poorer than the Western Shore, see Stiverson, *Poverty in a Land of Plenty*, appendix, pp. 146, 147.

26. *Minutes of the Methodist Conferences, 1773–1813*, passim.

27. All but one of the early membership records (class meeting records) of Methodist societies on the Peninsula have been lost. Nevertheless, the Methodism of these people has been established by the use of a number of sources, including Papenfuse, ed., *Biographical Dictionary of the Maryland Legislature*, vol. 1, passim; Trustees' Minutes, Bethel Methodist Church, Cecil County, Md., pp. 1, 3, Barratt's Chapel Archives; Asbury, *Journal*, passim; Emerson Wilson, *Forgotten Heroes of Delaware* (Cambridge, Mass., 1969), passim; Lednum, *The Rise of Methodism*, pp. 166, 167, 254–62, 416; as well as numerous other primary and secondary sources.

28. Asbury, *Journal*, passim; Colbert, Journal, 2:33. For a short list of some American Methodists of considerable wealth who lived outside the Peninsula, see Lednum, *The Rise of Methodism*, p. 167.

29. Colbert, Journal, 2:101, 34, 74, 46–47; Bangs, *Freeborn Garrettson*, p. 170; Allen manuscript, 3:36; Everett, "An Account of the Most Remarkable Occurrences," p. 608; Phoebus, *Beams of Light on Early Methodism*, p. 236; Great Choptank Parish Report, 1797, Maryland Diocesan Archives, Maryland Historical Society, Baltimore, Md.; Asbury, *Journal*, 1:695; J. D. C. Hanna, ed., *Centennial Services of Asbury Methodist Episcopal Church*

(Wilmington, Del., 1889), p. 145; Ware, *Sketches of the Life and Travels*, pp. 185, 186; Lednum, *The Rise of Methodism*, p. 57; Thomas Smith, *The Experience and the Ministerial Labor of Rev. Thomas Smith* (New York, 1848), pp. 68, 70. There is no evidence that the O'Kelly schism of 1792 had any impact on Peninsula Methodism.

30. Colbert, Journal, 2:99, 101, 113.

31. Robert W. Todd, "Complete Record, Historical and Statistical, of the Methodist Episcopal Church in the Town of Easton, Maryland, 1777–1877," manuscript, pp. 5, 6, St. Mark's U. M. Church, Easton, Md.; Asbury, *Journal*, 1:771, 772; Elizabeth Connor, *Methodist Trail Blazer, Philip Gatch* (Cincinnati, 1970), p. 44; Scharf, *History of Delaware*, 2:451, 639; Phoebus, "The Methodist Episcopal Church," p. 122.

32. *Minutes of the Methodist Conferences, 1773–1813*, pp. 241, 243, 292, 294; Richard Carwardine, *Transatlantic Revivalism* (Westport, Conn., 1978), p. 55; Isaac, "Evangelical Revolt," p. 359; Colbert, Journal, 2:88, 90, 93, 96, 113; Morgan, Memoir, pp. 14, 15, 19, 20.

33. This perception of God held by Methodist itinerants and lay people on the Peninsula is based on citations too numerous to list, found in journals, memoirs, and other sources. The Peninsula perception reflected the national perception of God, as found in John B. Boles, *The Great Revival, 1787–1805* (Lexington, Ky., 1972), pp. 30–34.

34. Bangs, *Freeborn Garrettson*, p. 170; Morgan, Memoir, p. 19; Smith, *Experience and Ministerial Labors*, pp. 68, 69, 88.

35. Boles, *The Great Revival*, pp. 87, 88; Colbert, Journal, 4:14, 15; Asbury, *Journal*, 2:234, 235, 3:327–29; Lednum, *The Rise of Methodism*, p. 233; Boehm, *Reminiscences*, pp. 44–47, 139.

36. Smith, *Experiences and Ministerial Labors*, pp. 97, 98; Ware, *Sketches of the Life and Travels*, p. 234; Asbury, *Journal*, 3:244; Allen Clark, "History of Wesley M. E. Church," typed manuscript, pp. 36–40, Hall of Records, Dover, Del.

37. Boehm, *Reminiscences*, pp. 135, 136; Todd, *Methodism on the Peninsula*, pp. 37, 38. Credit for the first altar call has been given to camp meetings in the West. However, Dr. Chandler's altar call predated those western camp meetings. For the older perspective on the altar call, see Carwardine, *Transatlantic Revivalism*, p. 13.

38. Boles, *The Great Revival*, p. 55; Lee, *Short History of the Methodists*, pp. 308, 309; Boehm, *Reminiscences*, pp. 128–32; John Emory to Wesley Woods, Centreville, Md., November 28, 1806, Archives, Lovely Lane U. M. Church, Baltimore, Md. Statistics compiled from *Minutes of the Methodist Conferences, 1773–1813*, passim. For examples of the effectiveness of the pre–camp-meetings techniques on the Eastern Shores of Virginia and Maryland, see William P. Chandler to Francis Asbury, *Journal*, 3:328–30.

39. Boehm, *Reminiscences*, pp. 128–32, 157; Lee, *Short History of the Methodists*, p. 308; Morgan, Memoir, pp. 37–40; Asbury, *Journal*, 3:330, 331; Todd, *Methodism of the Peninsula*, p. 13; Phoebus, "The Methodist Episcopal Church," pp. 124, 125; Mr. W. to editor, *Methodist Magazine*,

n.d., item no. 270, Ezekiel Cooper Collection, GTS. For the view that early Methodist preachers often exaggerated the size of audiences, see Lednum, *The Rise of Methodism*, p. 64. George L. Caley, *A History of Asbury Methodist Church, Smyrna* (Smyrna, Del., 1972), p. 27, maintains that the site of the first camp meeting was actually two miles west of Smyrna.

40. Boehm, *Reminiscences*, pp. 115, 147, 151; Asbury, *Journal*, 3:350, 351, 368; Colbert, Journal, 5–6:218; Phoebus, "The Methodist Episcopal Church," p. 125.

41. Legislative Papers, Petitions Misc., passim, Hall of Records, Dover, Del.; Augustus M. Schee, ed., *Laws of the State of Delaware*, 5:297, 298, 730; Baker, ed., *Those Incredible Methodists*, p. 96.

42. Morgan, Memoir, pp. 41–44; Mariner, *Revival's Children*, pp. 46–47; Asbury, *Journal*, 3:370; Andrew Manship, *Thirteens' Year Experience in the Itinerancy* (Philadelphia, 1881), p. 375; Joseph Everett to Ezekiel Cooper, Philadelphia, Pa., July 7, 1807, item no. 93, Ezekiel Cooper Collection, GTS; Elliott, "Unwritten History of Eastern Shore Methodism," no. 4; Adam Wallace, *The Parson of the Islands* (Baltimore, 1906), pp. 82, 83; Reverend Wicks to Bishop Thomas John Claggett, Snow Hill, Md., August 29, 1813, Maryland Diocesan Archives.

43. Asbury, *Journal*, 2:633, 668. Figures used in calculating the percentage of the Peninsula population that was Methodist were gleaned from U.S. Census Bureau Reports and Methodist Annual Reports carried in conference journals. Methodist dominance of the Peninsula was recognized by just about everyone. On April 9, 1800, for example, the Philadelphia newspaper *Aurora* admitted that even in Delaware, where Presbyterian influence was strong in New Castle County, Methodists were "the most numerous religious society."

Chapter 4: The Attractions of Methodism

1. Morgan, Memoir, pp. 20, 21.

2. Lednum, *The Rise of Methodism*, p. 418; Asbury, *Journal*, 1:470, 471, 387; Phoebus, *Beams of Light on Early Methodism*, p. 12; William Duke, *Observations on the Present State of Religion in Maryland* (Baltimore, 1795), p. 44; Isaac Davis, Autobiography, p. 1, Hall of Records, Dover, Del.; Joseph Everett, "An Account of the Most Remarkable Occurrences," p. 505; Elliott, "Unwritten History of Eastern Shore Methodism," nos. 5, 6; Wallace, *Parson of the Islands*, pp. 69, 88, 89; Smith, *Experience and Ministerial Labors*, pp. 72–78; Morgan, Memoir, pp. 2, 101, 102.

3. Barclay, *Early American Methodism*, 1:40; Edwards, *After Wesley*, p. 143; Lednum, *The Rise of Methodism*, pp. 56, 57, 417; Smith, *Experience and Ministerial Labors*, p. 105; James Mitchell, *The Life and Times of Levi Scott* (New York, 1885), p. 32; Bangs, *Freeborn Garrettson*, pp. 74, 218; Manship, *Thirteen Years' Experience in the Itinerancy*, p. 157; Asbury, *Journal*, 1:303, 496; Rankin, Diary, p. 160.

4. *Laws of Delaware*, 2:1218, 3:155; Edmund de S. Brunner and
Wilbur C. Hallenbeck, *American Society: Urban and Rural Patterns* (New York,
1955), p. 216; Brunner, *Village Communities*, (Garden City, N.Y., 1928),
pp. 211, 212; William J. Wade, *Sixteen Miles from Anywhere* (Georgetown,
Del., 1976), pp. 7, 11–12; Williams, *History of Wesley U. M. Church*, pp. 7–
8.

5. Reverend Henry Davis to Bishop John Claggett, Annapolis,
Md., June 13, 1816, Maryland Diocesan Archives; Proposals offered to
the Parishioners of St. Peter's Parish [Easton, Md.], May 1788, Maryland
Diocesan Archives; Smith, *Experience and Ministerial Labors*, p. 74; St. Ste-
phens Parish Vestry to Bishop James Kemp, Sassafras Neck, Cecil Co.,
Md., November 1816, Maryland Diocesan Archives; Asbury, *Journal*, 2:633;
Ethan Allen, *Clergy in Maryland of the Protestant Episcopal Church Since the
Independence of 1783* (Baltimore, 1860), pp. 5, 6; Mariner, *Revival's Children*,
p. 83; Charles A. Silliman, *The Episcopal Church in Delaware, 1785–1954* (Wil-
mington, Del., 1982), p. 22; *Minutes of Annual Conferences of the Methodist
Episcopal Church, 1773–1828*, p. 285; William Duke, *Observations on the Present
State of Religion in Maryland*, pp. 18–21; Coke, *Extracts of the Journals*, p. 18;
Morgan, Memoir, pp. 5, 6; Covington Messick to Vestry of Stepney Par-
ish, 1807, Hall of Records, Annapolis, Md. For specific examples of Meth-
odism pushing Episcopalianism out of most of Maryland's Eastern Shore,
see Reverend Henry Davis to Bishop Claggett, May 16, 1808; Reverend
William Wickes to Bishop Kemp, Princess Anne, Aug. 23, 1819; and
Reverend Purnell Smith to Bishop Kemp, May 27, 1820, in Maryland
Diocesan Archives.

6. Mariner, *Revival's Children*, p. 83; Lappen, *Presbyterians on Del-
marva*, p. 26; John W. Christie, "Presbyterianism in Delaware"; H. Clay
Reed, ed., *Delaware, A History of the First State*, 2:652; *Peninsula Methodist*
(Wilmington), March 21, 1896, p. 8.

7. Edwards, "Materials Towards a History of Baptists," p. 52;
Albert Henry Newman, *A History of the Baptist Church in the United States*
(New York, 1915), p. 273; Mariner, *Revival's Children*, pp. 2, 12–18, 28–
30, 86–87.

8. Duke, *Observations on the Present State of Religion in Maryland*, p. 36;
George B. Utley, *The Life and Times of Thomas John Claggett* (Chicago, 1913),
pp. 38, 39; Todd, "Complete Record of the Methodist Episcopal Church,"
p. 5; Asbury, *Journal*, 1:138, 584; Thomas L. McKenney, Chestertown,
Md., to Ezekiel Cooper, New York, N.Y., February 18, 1807, item no. 88,
Ezekiel Cooper Collection, GTS; Jane Herson, "Development of Methodism in Delaware," (M.A. thesis, University of Delaware, 1956), pp. 118,
119; Phoebus, "The Methodist Episcopal Church," p. 126; George Dashiell, *An Address to the Protestant Episcopal Church in Maryland* (n.p., 1816),
passim; Reverend William Duke to Reverend James Kemp, Elkton, Md.,
April 21, 1814, Maryland Diocesan Archives; Rightmyer, "Episcopate of
Bishop Kemp," *Historical Magazine of the Protestant Episcopal Church* (March
1959): 66–84.

9. Bangs, *Freeborn Garrettson*, p. 81; Asbury, *Journal*, 1:305, 306, 344; Asbury to Ezekiel Cooper, Bolinbroke, Talbot County, November 12, 1790, item no. 16, Ezekiel Cooper Collection, GTS; Benjamin Abbott, *The Experiences and Gospel Labours of the Rev. Benjamin Abbott*, ed. John Firth (New York, 1805), p. 215; Todd, "Complete Records of the Methodist Episcopal Church," p. 9; Colbert, Journal, 2:88, 89.

10. Colbert, Journal, 2:92, 37, 46; Smith, *Experience and Ministerial Labor*, p. 100; Asbury, *Journal*, 2:389; Ayres, Journal, April 1, 1786, January 9, 1786; Abbott, *Experience and Gospel Labours*, p. 106; Todd, *Methodism of the Peninsula*, pp. 61–62; Caley, *Asbury U. M. Church*, pp. 27, 30; Semmel, *The Methodist Revolution*, p. 89; Morgan, Memoir, p. 215.

11. Wallace, *Parson of the Islands*, p. 89.

12. The value system of eighteenth-century Delmarva seems to have paralleled the value system found in Virginia just prior to the American Revolution, according to Rhys Isaac in "Evangelical Revolt," pp. 345–68. The sources for the generalizations about the value system of the Delmarva Peninsula are too scattered and numerous to list here. Many, however, will be cited in chapter 6.

13. Lednum, *The Rise of Methodism*, pp. 166, 167, passim; Asbury, *Journal*, 1, passim; Freeborn Garrettson Collection, passim; "Memoir of Mrs. Anna Matilda Moore," *Methodist Magazine* (New York, 1828), 136, 137.

14. Papenfuse, ed., *Biographical Dictionary of the Maryland Legislature*, 1:308, 309; Lednum, *The Rise of Methodism*, p. 276; Smith, *Experience and Ministerial Labors*, p. 31; Cooper, *Substance of a Funeral Discourse*, p. 93; *Dictionary of American Biography*, "James Asheton Bayard," "Richard Bassett." For a slightly different story of the conversion of the Ennalls girls, see Bangs, *Freeborn Garrettson*, pp. 98, 99.

15. Freeborn Garrettson to Mr. Hopper [Hooper?], 1785, Freeborn Garrettson Collection; James Lackington, *Memoirs of James Lackington* (New York, 1796), p. 71. For a very negative reaction to Lackington's perspectives on Methodism, see Emory, *Life of The Rev. John Emory, D.D.*, (New York, 1841), p. 59. John A. Munroe, *Louis McLane: Federalist and Jacksonian* (New Brunswick, N.J., 1973), pp. 11, 12; Boehm, *Reminiscences*, pp. 151, 152; Luff, *Journal of the Life of Nathaniel Luff*, pp. 126, 127; Mariner, *Revival's Children*, p. 59; Elliott, "Unwritten History of Eastern Shore Methodism," nos. 6, 5.

16. Abbott, *Experiences and Gospel Labours*, p. 110; Lednum, *The Rise of Methodism*, pp. 274, 275; Smith, *Experience and the Ministerial Labors*, p. 97.

17. Davis, Autobiography, pp. 3, 6, 8–12; *Smyrna Times*, April 2, 1856; Lednum, *The Rise of Methodism*, p. 231; Caley, *History of Asbury United Methodist Church*, p. 39; Morgan, Memoir, p. 230; *Discipline of the Methodist Episcopal Church in America*, 5th ed., (New York, 1789), p. 49; Bangs, *A History of the Methodist Episcopal Church*, (New York, 1839), 1:214; Allen, manuscript, 3:36; Proceedings of Trustees in Salem M. E. Church, New

Castle County, Delaware, p. 7, Hall of Records, Dover, Del.; Trustee's Book, 1807–?, passim, Archives, Wesley U. M. Church, Georgetown, Del.; Papers relative to C. & J. Layton's claim against Wesley Chapel, passim, Archives, Wesley U. M. Church; Williams, *History of Wesley U. M. Church*, pp. 6, 7.

18. Semmel, *The Methodist Revolution*, p. 170; Boles, *The Great Revival*, pp. 166–69; Asbury, *Journal*, 1:335, 497, 612, 651, 2:635; Baker, *The History of Early New England Methodism*, pp. 16–19. The ability of Methodism to draw from the "middling sort" is supported by some concrete evidence. At a Methodist meeting in Smyrna, Delaware, in 1779, ten of those present can be categorized according to source of income: two cabinet makers, three land owners, two merchant-storekeepers, two tanners, and one ship-owner. In a study of Delaware silversmiths, only three who worked south of New Castle County from 1775–1820 can be categorized according to religion. One was a Quaker and two were Methodists. Caley, *History of Asbury United Methodist Church*, p. 25; Ruthanna Hindes, "Delaware Silversmiths, 1700–1850," *Delaware History*, 12 (October 1967): 270–71, 278–80. Terry David Bilhartz, "Urban Religion and the Second Great Awakening: A Religious Study of Baltimore, Maryland, 1790–1830," (Ph.D. diss., George Washington University, 1979), pp. 30–32, 39, 49–50, finds Methodists in Baltimore tending to be skilled artisans. For the view that Methodism drew primarily from the "lower sort" in the South and in New England respectively, see Boles, *The Great Revival*, pp. 169–70; and Baker, *The History of Early New England Methodism*, pp. 16–18.

19. Asbury, *Journal*, 1:497, 397; Morgan, Memoir, pp. 17–19, passim; Wallace, *Parson of the Islands*, pp. 27, 31, 58–59, passim.

20. Colbert, Journal, 2:111; Legislative Papers, Petitions Misc., folder 1, January 1826. The use of the prefix "brother" or "sister" is so common in the primary source materials that I will not cite the many sources.

21. State laws for the incorporation of individual church congregations limited voting rights to free, white adult males. These state laws reflected restrictions on women already in practice. See, for example, Dudley's Chapel Minutes of Board of Trustees, 1797–1900, p. 5. For examples of state-mandated voting restrictions in Maryland see Trustees' Minnutes, 1809–1847, pp. 6, 7, Archives, Zion U. M. Church, Cambridge, Md. See Trustees Book, 1807, Archives, Wesley U. M. Church, Georgetown, Del., for restrictions in Delaware. For a typical example of an all-female class meeting led by a male, see Smith, *Experience and Ministerial Labors*, p. 27. John Wesley, *The Works of the Rev. John Wesley*, ed. John Emory (New York, 1831), 5:235; *Discipline of the Methodist Episcopal Church*, p. 31; Charles Johnson, *The Frontier Camp Meeting* (Dallas, 1955), p. 46; John D. C. Hanna, ed., *Centennial Services of Asbury Methodist Episcopal Church*, pp. 140, 151; Harold Hancock, ed., "Alexander B. Cooper's Civil War Memoirs of Camden," *Delaware History* (Spring-Summer 1982): 59; Baker, *The History of Early New England Methodism*, p. 21; Lednum, *The Rise of*

Methodism, p. 270. Since early membership records for individual Methodist societies on the Peninsula—with the exception of Asbury Church, Wilmington—aren't extant, it is impossible to present a statistical breakdown of males vs. female members. However, Colbert, Journal, 4:60; Ayres, Journal, p. 15 and passim; Asbury M. E. Church (Wilmington) Records, vol. 5; and Terry David Bilhartz, "Urban Religion and the Second Great Awakening," p. 62, indicate that Methodists, on the Peninsula and on the west side of the Chesapeake, were overwhelmingly female. In the case of Asbury Church, Wilmington, women outnumbered men almost two to one.

22. Lednum, *The Rise of Methodism*, pp. 115, 267, 268, 273–75; *Queen Anne's Observer* (Centreville, Md.), July 13, 1939, sect. 2, p. 7; Munroe, *Louis McLane*, p. 11; Bangs, *Freeborn Garrettson*, pp. 99, 100, 129; Smith, *Experience and Ministerial Labors*, pp. 75, 99; John Munroe, ed., "James Hemphill's Account of a Visit to Maryland in 1802," *Delaware History*, 3:67; Allen manuscript, 3:36. For a good example of female piety, see Emory, *Life of John Emory*, passim.

23. Jeffrey Saver, "Edward O. Wilson, Father of a New Science," *Science Digest* (May 1982): 86; Hanna, ed., *Centennial Services of Asbury Methodist Episcopal Church*, p. 151; Morgan, Memoir, p. 102; "Memoir of Mrs. Anna Matilda Moore," p. 135; Davis, Autobiography, p. 7.

24. Smith, *The Experience and Ministerial Labors*, p. 99. For the behavior of Garrettson and other itinerants in the face of persecution, see chapter 2. For particularly interesting views on why more women than men joined churches in New England during the eighteenth and early nineteenth century, see Nancy F. Cott, *The Bonds of Womanhood: "Woman's Sphere" in New England, 1780–1835* (New Haven, Conn., 1977), pp. 126–59; and Laurel Thatcher Ulrich, *Good Wives: Image and Reality in the Lives of Women in Northern New England, 1650–1750* (New York, 1982), pp. 215–16.

25. Boehm, *Reminiscences*, pp. 59–60; Smith, *Experience and Ministerial Labors*, pp. 30, 31; Abbott, *Experience and Gospel Labours*, p. 109. A real opportunity for female leadership in Methodism opened up with the sectarian development of the Sunday school in the 1830s. See Mariner, *Revival's Children*, p. 82.

26. Lewis Baldwin, "Invisible Strands in African Methodism" (Ph.D. diss., Northwestern University, 1980), p. 53; Asbury, *Journal*, 1:732, 323, 696; Bangs, *Freeborn Garrettson*, p. 58; Colbert, Journal, 2:105, 107; 4:35, 37, 73, 44, 61, 63, 65, 67, 205; A. Tyndall, Concord M. E. Church, typed manuscript, p. 1, Hall of Records, Dover, Del.; Barratt's Chapel Record Book, pp. 6, 7; Morgan, Memoir, p. 39. Allen Clark, archivist at Barratt's Chapel, is convinced that blacks were forced to stand during services by the structural nature of the gallery used by blacks and reports of blacks being forced to stand during services elsewhere in the United States.

27. Figures on black and white Methodists were drawn from Conference journals. Percentages of blacks and whites who became Methodists

on the Peninsula in 1810 are tabulated from *Third U.S. Census (1810)* and *Minutes of Methodist Conferences, 1773–1813*. An examination of early census figures for the Peninsula indicates that approximately one-half of the total counted were sixteen and over and, therefore, eligible for church membership. Thus, I arrived at both blacks and whites, sixteen and over, by dividing total population by two.

Although it is impossible to break down black Methodists into free and enslaved categories, the number of black Methodists from counties in which most blacks were free doesn't show a distinctly different pattern from those counties in which most blacks were slaves. Therefore, it would seem that free and enslaved blacks were equally attracted to Peninsula Methodism prior to 1820.

28. Albert J. Raboteau, *Slave Religion: The Invisible Institution in the Antebellum South* (New York, 1978), p. 132; Mathews, *Slavery and Methodism*, pp. 1–24. Asbury, *Journal*, 1:273, 274, 582; For Asbury's opposition to slavery during the American Revolution, later edited out of his *Journal*, see Frank E. Maser, ed., "Discovery," *Methodist History* (January 1971): 35. Boehm, *Reminiscences*, pp. 26, 70; Allen manuscript, 3:35; Colbert, Journal, 2:104, 126, 216; 4:8, 41, 48; Morgan, Memoir, pp. 53, 54. For example of a Peninsula-born-and-raised-Methodist attacking slavery in newspapers outside the Peninsula, see Ezekiel Cooper's condemnation in *Virginia Gazette*, November 28, 1791, p. 2; *Maryland Gazette*, November 11, 1790, p. 3; December 2, 1790, pp. 2–3; December 30, 1790, p. 2; January 20, 1771, p. 2; and *Maryland Journal*, April 18, 1792.

29. Mathews, *Slavery and Methodism*, p. 24; Asbury, *Journal*, 1:274. There were occasional antislavery protests generated by Peninsula Methodism as the nineteenth century progressed. In 1826, for example, the Cambridge Circuit sent a request to the Methodist General Conference— a quadriennial conference of Methodism in the United States—to deny slaveholders the right to join the Methodist Episcopal Church. Mathews, *Slavery and Methodism*, p. 54. For Asbury's later temporizing on the issue of slavery see Rudolph, *Francis Asbury*, pp. 176–85.

30. Todd, *Methodism of the Peninsula*, pp. 183–85; Colbert, Journal, 4:49, 56, passim; 3:129; Asbury, *Journal*, 1:274, 655.

31. Did African culture and, in particular, African religion survive among American slaves? This has become a subject of considerable controversy among historians. Melville J. Herskovitz, in *The Myth of the Negro Past* (Boston, 1958), argued that the African heritage survived among American blacks despite the trauma of slavery. E. Franklin Frazier, in *The Negro Church in America* (New York, 1964) and in other works, maintains that the African in America was almost totally stripped of his culture by American slavery. A particularly stimulating treatment of the survival of African religious traits among American slaves can be found in Eugene D. Genovese, *Roll, Jordan, Roll: The World the Slaves Made* (New York, 1976), pp. 161–284. I have found the most satisfactory study of African religious remnants in white Christianity in Albert J. Raboteau's *Slave Religion*, pp. 43–92.

32. A. Chandler, *History of the Churches on the Delmar Circuit* (Wilmington, 1886), p. 10; Minutes of Board of Trustees, Asbury M. E. Church, Wilmington, Del., June 9, 1805; Barratt's Chapel Record Book, pp. 7–9.

33. Colbert, Journal, 4:74; Asbury M. E. Church, (Wilmington) Records, vol. 5; Munroe, *Federalist Delaware*, p. 219.

34. Folder no. 5, M. E. Black, Federal Writers' Project, Church Records; Asbury, *Journal*, 2:501; Asbury M. E. Church (Wilmington) vol. 5; Scharf, *History of Delaware*, 2:729, 730; Elizabeth Montgomery, *Reminiscences of Wilmington* (Philadelphia, 1851), p. 252; Baldwin, "Invisible Strands in African Methodism," pp. 62, 65. Cokesbury United Methodist Church, near Port Deposit, Cecil County, Maryland, claims to be the oldest black congregation in the United States—therefore older than Ezion—but the claim can't be documented.

35. Lednum, *The Rise of Methodism*, p. 380; Colbert, Journal, 4:51.

36. Daniel Blake Smith, *Inside the Great House: Planter Family Life in Eighteenth-Century Chesapeake Society* (Ithaca, N.Y., 1980), pp. 265–67; Phoebus, *Beams of Light on Early Methodism*, p. 12.

37. Watters, *Short Account of the Christian Experience*, p. 38; Bishop James Kemp to Reverend William Duke, Baltimore, September 19, 1815, Maryland Diocesan Archives (Kemp had observed Peninsula Methodism while Episcopal rector in Dorchester County for nineteen years); Asbury, *Journal*, 2:388, 1:302; Davis, Autobiography, pp. 2, 7, 8, 10, 14; Emory, *Life of John Emory*, p. 12; William Coulter to Ezekiel Cooper, Dorchester Co., Md., March 29, 1800, no. 63, Ezekiel Cooper Collection, MCDU; Lednum, *The Rise of Methodism*, p. 229; Robert Robinson and Daniel Costen, *Old Country Churches of Sussex County*, (Georgetown, Del., 1977), p. 37.

Chapter 5: The Broadcasters of Methodism

1. Quote is from Hallman, *Garden of Methodism*, p. 18. Figures on Methodist itinerants on the Peninsula are compiled primarily from Hallman, *Garden of Methodism*, pp. 56–92, and *Minutes of the Annual Conferences of the Methodist Episcopal Church, 1773–1828* (New York, 1840), passim. Of the other fifty-five itinerants whose birthplaces can be identified, thirty-five were born in America, ten in Ireland, eight in England, one in Wales, and one in Scotland.

2. Watters, *A Short Account of the Christian Experiences*, pp. 38–39; Asbury, *Journal*, 1:333, 269; Ware, *Sketches of the Life and Travels*, p. 94; Todd, "Complete Records of the Methodist Episcopal Church," p. 1; Robert Baird, *Religion in the United States of America* (Glasgow, 1844), pp. 434–41; Cooper, *Substance of a Funeral Discourse*, p. 117. For a perspective on illiteracy in 1790 in Pennsylvania and Virginia, see Kenneth A. Lockridge, *Literacy in Colonial New England*, (New York, 1974), p. 77.

3. Barclay, *Early American Methodism*, 1:33; Boehm, *Reminiscences*, p. 157; Asbury, *Journal*, 1:392, 293; Emory, *Life of John Emory*, pp. 13–52; Colbert, Journal, 2:42, 73, 76, 77, 113, 3:137.

4. Ezekiel Cooper, Notebook, unpaginated, MCDU; Smith, *Experiences and Ministerial Labors*, pp. 9–11. For examples of Peninsula itinerants

developing a heightened sensitivity of death prior to their conversion experience, see Sprague, ed., *Annals of the American Pulpit*, 7:34, 35, 119; Bangs, *Freeborn Garrettson*, pp. 30, 33; Phoebus, *Light on Early Methodism*, p. 16. For examples of Methodist preachers who served the Peninsula, giving the specific date and place of the conversion experience, see Emory, *Life of John Emory*, pp. 27, 28; Luff, *Journal of the Life of Nathaniel Luff*, p. 129; Everett, "An Account of the Most Remarkable Occurrences," pp. 510, 560, 561; Bangs, *Freeborn Garrettson*, pp. 38–40.

5. Everett, "An Account of the Most Remarkable Occurrences," pp. 510, 555, 557, 560, 561; Mitchell, *Life and Times of Levi Scott*, p. 36. Although Everett's first conversion occurred in 1763, seven years before Methodism came to the Peninsula, it closely resembled his second conversion experience in 1778, which made him a Methodist.

6. Williams, *History of Wesley U.M. Church*, p. 9; Lednum, *The Rise of Methodism*, p. 88, 326; Emory, *Life of John Emory*, pp. 43, 44; Wallace, *Parson of the Islands*, p. 172; Arthur A. Walls, *History of Dudley's Chapel* (microfilm), p. 11, Queen Anne's Charge and Sudlersville Charge Church Records, Hall of Records, Annapolis, Md.; *Minutes of Annual Conferences*, vols. 1 & 2, passim; Everett, "An Account of the Most Remarkable Occurrences," p. 604; Hallman, *Garden of Methodism*, p. 375.

7. Emory, *Life of John Emory*, pp. 37, 38, 34; Everett, "An Account of the Most Remarkable Occurrences," pp. 604, 605; Asbury, *Journal*, 1:389; Ware, *Sketches of the Life and Travels*, p. 74; Bangs, *History of the Methodist Episcopal Church, 1766–1792*, 1:189, 190, 177–84; Colbert, Journal, 2:118; *Minutes of Methodist Conferences, 1773–1813*, pp. 262, 263. For the lives of Emory and Scott, see Emory, *Life of John Emory*, and Mitchell, *Life and Times of Levi Scott*.

8. Barclay, *Early American Methodism*, 2:289–99; Smith, *Experience and Ministerial Labors*, p. 94; Main, *Social Structure of Revolutionary America*, pp. 70, 71, 77; Lednum, *The Rise of Methodism*, pp. 304, 305, 246, 247; Emory, *Life of John Emory*, p. 61; Norwood, *Story of American Methodism*, p. 139. For an historical perspective on itinerants' salaries, see Michael J. Nickerson, "Historical Relationships of Itinerancy and Salary," *Methodist History* (October 1982): 43–59.

9. Everett, "An Account of the Most Remarkable Occurrences," p. 607; Boehm, *Reminiscences*, p. 27; Norwood, *Story of American Methodism*, p. 139; Colbert, Journal, 4:155.

10. Ayres, Journal, passim; Rankin, Diary, pp. 136, 142; Colbert, Journal, 5–6: 61, 62, 64; Wesley quoted in D. D. Thompson, *John Wesley as Social Reformer* (Freeport, N.Y., 1971), p. 28; Asbury, Journal, 3:19; Bangs, *History of the Methodist Episcopal Church*, 1:181. For a brief but important discussion of the relationships between southern evangelists and women, see Mathews, *Religion in the Old South*, pp. 105, 106.

11. Lednum, *The Rise of Methodism*, p. 196; Morgan, Memoir, pp. 59, 83; *Minutes of Methodist Conferences, 1773–1813*, passim; Chandler, *History of Churches on Delmarva Circuit*, pp. 10, 11; Todd, "Complete Record of the

Methodist Episcopal Church," p. 10; Caley, *History of Asbury U.M. Church*, p. 28.

12. Williams, *History of Wesley U. M. Church*, p. 10; Ware, *Sketches of the Life and Travels*, p. 83; Asbury, *Journal*, 1:524 n., 293, 303; Ayres, Journal, December 13, 1785; Colbert, Journal, 4:5; Lednum, *The Rise of Methodism*, p. 279; Todd, "Complete Record of the Methodist Episcopal Church," p. 10; *Minutes of Methodist Conferences, 1773–1813*, p. 262; Smith, *Experience and Ministerial Labors*, p. 72.

13. Turner, ed., *Some Records of Sussex County*, p. 240; Samuel Tingley to Secretary, S.P.G., New York, March 5, 1782, Morris Library, University of Delaware; Abbott, *The Experience and Gospel Labours*, p. 212; Ayres, Journal, December 15, 1785; Boehm, *Reminiscences*, pp. 440, 79, 80, 425.

14. Asbury, *Journal*, 1:325, 330; Ayres, Journal, September 1785; Colbert, Journal, 2:67, 68, 94.

15. For a typical sampling of motivations of Peninsula itinerants, see Todd, *Methodism of the Peninsula*, p. 59; Colbert, Journal, 2:49; Luff, *Journal of the Life of Nathanial Luff*, p. 129; Barclay, *Early American Methodism*, 1: xvi; Asbury, *Journal*, 1:330; George Roberts, *The Substance of a Sermon Now Enlarged* (Baltimore, 1807), p. 72; Wallace, *Parson of the Islands*, p. 87; Watters, *Short Account of the Christian Experience*, pp. 38, 39.

16. *Minutes of the Methodist Conferences, 1773–1813*, passim; Norwood, *Story of American Methodism*, p. 137; Morgan, Memoir, p. 84; Boehm, *Reminiscences*, p. 159; Lednum, *The Rise of Methodism*, p. 331.

17. Boehm, *Reminiscences*, pp. 71, 48, 133; Asbury, *Journal*, 1:274; Pilmore, *Journal of Joseph Pilmore*, p. 84; Ware, *Sketches of the Life and Travels*, p. 81; Everett, "An Account of the Most Remarkable Occurrences," p. 562; Wallace, *Parson of the Islands*, p. 169; Colbert, Journal, 4:3, 75.

18. Colbert, Journal, 3:126, 131, 134, 4:78; Ayres, Journal, March 19, 1786; Morgan, Memoir, pp. 44, 45; Lorenzo Dow, *Travels and Labors of Lorenzo Dow*, p. 172; Boehm, *Reminiscences*, pp. 125, 126; Hulbert Footner, *Rivers of the Eastern Shore* (New York, 1954), pp. 78, 79. See series of letters in Smyrna Circuit Folder, Hall of Records, Dover, Del., for other charges against Chandler. In his memoir, William Morgan incorrectly wrote that the eclipse of the sun took place in 1807 rather than in 1806. For a slightly different but secondary-source account of the impact of the eclipse on that camp meeting, see Elijah Hitch, *Historical Sketch of Moore's Chapel* (Philadelphia, 1863), pp. 23, 24.

19. Jonathan Crowther, *True and Complete Portraiture of Methodism* (New York, 1813), pp. 218, 219; Bilhartz, "Urban Religion and the Second Great Awakening," pp. 245, 246; William Nash Wade, "A History of Public Worship in the Methodist Episcopal Church . . . 1784 to 1905," (Ph.D. diss., University of Notre Dame, 1981), p. 96; Smith, *Experiences and Ministerial Labors*, pp. 296, 297.

20. Isaac, "Evangelical Revolt," p. 355; Duke, *Observations on the Present State of Religion in Maryland*, p. 26; Crawther, *True and Complete Portraiture of Methodism*, p. 220; *Methodist Magazine* (New York, 1820), p. 145;

Lednum, *The Rise of Methodism*, p. 22; Boehm, *Reminiscences*, p. 443; *A Pocket Hymn Book* (Philadelphia, 1797), p. i; Phoebus, *Beams of Light on Early Methodism*, p. 247; Clark, "History of Wesley United Methodist Church, Dover, Del.," p. 46; Wallace, *Parson of the Islands*, pp. 88, 124, 270.

21. Crowther, *True and Complete Portraiture of Methodism*, pp. 218, 220, 225; Bangs, *History of the Methodist Episcopal Church*, p. 190; Boles, *The Great Revival*, p. 111; Smith, *Experience and Ministerial Labors*, p. 77; Morgan, Memoir, pp. 26, 25; Abbott, *Experiences and Gospel Labours*, p. 110.

22. Wallace, *Parson of the Islands*, p. 164; Boehm, *Reminiscences*, 439; Levi Scott, "Semi-Centennial Sermon," *Annual Minutes of the Wilmington Conferences* (Wilmington, 1876), p. 76; Smith, *Experience and Ministerial Labors*, p. 34; *Discipline of the Methodist Episcopal Church in America*, p. 7; James Penn Pilkington, *The Methodist Publishing House*, (New York, 1968), 1:25, 28, 36, 50, 103; Evald Rink, *Printing in Delaware, 1761–1800*, (Wilmington, Del., 1969), p. 73; Asbury, *Journal*, 1:330.

23. Boehm, *Reminiscences*, p. 74; Colbert, Journal, 3:143; 4:73; 2:56; Watters, *Short Account of the Christian Experience*, p. 41.

24. Semmel, *The Methodist Revolution*, p. 171; Frederick A. Norwood, *Church Membership in the Methodist Tradition* (Nashville, 1958), p. 106; Colbert, Journal, 2:67.

25. *Discipline of the Methodist Episcopal Church*, pp. 5, 9; Wallace, *Parson of the Islands*, pp. 161–80, passim; Morgan, Memoir, pp. 76, 77; Colbert, Journal, 2:43, 58; Todd, *Methodism of the Peninsula*, pp. 155, 176, 177.

26. Asbury, *Journal*, 1:298, 413; Coke, *Extracts of the Journals*, p. 18; Colbert, Journal, 5–6: 44, 61, 63, 65, 67; Lednum, *The Rise of Methodism*, pp. 281, 282.

27. Norwood, *Story of American Methodism*, p. 168; Colbert, Journal, 2:61; 4:1; 5–6: 205; Baldwin, "Invisible Strands in African Methodism," pp. 35, 8; Richard Allen, *The Life Experience and Gospel Labors of the Rt. Rev. Richard Allen* (Nashville, 1960), pp. 1–36; Asbury, *Journal*, 1:310; Pauline A. Young, "The Negro in Delaware, Past and Present," ed. H. Clay Reed, *Delaware, A History of the First State*, pp. 604, 605.

Professor Gary Nash of U.C.L.A. has discovered in Manumission Book A, p. 2, Papers of Pennsylvania Abolitionist Society, Historical Society of Pennsylvania, Philadelphia, Pa., that Allen's master was Stokely Sturgis, not "Mr. Stokeley" as Allen indicated in Allen, *The Life Experiences and Gospel Labor*, pp. 5, 6, 16, 17. Professor Nash has also discovered that Allen did some extensive traveling beyond the Philadelphia-Baltimore area. See Josiah Grover, Benjamin Grover, and Nicholas Dorsey, Baltimore, October 20, 1785, contained in testimonial from Thomas Attmore, September 20, 1787, Papers of Pennsylvania Abolitionist Society.

Chapter 6: The Impact of Methodism

1. Samuel Tingley to Secretary, S.P.G., New York, March 15, 1782, transcript, S.P.G. Collection, Series B, vol. 21, pt. 2, Morris Library, University of Delaware; Smith, *Experience and Ministerial Labors*, p. 59; Everett,

"An Account of the Most Remarkable Occurrences," p. 507; Lackington, *Memoirs of James Lackington*, pp. 61, 65; Morgan, Memoir, p. 1; Semmel, *The Methodist Revolution*, pp. 98–101.

2. Everett, "An Account of the Most Remarkable Occurrences," pp. 558–60; *Minutes of Methodist Conferences, 1773–1813*, p. 278; Lednum, *The Rise of Methodism*, pp. 264, 265, 342; Asbury, *Journal*, 1:523; Smith, *Experience and Ministerial Labors*, pp. 73–78; Mariner, *Revival's Children*, pp. 59, 60; Elliott, "Unwritten History of Eastern Shore Methodism," no. 5; The Reverend James Kemp to Mrs. Mary Goldsborough, Great Choptank Parish, Dorchester Co., Md (1811?), Maryland Diocesan Archives; Duke, *Observations on the Present State of Religion in Maryland*, p. 30; Hulbert Footner, *Rivers of the Eastern Shore*, p. 104; Luff, *Journal of the Life of Nathaniel Luff*, p. 33; Asbury, *Journal*, 3:343. For a brief discussion of the strange phenomenon of opposites attracting see Isaac, "Evangelical Revolt," p. 348.

3. Thomas Coke and Francis Asbury, *Discipline of 1796*, in Norwood, *Church Membership in the Methodist Tradition*, appendix, p. 135, and passim.

4. Baker, *Introduction to the History of Early New England Methodism*, p. 68; Edwards, *After Wesley*, pp. 135, 136; Coke and Asbury, *Discipline of 1796*, in Norwood, *Church Membership in the Methodist Tradition*, appendix, p. 135; Asbury, *Journal*, 1:447 n.; Davis, Autobiography, p. 11; Boehm, *Reminiscences*, pp. 427–29, 124; Smith, *Experience and Ministerial Labors*, p. 85; Bangs, *Freeborn Garrettson*, pp. 79, 94; *Discipline* (New York, 1789), p. 25; Lednum, *The Rise of Methodism*, pp. 255, 92; Colbert, Journal, 4:72.

5. Wallace, *Parson of the Islands*, pp. 100, 101; *Discipline* (1789), pp. 15, 29; Asbury, *Journal*, 1:613; Rudolph, *Francis Asbury*, p. 141–43; Morgan, Memoir, p. 82.

6. Barclay, *Early American Methodism*, 2:26–38; *Minutes of Methodist Conferences, 1773–1813*, passim; *Discipline* (1785), p. 10; Asbury, *Journal*, 1:653, 2:239.

7. Abstract of several letters from Henry Baley to Allen McLane, Box 38, Folder 23, Allen McLane Collection, Historical Society of Delaware, Wilmington, Del.; Davis, Autobiography, p. 11; Morgan, Memoir, 429; Wallace, *Parson of the Islands*, pp. 58, 59, 209–14; Barclay, *Early American Methodism*, 2:31, 35; *Minutes of Methodist Conferences, 1773–1813*, p. 8; Lednum, *The Rise of Methodism*, pp. 281–82; Smyrna Circuit folder, 1783–1829, passim.

8. Asbury, *Journal*, 1:391; Pilmore, *Journals of Joseph Pilmore*, p. 84; Rankin, Diary, p. 107; Colbert, Journal, 2:119; Baker, *Introduction to the History of Early New England Methodism*, pp. 61–66; Barclay, *Early American Methodism*, 2:31; Morgan, Memoir, pp. 6, 7, 14, 16.

9. Morgan, Memoir, pp. 17, 18, 33, 208–11; Charles H. Bohner, "Rum and Reform: Temperance in Delaware Politics," *Delaware History* (September 1953): 238–43; Norwood, *Story of American Methodism*, p. 349.

10. Edwards, *After Wesley*, p. 133, 134; Lednum, *The Rise of Methodism*, p. 259; Asbury, *Journal*, 1:613.

11. Edwards, *After Wesley*, pp. 128–30, 132–37; Wallace, *Parson of the Islands*, p. 201; Asbury, *Journal*, 1:115; Emory, *Life of John Emory*, pp. 30, 31, 24; Mariner, *Revival's Children*, p. 59; Elliott, "Unwritten History of Eastern Shore Methodism," no. 5; Lednum, *The Rise of Methodism*, p. 350, 342–344, 341; Thompson, *John Wesley as Social Reformer*, p. 27.

12. Edwards, *After Wesley*, p. 130; Mitchell, *Life and Times of Levi Scott*, p. 35; Hancock, ed., "Alexander B. Cooper's Civil War Memoirs of Camden," p. 59; Morgan, Memoir, p. 22; Wallace, *Parson of the Islands*, pp. 193–95; Colbert, Journal, 4:81, 5–6: 35.

13. Thompson, *John Wesley As Social Reformer*, p. 27; Edwards, *After Wesley*, p. 137; Emory, *Life of John Emory*, p. 35; Everett, "An Account of the Remarkable Occurrences," p. 604; Morgan, Memoir, pp. 204, 205; Colbert, Journal, 3:137.

14. Luff, *Journal of the Life of Nathanial Luff*, p. 37; Bangs, *Freeborn Garrettson*, p. 83; Boehm, *Reminiscences*, pp. 169, 170; Hallman, *Garden of Methodism*, p. 257.

15. *First Census of the United States, 1790*, passim; *Fourth Census of the United States, 1820*, passim; Morgan, Memoir, pp. 83, 34, title page; Elliott, "Unwritten History of Eastern Shore Methodism," no. 3; Papenfuse, ed., *Biographical Dictionary of the Maryland Legislature*, 1:308, 309, 460, 178; Wallace, *Parson of the Islands*, passim; Gregory A. Stiverson, "Deal Island: Records Relating to the Study of a Maryland Community," Second Conference on Maryland History, (May 24–26, 1978), doc. 8.

16. Boehm, *Reminiscences*, p. 69; Everett; "An Account of the Most Remarkable Occurrences," p. 609.

17. Morgan, Memoir, pp. 53, 54; extract from Journal of the Philadelphia Annual Conference, Easton, Md., April 20, 1810, in Journal of the Quarterly Conference of the Accomack Circuit, June 4–5, 1814; Whitelaw, *Virginia's Eastern Shore*, 2:869; Asbury, *Journal*, 1:582; Kenneth Carroll, "Religious Influences on the Manumissions of Slaves in Caroline, Dorchester, and Talbot Counties," *Maryland Historiccal Magazine* (June 1961): 187–197; Smith, *Experience and Ministerial Labors*, p. 113. The first *Discipline* of the Methodist Episcopal Church called for expulsion of slave holders but, because of predictable southern opposition, this rule was suspended within six months. See Barclay, *Early American Methodism*, 2:71–74.

18. Mathews, *Slavery and Methodism*, p. 9; Colbert, Journal, 4:7, 12; Boehm, *Reminiscenses*, p. 69; Barclay, *Early American Methodism*, 2:80, 81; Mattison, *Impending Crisis of 1860*, p. 24–28; James Essig, *The Bonds of Wickedness* (Phlladelphia, 1982), p. 120; extract from Journal of the Philadelphia Annual Conference, April 14, 1814, in the Journal of the Quarterly Conference of the Accomack Circuit, June 4–5, 1814.

19. Morgan, Memoir, p. 220; Scharf, *History of Delaware*, 2:827; Barratt, *Barratt's Chapel and Methodism*, pp. 41–43; Wilson, *Forgotten Heroes of Delaware*, p. 71; Norman A. Moore, Jr., "The Antislavery Movement in Delaware" (M.A. thesis, University of Delaware, 1965), pp. 22, 23, 40, 56, 64–66, 74, 81, 83, 84, 89, 91, 93, 94, 97, 100; Williams, *History of Wesley U.M. Church*, p. 11; Munroe, *History of Delaware*, pp. 97, 98; Munroe, *Federalist Delaware*, pp. 217, 218.

20. Lednum, *The Rise of Methodism*, p. 341 n.; Elliott, "Unwritten History of Eastern Shore Methodism," no. 4; William Baskerville Hamilton, *Thomas Rodney, Revolutionary and Builder of the West*, (Durham, N.C., 1953), p. 55; Smith, *Experience and Ministerial Labors*, p. 82; Rankin, Diary, pp. 136, 190; Tench Tilghman to Bishop Kemp, Dorchester County, November 26, 1815, Maryland Diocesan Archives. For further evidence that Methodists made "good" slaves, see Allen, *Life Experience and Gospel Labors*, p. 17.

21. Colbert, Journal, 2:84; Records of Asbury M. E. Church (Wilmington) vol. 5; Munroe, *Federalist Delaware*, p. 220.

Did those Peninsula Methodists who refused to free their slaves treat them more humanely than did non-Methodists? Certainly the experience of black abolitionist Frederick Douglas (although he was reporting on conditions more than a decade later than the period of this study) doesn't support this conclusion. In Talbot County in 1834 the sixteen-year-old Douglas was rented out by his master to Edward Covey, a notorious "slave breaker" who professed to be a devout Methodist. Although Douglas had never felt the pain and humiliation of the lash before, Covey brutally whipped him at least once a week. Nathan Irwin Huggins, *Slave and Citizen: The Life of Frederick Douglas* (Boston, 1980), p. 9; Irving Mark and E. L. Schwaab, eds., *The Faith of Our Fathers* (New York, 1952), pp. 157–59.

22. Morgan, Memoir, p. 54; Mathews, *Slavery and Methodism*, p. 54; Mattison, *Impending Crisis of 1860*, pp. 28, 25; Journal of Quarterly Conferences of the Accomack Circuit, 1804–1867, March 13, 1824. For a feeling for the antiabolitionist sentiment that surged through Peninsula Methodism after the 1820s, see Todd, *Methodism of the Peninsula*, passim; Mattison, *Impending Crisis of 1860*, p. 28.

23. Lednum, *The Rise of Methodism*, p. 350; Asbury, *Journal*, 2:668. Robert Wright was U.S. senator, 1801–6, governor of Maryland, 1806–9, and U.S. congressman, 1810–17, 1821–23. Scharf, *History of Maryland*, 2:622.

24. John 17:16; Rom. 12: 2; Titus 2:4; 2 Cor. 6:14; Norwood, *Church Membership in the Methodist Tradition*, p. 66; John Munroe, ed., "James Hemphill's Account of a Visit to Maryland in 1802," *Delaware History* (March 1948): 67.

25. Rankin, Diary, p. 136; Caesar Augustus Rodney memo on case of James Payne, September 24, 1802, H.F. Brown Collection, box 23, no. 5, Historical Society of Delaware, Wilmington, Del.; Edwards, *After Wesley*, p. 118; Asbury, *Journal*, 1:653, 654.

26. Statements dated August 3, 18, 1818, Smyrna Circuit folder, 1783–1829; Caesar August Rodney memo, September 24, 1802, H. F. Brown Collection, box 23, no. 5; Robert Ayres, Journal, October 12, 1785; Caleb Rodney Case, notes, Ezekiel Cooper Collection, MCDU; Caleb Layton to Ezekiel Cooper, Georgetown, April 4, 1826, Ezekiel Cooper Collection, MCDU.

27. Boehm, *Reminiscences*, pp. 442, 443, 447; Colbert, Journal, 4:36, 11; 3:131, Lednum, *The Rise of Methodism*, p. 350.

28. Rudolph, *Francis Asbury*, p. 32; Asbury, *Journal*, 1:299, 696; Morgan, Memoir, pp. 91–93.

29. Ridgway, *Community Leadership in Maryland, 1790–1840*, p. 33. For the willingness of Delaware politicians of this era to portray the opposition in the most unfavorable light, see Munroe, *Federalist Delaware*, p. 233. For the susceptibility of evangelical Christians to the oral message and its corresponding use by politicians, see Harry S. Stout, "Religion, Communication, and the Ideological Origins of the American Revolution," *William and Mary Quarterly* (October 1977): 519–41.

30. For specific examples of the traditional involvement of Methodist Peninsula gentry in the political arena prior to conversion, see Papenfuse, ed., *Biograhical Dictionary of the Maryland Legislature*, vols. 1, 2, passim. At least fifteen Eastern Shore gentry, prior to conversion to Methodism, served in Maryland's legislature during and shortly after the American Revolution.

31. Papenfuse, ed., *Biographical Dictionary of the Maryland Legislature*, vol. 1, passim; Davis, Autobiography, passim; Wilson, *Forgotten Heroes of Delaware*, p. 71; Johnson, ed., *Dictionary of American Biography*, s.v. "Richard Bassett." Unlike the General and Annual Conferences, the Quarterly Meetings on the Peninsula did allow for some lay participation. See Elliott, "Unwritten History of Eastern Shore Methodism," no. 7.

32. Ridgway, *Community Leadership in Maryland, 1790–1840*, p. 33; Barclay, *Early American Methodism*, 1:53, 54; Mills, *Bishops by Ballot*, pp. 195, 196, 208; Rudolph, *Francis Asbury*, p. 67.

33. Lee, *Short History of the Methodists*, pp. 149–59; Barclay, *Early American Methodism*, 1:160, 161; Asbury, *Journal*, 1:650.

34. Barclay, *Early American Methodism*, 1:162, 163; Norwood, *Story of American Methodism*, pp. 181–84; Morgan, Memoir, pp. 224–29, 243. When the Methodist Protestant and the Methodist Episcopal churches were reunited in 1939, on the Peninsula there were approximately 11,000 Methodist Protestants and approximately 53,000 Methodist Episcopals. Hallman, *Garden of Methodism*, p. 18.

35. Munroe, *Federalist Delaware*, pp. 238–41; Munroe, *Louis McLane*, p. 19; Morgan, Memoir, p. 92; Leon deValinger, ed., *A Calendar of the Ridgely Family Papers*, (Milford, De., 19 1:290; Barratt, *Barratt's Chapel and Methodism*, p. 35; *Aurora* (Philadelphia), April 8, 9, 1800. One leading Delaware Methodist who left the Federalists for the Democratic-Republicans was Isaac Davis of Smyrna. Davis, Autobiography, pp. 5, 6.

36. Thomas Rodney to ?, Kent County, Delaware, April 1800, Church Letters, Historical Society of Delaware; James H. Broussard, *The Southern Federalist, 1800–1816*, (Baton Rouge, La., 1978), p. 393; John A. Munroe, *History of Delaware*, (Newark, 1979), p. 103.

37. Duke, *Observations on the Present State of Religion in Maryland*, pp. 36, 37; Ridgway, *Community Leadership in Maryland, 1790–1840*, pp. 29, 322–30; Reverend Joseph Bend to the Reverend William Duke, November 3, 1798, Maryland Diocesan Archives; *Journal of a Convention of the Protestant Episcopal*

Church in the State of Maryland, 1807 (Baltimore, 1807), p. 12; Phoebus, *Beams of Light on Early Methodism in America*, p. 24. For information on William Hindman, see Papenfuse, ed., *Biographical Dictionary of the Maryland Legislature*, 1. Methodists in New England also put aside their uneasiness concerning political involvement because of the issue of tax support for churches. Generally, because the Democratic-Republican party was for disestablishment, New England Methodists supported the party of Jefferson. Baker, *The History of Early New England Methodism*, p. 45.

38. Ann Ridgely to ?, Dover, May 10, 1798; Ann Ridgely to Mrs. Ann Ridgely, Dover, July 29, 1798, Ridgely Papers, Hall of Records, Dover, De.; Luff, *Journal of the Life of Nathaniel Luff*, p. 122.

39. Reverend James Kemp to Mrs. Mary Goldsborough, Great Choptank Parish, (ca. 1811), Maryland Diocesan Archives; Boehm, *Reminiscences*, p. 70.

40. Morgan, Memoir, pp. 28–31; Boehm, *Reminiscences*, p. 71; Luff, *Journal of the Life of Nathaniel Luff*, p. 33.

Selected Bibliography

Primary Sources

A. Manuscripts

Annapolis, Md. Hall of Records
    Ethan Allen, St. Peter's Parish in Talbot County Records, vol. 3.
    Minutes of Board of Trustees of Dudley's Chapel, Queen Anne's County, Maryland, 1794–1900.
Baltimore, Md. Maryland Historical Society.
    Maryland Diocesan Archives.
    ———. Lovely Lane U. M. Church.
    John Emory letters.
    John Littlejohn Journal, typed copy.
Cambridge, Md. Zion U. M. Church.
    Zion M. E. Church Trustees' Minutes, 1809–47.
Dover, Del. Hall of Records.
    Asbury Methodist (Wilmington) Records, vol. 5. Asbury's records, as well as other Methodist material, are in the process of being moved to Barratt's Chapel, Frederica, Del.
    Isaac Davis Autobiography. A typed copy is in the possession of Mrs. James McNeal, Bethany Beach, Del.
    Legislative Papers, Petitions Miscellaneous.
    Methodist Episcopal, Black, folder no. 5, Federal Writers' Project, Church Records.
    William Morgan's Memoir of His Own Life.
    Proceedings of Trustees of Salem M. E. Church, New Castle County, Del.
    Smyrna Circuit Folder, 1783–1829.

Evanston, Il. United Library, Garrett Theological Seminary.
  Ezekiel Cooper Collection.
Frederica, Del. Barratt's Chapel.
  Asbury M. E. Church (Wilmington) Minutes of Board of
    Trustees.
  Barratt's Chapel Record Book.
  Bethel Methodist Church Trustees' Minutes, Cecil County.
  Thoroughfare Neck M. E. Church (New Castle County)
    Trustees' Minutes.
Georgetown, Del. Wesley U. M. Church.
  Wesley M. E. Church Trustees' Book, 1807–?
Madison, N.J. Drew University, Methodist Collection.
  Ezekiel Cooper Collection.
  Freeborn Garrettson Collection.
  Philip Gatch Autobiography, on microfilm.
  Thomas Rankin Diary, typed copy. Original is at United
    Library, Garrett Theological Seminary, Evanston, Il.
Newark, Del. University of Delaware, Morris Library.
  Society for Propagation of the Gospel Letters. See also Free-
    born Garrettson's personal copy of his printed journal with
    corrections in his own hand.
Philadelphia, Pa. St. George's U. M. Church.
  William Colbert's Journal, typed copy. Original at United
    Library, Garrett Theological Seminary, Evanston, Il.
———. Presbyterian Historical Society.
  Lewes Presbytery Records, 1758–1810.
Pittsburgh, Pa. Historical Society of Western Pennsylvania.
  Robert Ayres Journal.
Washington, D.C. Library of Congress.
  Thomas Haskins's Diaries.
Wilmington, Del. Historical Society of Delaware.
  Allen McLane Collection.
  H. F. Brown Collection.
  Church Letters Collection.
  Thomas Rodney Collection.
Vienna Va. In possession of the Rev. Dr. Kirk Mariner.
  Journal of Quarterly Conference of the Accomack
    Circuit (Va.), 1804–67, typed copy.

B. Newspapers

Aurora (Philadelphia, Pa.)
Delaware Gazette (Wilmington, Del.)
Pennsylvania Gazette (Philadelphia, Pa.)

C. Periodicals

Arminian Magazine
Methodist Magazine

D. Other Printed Primary Source Material

Abbott, Benjamin. *The Experiences and Gospel Labours of the Rev. Benjamin Abbott.* Edited by John Firth. New York: Methodist Church, 1805.

Allen, Ethan. *Protestant Episcopal Church Convention in Maryland of 1780, 81, 82, 83.* Baltimore: no publisher given, 1878. Copies in Maryland Diocesan Archives, Maryland Historical Society, Baltimore.

Allen, Richard. *The Life Experience and Gospel Labors of the Rt. Rev. Richard Allen.* Nashville: Abingdon Press, 1960.

Asbury, Francis. *Journal and Letters of Francis Asbury,* 3 vols. Edited by Elmer Clark. Nashville: Abingdon Press, 1958.

Boehm, Henry. *Reminiscences, Historical and Biographical, of Sixty-Four Years in the Ministry.* New York: Carlton and Porter, 1865.

Census of the United States, 1790, 1800, 1810, 1820.

Christie, John W. "Newly Discovered Letters of George Whitefield, 1745–46" *Journal of Presbyterian Historical Society* (September 1954): 160–164; (December 1954): 259–266.

Coke, Thomas. *Extracts From the Journals of the Rev. Dr. Coke's Five Visits to America.* London: G. Whitefield, 1793.

Coke, Thomas. "The Journal of Bishop Coke." *Arminian Magazine* (1789): 242–244, 286–290.

Cooper, Ezekiel. *The Substance of a Funeral Discourse . . . on the Death of Francis Asbury.* Philadelphia: Jonathan Pounder, 1819.

Crowther, Jonathan. *True and Complete Portraiture of Methodism.* New York: Daniel Hitt and Thomas Ware, 1813.

Dashiell, George. *An Address to the Protestant Episcopal Church in Maryland.* No place, publisher or date given. Copy can be found in Maryland Historical Society, Baltimore, Md.

deValinger, Leon, Jr., ed. *A Calendar of Ridgely Family Letters.* 2 vols. Milford, Del.: Milford Chronicle Publishing Co, 1948.

Discipline of the Methodist Episcopal Church in America, 5th ed. New York: William Ross, 1789.

Dow, Lorenzo. *Travels and Labors of Lorenzo Dow.* New York: Richard C. Valentine, 1855.

Duke, William. *Observations on the Present State of Religion in Maryland.* Baltimore: Samuel and John Adams, 1795.

Evans, William and Thomas, ed. "Memoir of Martha Routh." *The Friends Library.* Vol. 12. Philadelphia: no publisher given, 1848.

Everett, Joseph. "An Account of the Most Remarkable Occurrences of the Life of Joseph Everett." *Arminian Magazine* (1790): 505–11, 555–62, 601–9.

Franklin, Benjamin. *The Autobiography and Other Writings.* Edited by L. Jesse Lemisch. New York: New American Library, 1961.

Garrettson, Freeborn. *The Experience and Travels of Mr. Freeborn Garrettson.* Philadelphia: Joseph Crukshank, 1791.

Hancock, Harold, ed. "Alexander B. Cooper's Civil War Memoirs of Camden." *Delaware History* (Spring–Summer 1982): 50–72.

Journal of a Convention of the Protestant Episcopal Church in the State of Maryland, 1807. Baltimore: no publisher given, 1807.

Klett, Guy S., ed. *Minutes of the Presbyterian Church of America.* Philadelphia: Presbyterian Historical Society, 1976.

Lackington, James. *Memoirs of James Lackington.* New York: J. Fellows, 1796.

Lee, Jesse. *A Short History of the Methodists.* Baltimore: Megill and Clime, 1810.

Luff, Nathaniel. *Journal of the Life of Nathaniel Luff, M.D.* New York: Clark and Sickles, 1848.

Manship, Andrew. *Thirteen Years Experience in the Itinerancy.* Philadelphia: Methodist Episcopal Book and Publishing House, 1881.

"Memoir of Mrs. Anna Matilda Moore." *Methodist Magazine* (1828): 136–37.

Mifflin, Benjamin. "Journal of a Journey from Philadelphia to the Cedar Swamps and Back, 1764." *Pennsylvania Magazine of History and Biography*, 40 (1928).

Minutes of Annual Conferences of the Methodist Episcopal Church, 1773–1828. New York: T. Mason and G. Lane, 1840.

Minutes of the Methodist Conferences Annually Held in America; From 1773 to 1813. New York: Daniel Hitt and Thomas Ware, 1813.

Montgomery, Elizabeth. *Reminiscences of Wilmington.* Philadelphia: Collins, 1851.

Munroe, John A., ed. "James Hemphill's Account of a Visit to Maryland in 1802." *Delaware History* (September 1948): 61–78.

Perry, William Stevens, ed. *Historical Collections Relating to the American Colonial Church.* Vol. 4, *Maryland* and Vol. 5, *Delaware.* Hartford: Church Press Co., 1878.

Perry, William Stevens, ed. *Historical Collections Relating to the American Colonial Church.* Vol. 2, *Pennsylvania.* New York: A.M.S. Press, 1969.

Phoebus, George A. *Beams of Light on Early Methodism in America. Chiefly Drawn from the Diary, Letters, Manuscripts, Documents and Original Tracts of the Rev. Ezekiel Cooper.* New York: Phillips and Hunt, 1887.

Pilmore, Joseph. *Journal of Joseph Pilmore.* Edited by Frederick Maser and Howard T. Maag. Philadelphia: Message Pub Co., 1959.

Scott, Levi. "Semi-Centennial Sermon." *Minutes of Eighth Annual Session of M. E. Church.* Wilmington, Del.: James and Webb, 1876.

Smith, Thomas. *The Experience and the Ministerial Labor of Rev. Thomas Smith . . . compiled chiefly from his Journal by Rev. David Dailey.* Edited by George Peck. New York: Lane and Tippett, 1848.

Stiverson, Gregory A. "Deal Island: Records Relating to the Study of a Maryland Community." Xeroxed copy. Presented at Second Conference on Maryland History (May 24–28, 1978).

Turner, C. H. B., ed. *Some Records of Sussex County.* Philadelphia: Allen, Lane and Scott, 1909.

Ware, Thomas. *Sketches of the Life and Travels of Rev. Thomas Ware.* New York: Lane and Sanford, 1842.

Watters, William. *A Short Account of the Christian Experience and Ministerial Labours of William Watters.* Alexandria, Va.: S. Snowden, 1806.

Whitefield, George. *George Whitefield's Journals.* Edited by Iain Murray. London: Banner of Truth Trust, 1960.

Woolman, John. *The Journal of John Woolman.* Gloucester, Mass.: Peter Smith, 1971.

Secondary Sources

A. Unpublished Manuscripts

Clark, Allen. "History of Wesley Methodist Episcopal Church, Dover, Delaware." Hall of Records, Dover, Del.

Elliott, John Wesley Andros. "Unwritten History of Eastern Shore Methodism." In possession of the Rev. Kirk Mariner, Vienna, Va.

Nash, Gary. "To Rise Out of the Dust: Absalom Jones and the African Church of Philadelphia, 1785–1795." Paper given before Philadelphia Center for Early American Studies Seminar, Philadelphia, September 24, 1982.

Todd, Robert W. "Complete Record, Historical and Statistical, of the Methodist Episcopal Church in the Town of Easton, Maryland, 1777–1877." Archives, St. Mark's U. M. Church, Easton, Md.

Tyndall, A. "Concord M. E. Church." Hall of Records, Dover, Del.

Walls, Arthur A. "History of Dudley's Chapel" Microfilm ed. Queen Anne's Charge and Sudlersville Charge Church Records. Hall of Records, Annapolis.

Withgott, Margaret. "Migration from the Eastern Shore to Ohio." Typed copy in file folder no. 276, Maryland Room, Dorchester County Library, Cambridge, Md.

B. Dissertations and Theses

Baldwin, Lewis. "Invisible Strands in African Methodism." Ph.D. dissertation, Northwestern University, 1980.

Bilhartz, Terry David. "Urban Religion and the Second Great Awakening: A Religious Study of Baltimore, Maryland, 1790–1830." Ph.D. dissertation, George Washington University, 1979.

Herson, Jane. "The Development of Methodism in Delaware, 1739–1830." M.A. thesis, University of Delaware, 1956.

May, James W. "From Revival Movement to Denomination: A Re-Examination of the Beginnings of Methodism." Ph.D. dissertation, Columbia University, 1962.

Moore, Norman A., Jr. "The Antislavery Movement in Delaware." M.A. thesis, University of Delaware, 1965.

Simpson, Robert Drew. "Freeborn Garrettson, American Methodist Pioneer." Ph.D. dissertation, Drew University, 1954.

vanVoorst, Carol Lee. "The Anglican Clergy in Maryland, 1692–1776." Ph.D. dissertation, Princeton University, 1978.

Wade, William Nash. "A History of Public Worship in the Methodist Episcopal Church . . 1784 to 1905." Ph.D. dissertation, University of Notre Dame, 1981.

C. Published Works

Allen, Ethan. *Clergy in Maryland of the Protestant Episcopal Church Since the Independence of 1783*. Baltimore: James S. Walters, 1860.

Baker, Frank. *From Wesley to Asbury*. Durham: Duke University Press, 1976.

Baker, George C. *An Introduction to the History of Early New England Methodism, 1789–1839.* Durham: Duke University Press, 1941.

Baker, Gordon Pratt. *Those Incredible Methodists.* Baltimore: The Baltimore Conference, 1972.

Bangs, Nathan. *History of the Methodist Episcopal Church.* 2 vols. New York: T. Mason and G. Lane, 1839.

Bangs, Nathan. *The Life of the Rev. Freeborn Garrettson.* New York: Carlton and Porter, 1832.

Barclay, Wade Crawford. *Early American Methodism, 1769–1844.* Vol. 1. New York: Board of Missions and Church Extension of the Methodist Church, 1952.

Barratt, Norris S. *Barratt's Chapel and Methodism.* Wilmington, Del.: Historical Society of Delaware, 1911.

Belden, Albert D. *George Whitefield: The Awakener.* New York: Macmillan, 1953.

Bohner, Charles H. "Rum and Reform: Temperance in Delaware Politics," *Delaware History* (September 1953): 238–243.

Boles, John B. *The Great Revival, 1787–1805.* Lexington: University of Kentucky Press, 1972.

Bradley, Patricia Hayes. "Mark the Perfect . . . Freeborn Garrettson Speaks for Methodism." *Methodist History* (April 1978): 115–27.

Brunner, Edmund de S. *Village Communities.* Garden City, N.Y.: Doubleday, Doran, 1928.

Brunner, Edmund de S., and Hallenback, Wilbur C. *American Society: Urban and Rural Patterns.* New York: Harper, 1955.

Caley, George L. *A History of Asbury United Methodist Church, Smyrna, Del.* Smyrna: Shore Quality Press, 1972.

Carroll, Kenneth. "The Influence of John Woolman on Joseph Nichols and the Nicholites." *Then and Now: Quaker Essays, Historical and Contemporary*, edited by Anna Brinton. Philadelphia: University of Pennsylvania Press, 1960.

Carroll, Kenneth. *Joseph Nichols and the Nicholites.* Easton, Pa.: Easton Publishing Co., 1962.

Carroll, Kenneth. *Quakerism on the Eastern Shore.* Baltimore: Maryland Historical Society, 1970.

Carroll, Kenneth. "Religious Influences on the Manumission of Slaves in Caroline, Dorchester and Talbot Counties." *Maryland Historical Magazine* (June 1961): 176–97.

Carwardine, Richard. *Transatlantic Revivalism: Popular Evangelicalism in Britain and America, 1790–1865.* Westport, Conn.: Greenwood Press, 1978.

Clemens, Paul G. E. *The Atlantic Economy and Colonial Maryland's Eastern Shore.* Ithaca, N.Y.: Cornell Unviersity Press, 1980.

Conrad, Henry C. *History of the State of Delaware.* Vol. 2. Wilmington, Del.: published by the author, 1908.

Conrad, Henry C. "Samuel White and his Father, Thomas White." *Historical and Biographical Papers, Historical Society of Delaware.* Vol. 4. Wilmington, Del.: John M. Rogers Press, n.d.

Downing, Mary Catherine. *Sydenham Thorne: Clergyman and Founder.* Milford, Del.: Milford Historical Society, 1974.

Edwards, Maldwyn. *After Wesley: A Study of the Social and Political Influence of Methodism in the Middle Period.* London: Epworth Press, 1935.

Edwards, Morgan. "Materials Toward a History of the Baptists in Delaware State." *Pennsylvania Magazine of History and Biography* 9 (1885): 47–51.

Emory, Robert. *The Life of the Rev. John Emory, D.D.* New York: George Lane, 1841.

Essig, James. *The Bonds of Wickedness.* Philadelphia: Temple University Press, 1982.

Faulkner, John Alfred. *Burning Questions in Historic Christianity.* New York: Abingdon Press, 1930.

Faulkner, John Alfred. *The Methodists.* New York: Methodist Book Concern, 1913.

Footner, Hulbert. *Rivers of the Eastern Shore.* New York: Farrar and Rinehart, 1944.

Gaustad, Edwin Scott. *Historical Atlas of Religion in America.* New York: Harper and Row, 1962.

Genovese, Eugene D. *Roll, Jordan, Roll: The World the Slaves Made.* New York: Vintage Books, 1976.

Gewehr, Wesley M. *The Great Awakening in Virginia.* Durham, N.C.: Duke University Press, 1930.

Halevy, Elie. *The Birth of Methodism in England.* Edited by Bernard Semmel. Chicago: University of Chicago Press, 1971.

Hallman, E. C. *The Garden of Methodism.* No place given: published at request of Peninsula Annual Conference of the Methodist Church, 1948.

Hallman, E. C. *History of the Centenary Methodist Church.* Laurel, Del.: no publisher given, 1942.

Hallman, E. C. "Methodism in Delaware." *Delaware, A History of the First State.* Vol. 2. Edited by H. Clay Reed. New York: Lewis Historical Publishing Co., 1947.

Hancock, Harold B. *The Loyalists of Revolutionary Delaware.* Newark, Del.: University of Delaware Press, 1977.

Hanna, J. D. C., ed. *Centennial Services of Asbury Methodist Episcopal Church*. Wilmington, Del.: Delaware Printing Co., 1889.

Hartdagen, Gerald E. "The Vestries and Morals in Colonial Maryland," *Maryland Historical Magazine* 60 (1868): 360–78.

Hoffman, Ronald. *A Spirit of Dissension: Economics, Politics and Revolution in Maryland*. Balitmore: John Hopkins University Press, 1975.

Isaac, Rhys. "Evangelical Revolt: The Nature of the Baptist Challenge to the Traditional Order in Virginia." *William and Mary Quarterly* (July 1974): 345–68.

Isaac, Rhys. *The Transformation of Virginia, 1740–1790*. Chapel Hill, N.C.: University of North Carolina Press, 1982.

Lappen, James H. *Presbyterians on Delmarva, The History of the New Castle Presbytery*. No place or publisher given, 1972.

Lednum, John. *A History of the Rise of Methodism in America*. Philadelphia: published by the author, 1859.

Main, Jackson Turner. *The Social Structure of Revolutionary America*. Princeton: Princeton University Press, 1965.

Mariner, Kirk. *Revival's Children: A Religious History of Virginia's Eastern Shore*. Salisbury, Md.: Peninsula Press, 1979.

Mathews, Donald G. *Religion in the Old South*. Chicago: University of Chicago Press, 1977.

Mathews, Donald G. *Slavery and Methodism: A Chapter in American Morality, 1780–1840*. Princeton: Princeton University Press, 1965.

Mattison, H. *The Impending Crisis of 1860: Or the Present Connection of the Methodist Episcopal Church with Slavery, And Our Duty in Regard to It*. New York: Mason, 1859.

Maxson, Charles Hartshorn. *The Great Awakening in the Middle Colonies*. Chicago: University of Chicago Press, 1920.

May, James W. "Francis Asbury and Thomas White: A Refugee and His Tory Patron," *Methodist History* (April 1976): 141–64.

Mills, Frederick M. *Bishops by Ballot, An Eighteenth Century Ecclesiastical Revolution*. New York: Oxford University Press, 1978.

Mitchell, James. *The Life and Times of Levi Scott*. New York: Phillips and Hunt, 1885.

M'Lean, John. *Sketch of Rev. Philip Gatch*. Cincinnati: Swormstedt and Poe, 1854.

Munroe, John A. *Colonial Delaware: A History*. Millwood, N.Y.: KTO Press, 1978.

Munroe, John A. *Federalist Delaware*. New Brunswick: Rutgers University Press, 1954.

Munroe, John A. *Louis McLane, Federalist and Jacksonian*. New Brunswick: Rutgers University Press, 1973.

Munroe, John A. "Reflections on Delaware and the American Revolution." *Delaware History* (Spring-Summer 1976): 1–11.

Norwood, Frederick A. *Church Membership in the Methodist Tradition.* Nashville: Methodist Publishing House, 1958.

Norwood, Frederick A. *The Story of American Methodism.* New York: Abingdon Press, Nashville, 1974.

Nybakken, Elizabeth I. "New Light on the Old Side: Irish Influences on Colonial Presbyterianism." *Journal of American History* (March 1982): 813–32.

Papenfuse, Edward C., ed. *A Biographical Dictionary of the Maryland Legislature, 1635–1789.* 2 vols. Baltimore: Johns Hopkins University Press, 1979.

Pattison, Robert. "The Life and Character of Richard Bassett." *Papers of Historical Society of Delaware.* Vol. 29. Wilmington: Historical Society of Delaware, 1900.

Phoebus, George A. "The Methodist Episcopal Church." *Historical and Biographical Encyclopedia of Delaware*, edited by J. M. McCarter and B. F. Jackson. Wilmington, Del.: Aldine Publishing and Engraving Co., 1882.

Pilkington, James Penn. *The Methodist Publishing House.* Vol. 1. New York: Abingdon Press, 1968.

Raboteau, Albert J. *Slave Religion: The Invisible Institution in the Antebellum South.* New York: Oxford University Press, 1978.

Ridgway, Whitman. *Community Leadership in Maryland, 1790–1840.* Chapel Hill: University of North Carolina Press, 1979.

Rightmyer, Nelson Waite. *The Anglican Church in Delaware.* Philadelphia: Church Historical Society, 1947.

Rightmyer, Nelson Waite. "The Episcopate of Bishop Kemp." *Historical Magazine of the Protestant Episcopal Church* (March 1959): 66–84.

Rightmyer, Nelson Waite. *Maryland's Established Church.* Baltimore: The Church Historical Society for the Diocese of Maryland, 1956.

Rudolph, L. C. *Francis Asbury.* Nashville: Abingdon Press, 1966.

Saver, Jeffrey. "Edward O. Wilson, Father of a New Science." *Science Digest* (May 1982): 84–87.

Scharf, J. Thomas. *History of Delaware, 1609–1828.* 2 vols. Philadelphia: L. J. Richards and Co., 1888.

Scharf, J. Thomas. *History of Maryland.* 3 vols. Hatboro, Pa.: Tradition Press, 1967.

Semmel, Bernard. *The Methodist Revolution.* New York: Basic Books Inc., 1973.

Silliman, Charles A. *The Episcopal Church in Delaware, 1785–1954.* Wilmington, Del.: Diocese of Delaware, 1982.

Skaggs, David C., and Hartdagen, Gerald E. "Sinners and Saints, Anglican Clerical Conduct in Colonial Maryland." *Historical Magazine of the Protestant Episcopal Church* (June 1978): 177–95.

Smith, Daniel Blake. *Inside the Great House: Planter Family Life in Eighteenth-Century Chesapeake Society.* Ithaca: Cornell University Press, 1980.

Sprague, William B., ed. *Annals of the American Pulpit, Methodist.* New York: Robert Carter and Brothers, 1856.

Sprague, William B., ed. *Annals of the American Pulpit, Episcopalians.* New York: Robert Carter and Brothers, 1859.

Stevens, Abel. *A Compendious History of American Methodism.* New York: Carlton and Porter, 1867.

Stiverson, Gregory A. *Poverty in a Land of Plenty; Tenancy in Eighteenth Century Maryland.* Baltimore: Johns Hopkins University Press, 1977.

Stout, Harry S. "Religious Communication, and the Ideological Origins of the American Revolution." *William and Mary Quarterly* (October 1977): 519–41.

Thompson, D. D. *John Wesley as Social Reformer.* Freeport, N.Y.: Books for Libraries Press, 1971.

Todd, R. W. *Methodism of the Peninsula.* Philadelphia: Methodist Episcopal Book Room, 1886.

Tolles, Frederick B. "Quietism vs. Enthusiasm: The Philadelphia Quakers and the Great Awakening." *Pennsylvania Magazine of History and Biography* (January 1945): 26–38.

Trinterud, Leonard. *The Forming of an American Tradition.* Philadelphia: Westminster Press, 1949.

Tyerman, Luke. *The Life of the Rev. George Whitefield.* Vol. 2. London: Hodder and Stoughton, 1890.

Utley, George B. *The Life and Times of Thomas John Claggett.* Chicago: R. R. Donnelley and Sons, 1913.

Wallace, Adam. *The Parson of the Islands.* Baltimore: Thomas and Evans, 1906.

Weis, Frederick Lewis. *The Colonial Clergy of Maryland, Delaware and Georgia.* Lancaster, Mass.: Society of Descendents of Colonial Clergy, 1950.

Williams, William H. *A History of Wesley U. M. Church, Georgetown, Del., 1779–1978.* Georgetown, Del.: Countian Press, 1978.

Zebley, Frank. *The Churches of Delaware.* Wilmington: At author's expense, 1947.

Index

Abbott, Benjamin, 110
Abolitionism, 8, 44, 112, 113, 161–68
Accomac, Va., 75
Adams, James, 140
Adams, John, 23, 172, 176
African Methodist Episcopal Church, 118, 146
African Union Methodist Protestant Church, 116
Agriculture, 72
Airey, Henry, 36–38, 71, 74, 100, 163
Alcohol, 77, 78, 85, 86, 93, 98, 104, 106, 151–55
Allen, Richard, 118, 145, 146
Altar call, 80, 81
American Protestant Episcopal Church, 58, 67, 73, 90, 92–94, 96, 97, 132, 133, 137, 147, 148, 154, 168, 175–78
  evangelicals, 95
American Revolution, xi, 39–48
Amusements, 98, 99, 155–57
Anderson, Dr. James, 74, 150
Anglican Church, 1, 4, 5, 13–18, 74, 89, 90, 99, 147, 148
  Kent Co., a case study, 16, 17
Annamessex Chapel, Somerset Co., Md., 71
Anticlericalism, 15
Appoquinimi (St. Anne's), New Castle Co., Del., 6
Arminianism, 14, 21, 32, 94, 123, 134
Asbury Church, Wilmington, 75, 108, 109, 115, 116, 137
Asbury, Francis, xi, 7, 10, 25–28, 30, 36–38, 41, 42, 44–58, 60, 64–69, 76, 79, 84, 87, 91, 96, 97, 105, 107, 111, 112, 122, 123, 126, 129–31, 132, 137, 144, 145, 148, 152, 155, 162, 168, 172, 173
Asceticism, 10
Attractions of Methodism, 89–120

Authoritarian polity, 172–74
Ayres, Robert, 59, 132, 170

Back Creek (Bethel Chapel), Cecil Co., Md., 81
Baker, Daniel, 142
Baker, Elijah, 93–95
Baley, Henry, 152
Baltimore, Lord, 13, 14
Banning, Henry, 74, 163, 172
Baptists, 12, 13, 54, 77, 93–96, 154, 168
Barbon, Thomas, 152, 153
Barratt, Andrew, 162, 172, 174
Barratt, Philip, 64, 66, 74
Barratt, Widow, 66–68
Barratt's Chapel, 59, 64–69, 101, 115
Bassett, Ann Ennalls, 99, 100
Bassett, Richard, 57, 62, 74, 80, 86, 99–101, 108, 150, 164, 165, 172, 174, 175
Bateman, James, 116
Bayard, Ann Bassett, 100
Bayard, James, 100
Becket, William, 256
Benezet, Anthony, 112
Benson, James, 74, 172
"Better sort," 99–102, 105, 107, 119, 122, 149, 150. *See also* gentry
Blackiston Chapel, 64
Blackiston, Ebenezer, 169
Blacks, xiii, 44, 100, 111–19. *See also* 199n27, 200n31
  black preachers, 143–46
  statistics, 111–12
Bloxam, Argil, 142
Bluett, Thomas, 15
Boardman, Richard, 23, 50, 91
Boehm, Henry, xi, 84, 110, 131, 140, 159, 161–63, 177, 178
Bohemia Manor, 4, 7, 26, 28

Bolingbrook Chapel, 71
Bordley, James, 74, 172
"Born again," 4, 11, 21, 138, 147
Bouchell, Dr. Sluyter, 74
Boyer, Caleb, 128
Bridgetown Chapel, 60
Brown, John, 33
Brown, White, 69, 73
Brown's Chapel, 72, 105
Bruff, Rachel, 100
Bruff, William, 74, 160, 172
Burton, Thomas, 74, 90, 108, 148, 156, 165
Burton's Chapel, 148

Calvinism, 4, 14, 19, 95, 148
Cambridge, 37, 38, 61, 71, 99, 149, 167
Camden, Del., 108
Camp meetings, 57, 80–87, 100
Cape Henlopen, 152, 169
Catholics, 16, 97
Centreville, Md., 122, 155, 156
Chambers, John, 86
Chandler, Thomas, 14
Chandler, Dr. William, 81–84, 86, 122, 133, 135, 136
Chapel Branch Camp Meeting, 82–85
Chestertown, Md., 71, 72, 91, 109, 122, 150
Chew, Thomas, 36, 130
Church Hill, Md., 71
Christiana, Del., 2, 6, 28
Christmas Conference, 68
Circuit riders. *See* itinerants
Circuits, 21
Clow, Chaney, 40, 41
Coke, Thomas, 57, 61–72, 93, 143, 173
Colbert, William, 75, 77, 79, 96, 123, 131, 132, 135, 140, 141, 151, 157, 163, 166
Collins, John, 142
Concord, Sussex Co., Del., 111, 142
Congregationalists, 2
Conoway, Levin, 160
Conversion, 123, 124, 155, 156
Cooper, Ezekiel, 30, 90, 100, 119, 122, 176
Cooper, John, 33
Cornwall, England, 169
Cornwallis, Gen., 58
Coulter, Sarah, 120
Cox, Philip, 128
Crapper, Polly, 170
Crime, 169
Cromwell, Joseph, 52, 121, 153

Dame's Quarter, 149
Damned Quarter, 149
Dartmouth, Lord, 40
Davis, Isaac, 90, 103, 104, 120, 152, 165, 172
Davis, Lemuel, 74

Deacon, 127
Deal Island, 149
Death, 119, 120, 123, 124
Deism, 96
Delmarva Peninsula, xii, xiii
Democratic-Republicans, 171, 174, 175
Demographics, 91, 92
Devil's Island, 149
Disestablishment, 39, 50, 54
Dixon, Nathaniel, 163
Dover, Del., 7, 15, 48, 51, 60, 62, 64, 69, 80, 84, 91, 137, 174
Dow, Lorenzo, 136
Downes, Henry, 36, 74
Downing, William, 74
Dress, 150, 151
Dudley, Joshua, 38, 41
Dudley's Chapel, Queen Anne's County, Md., 64
Duke, William, 95
"Dull times," 74

Easton, Md., 35, 36, 37, 48, 76, 162
Eating, 151
Eclipse of sun, 135
Economic insurance, 106
Edwards, Jonathan, 2
Elder, 127
Elkton, Md., 91, 95
English (ancestry), xii, 12, 13, 22, 90, 175, 176
"Enthusiasm," 2, 9, 11, 18, 19, 21, 34, 61, 79, 100, 114, 115
Embury, Philip, 23
Emory, Charles, 172
Emory, John, 81, 120, 122, 124–27, 156, 157
Emory, Robert, 74, 108, 120, 126
Emory, Thomas, 142
Ennalls, Ann. *See* Ann Ennalls Bassett
Ennalls, Bartholomew, 148
Ennalls, Catherine, 99, 100
Ennalls, Henry, 74, 100, 102, 160, 172
Ennalls, Mary, 99
Ennalls, Sarah, 110
Episcopalians. *See* American Protestant Episcopal Church
Ethnic factor, 89, 90
Everett, Joseph, 14, 41, 47, 90, 112, 113, 124, 126, 133, 134, 148, 157
Ezion Church, Wilmington, Del., 116, 118

Family, 170
Federalists, 171, 174–76
First Methodist chapel, 28
First Methodist society, 6, 28
Fluvanna schism, 49, 53–55, 99
Fogwell, John, 47, 48, 122

Franklin, Benjamin, 2, 123, 158
Frazier, William, 74
French Revolution, 105, 107
Freud, Sigmund, 130
Furness, Robert, 27

Gabriel (angel), 136
Garden of Methodism, xi, xiii
Garrettson, Freeborn, 27, 30–38, 41, 44, 48, 53, 55, 57, 62, 64, 67–69, 79, 95, 111, 118, 122, 128, 145, 150, 158
Gatch, Philip, 28, 29, 51, 76
Gentry, xiii, 14, 32, 39, 64, 74, 98–102, 107, 131, 148–50, 153, 168, 172
Georgetown, Del., 91, 92, 104, 106, 171
Gewehr, Wesley, 17
Gill, William, 126
Goldsboro, Robert, 171
Great Awakening, 1–13, 119
"Great Pig Issue," 91, 92
Greenwood, Del., 96, 120
Green's Chapel, Kent Co., Del., 109

Hair style, 150
Halevy, Elie, 22
Hargus, J. R., 152, 169
Harrington, Philip, 74
Harris, Benton, 74
Harris, James, 10
Harrison, Thomas, 74
Hart, Joseph, 138
Hartley, Joseph, 35–38, 41, 48
Haskins, Thomas, 122, 124
Heck, Barbara, 23
Hemphill, James, 168
Hersey, Solomon, 27, 28
Hillsboro, Md., 76
Hindman, William, 74, 172, 176
Hopkins, Lambert, 17
Hopper, William, 74, 160, 174
Horses, 131
Hosier, Harry, 69, 111, 143, 145, 153
Hudson, Daniel, 164
Hudson, James, 170
Hymns. *See* music
Hynson (Hinson), Carvil, 28, 166
Hynson's Chapel. *See* Kent Chapel

Inglis, Charles, 9, 16, 17
Itinerants, 121–45
    celibacy, 129
    conversion, 123, 124
    disciplinarian, 140, 141
    education, 121–23
    image, 139, 140
    marriage, 126
    preaching, 83, 132–37
    relations with women, 126, 129, 130
    salary, 127
    singing, 137–39

Jarratt, Devereaux, 17, 53
Jefferson, Thomas, 175
Jeffry, 145, 146
Jewelry, 150
Jones, Joseph, 95
Jones Neck, Del., 10

Keene, Samuel, 51, 119
Kellam, James, 86
Kemp, James, 149, 176–78
Kennard, George, 168
Kent Chapel (Hynson's Chapel), 28, 60, 72
Kent Island, 33–71
King, John, 25–28, 122

Lackington, James, 100
Laurel, Del., 33, 84, 86, 95, 135, 161
Lawrenson, Lawrence, 126, 134, 135, 142
Laws, Elijah, 148
Laws, John, 120
Laws, Rhoda, 156
Layfield, George, 94–96
Lednum, John, xi
Lee, Jesse, 56, 82, 84
Lee, Thomas, 38
Lewes, Del., 1, 2, 4, 6, 7, 34, 35, 77, 78, 93, 130, 147, 152, 169–71
Line Chapel, Sussex Co., Del., 71
Littlejohn, John, 40
Local preachers, 141–43
Lovely Lane Chapel, 68
"Lower sort," 14, 21, 32, 98, 102, 105–7, 112, 119, 122, 150, 198n18
Loyalty oath, 35, 41, 44, 46, 50
Luff, Nathaniel, 72, 149, 158, 176, 178
Lyon, Richard, 130, 165

McLane, Allen, 74, 101, 102, 108, 152, 164, 165
Magaw, Samuel, 17, 18, 25, 51–53, 60, 62
Malaria, 131–32
Mariner, Kirk, 94
Meekins, Joseph, 164
Methodism and other faiths, 94–97
Methodist heritage, 19–22
Methodist personality, 177–78
Methodist Protestants, 174
Methodists, a socio-economic analysis, 105
"Middling sort," 14, 21, 32, 98, 102–5, 107, 119, 122, 150, 198n18
Mifflin, Benjamin, 11
Milford, Del., 57, 74, 75, 77, 81, 103, 141, 166, 170

Mitchell, Hester, 90
Mitchell, Josiah, 90
Mitchell, Nancy, 109
Moore, Anna Matilda, 109
Moore, James, 131
Moore, William, 55
Moravians, 12
Morgan, George, 106
Morgan, William, 77–79, 83, 84, 86, 89, 90, 97, 106, 138, 139, 142, 151, 152, 154, 156, 157–61, 164, 167, 171, 174, 177
Munroe, John, 43
Music, 102, 137–40, 156–57

Naylor, James, 9, 11
Neill, Hugh, 17, 18, 51–53, 60
New Castle (town), Del., 2, 3, 6, 28, 40, 91
"New Man," 147–49
New Side (New Light), 5–7, 11, 19
Newton, Christina, 156
Nicholites, 7–10, 16, 97, 112
Nichols, Joseph, 7–10, 79, 98
North East, Md., 2
Northwest Fork Hundred, Sussex Co., Del., 106
Nottingham, Md., 2
Nutter, David, 74

Ohio, 72, 73
O'Kelly, James, 173, 174
"Old Methodism," 49–56, 58, 61, 62, 66, 99, 172, 174, 179
Old Side (Old Light), 5, 7, 11
Old Union (African Union Church), Wilmington, 116, 118
Oliver, 86
Onancock, Va., 96

Pacifism, 30, 37, 41–43, 50, 176
Paine, Thomas, 96
Paramore, Thomas, 74
Parks, Charles, 156
Parks, John, 156
Parramore, William, 162
Payne, James, 169
Perfectionism, 21, 134, 148
Persecution, 32–38, 43, 44, 148, 167
Petticord, Caleb, 38, 148
Pilmore, Joseph, 23, 25, 26, 28, 50, 52, 61, 91, 134
Political involvement, 170–76
Poor whites *See* lower sort
Poverty
    itinerants, 127, 128
    lay Methodists, 104, 107
Predestination, 14, 94, 148
Prejudice, 115, 166, 167

Preparatory Conference of 1779, 54
Presbyterians, 2, 4–7, 11–13, 16–19, 87, 93, 95, 154, 168
Presiding elder, 127
Priestly, Joseph, 22
Pungateague, Va., 81, 96

Quakers, 8–11, 16, 96, 97, 112, 113, 151, 163, 168
Quantico Chapel, 71
Quantico, Va., 35

Raboteau, Albert, 114
Randle, John, 26, 28
Rankin, Thomas, 42–44, 46, 47, 51, 166, 169
Read, Robert, 51
Redden, Stephen, 177
Reedy Island, 4
Revival techniques, 79–84
Ridgely, Dr. Abraham, 74, 80, 174
Roberts, Robert, 132
Robertson, Roger, 163
Rodda, Martin, 40, 46
Rodney, Caesar, 38, 40, 41
Rodney, Caesar Augustus, 169
Rodney, Caleb, 164, 165
Roe, Samuel, 39
Rogers, Mrs., 108
Rollins, Isaac, 27
Roman Catholics. *See* Catholics
Ross, George, 7
Rush, Dr. Benjamin, 122
Russell, William, 164

Sacraments, 16, 22, 49, 51, 66
St. George's (town), Del., 4
St. George's Church, Philadelphia, Pa., 64, 146
St. Johnstown, Del., 120
St. Martin's, Md., 1135
St. Paul's Church, Philadelphia, Pa. , 17, 18, 25, 52, 61, 62
Salisbury, Md., 35
Salvation, 4, 118–20, 138
Saul of Tarsus, 148
Scot, Levi, 91, 124, 127
Scotch Irish, xiii, 5, 12, 13
Second Great Awakening, 76–87, 111
Segregation, 83, 107, 111
Semmel, Bernard, 22
Seymour, William, 86
Shankland, Rhoades, 74
Sharp, Solomon, 124, 133
Sharpless, Abraham, 159
"Shouting," 138, 139
Sin, 14, 77, 78, 80, 149, 150
Skillington, 60, 61

Slave trade, 163, 164
Slavery, xiii, 112–14, 161–68
Smallpox, 76, 124
Smith, Thomas, 123, 124, 128, 129, 131, 137, 150, 166
Smith, William, 61
Smyrna, Del. (Duck Creek Crossroads), 12, 57, 60, 62, 80–84, 104, 118, 129, 130, 152, 153, 168, 169, 173
Snow Hill, Md., 87, 163
Society, 21
Society for the Propagation of the Gospel, 13, 17
Sociobiology, 108
Spencer, Peter, 116–18, 142, 145, 146, 173
Sports, 98, 99, 155, 156
Spry, Christopher, 123
Statistics, 43, 49, 56, 58–60, 73, 74, 76, 77, 81, 82, 87, 94
Stevens, Abel, 68
Strawbridge, Robert, 22, 26, 30, 50, 137
Sturgis, Stokeley, 145

Tangier Island, 90, 106, 152
Tax support, 13, 94, 95, 175, 176
Taylor, Major, 153
Taylor, Thomas, 22, 23
Temperance, 104, 106, 151–55
Tennent, Charles, 5
Tennent, William, 2, 5
Thelwell, John, 167
Thomas, Joshua, 90, 106, 132, 133, 138, 141, 142, 151, 152, 161
Thompson, Abraham, 145, 146
Thorne, Sydenham, 17, 18, 51–53, 60
Tilgham, Tench, 166
Tingley, Samuel, 34, 52, 146
Tories, xi, 32, 33, 39–42, 44, 46, 47
Tuckahoe Chapel, 71
Tuckahoe Neck, 30, 76
Tumlin, Mary, 8
Tumlin, Nathaniel, 8

Union American Methodist Episcopal Church, 116
"Union" revival meetings (Dover, Del.), 80

Value system, 97–99
Varick, James, 145
Veasey, Thomas, 62

Vestry, 13, 14, 17
Virginia's Eastern Shore, 38, 39

Ware, Thomas, 48, 60, 61, 126, 127, 134
Washington College, 122
Washington, George, 50, 58
Watters, William, 28, 44, 51, 54, 55, 140
Wealth, 104, 105, 157–61
Webb, Capt. Thomas, 23, 24, 26, 28, 51
Webster, Richard, 27
Welsh, 12, 13
Welsh Tract Baptist Church, 12, 13, 93
Wesley, Charles, 1, 137, 138, 140
Wesley, John, 1, 19–23, 39, 42, 47, 54, 55, 61, 62, 67, 68, 92, 97, 112, 136, 139, 150, 151, 153, 172
Westward migration, 72, 73, 105, 106, 122, 130
Whatcoat, Richard, 62, 64, 66, 69
White Clay Creek, Del., 2, 5, 7
White Haven, Md., 152
White, Mary, 46, 107, 110
White, Thomas, xi, 36, 37, 46–48, 58, 74, 108
Whitefield, George, 1–7, 12, 19, 22, 33, 79, 98, 119
White's Chapel, 64, 65, 69
Williams, Ezekiel, 74
Williams, Robert, 23, 26, 53
Williams, William, 124
Willis, Henry, 39
Wilmington, Del., 2, 26–28, 40, 75, 76, 91, 107, 115, 116, 137, 140, 145, 152
Wilson, Edward, 108
Wilson, Matthew, 34
Wiltbank, John, 74
Wolf, Dr. Jacob, 171
Wolf, J., 34, 35
Women, 83, 107–11, 126, 129, 130, 198n21
Woolman, John, 8, 11
Work ethic, 9, 10, 104, 106, 157–61
Worton Chapel, Kent Co., Md., 72
Wright, Richard, 26
Wright, Robert, 167
Wyatt, Joseph, 126
Wye Mills, 84, 85

XYZ Affair, 176

Yellow fever, 75, 76
Yorktown, battle of, 58